Values and Principles in Union Foreign Policy

C000062858

As a fresh examination of the values and principles that inform EU Foreign Policy, this book presents a clear and close reading of the EU as an international actor.

This up-to-date volume explores the implications of these values and principles on the construction of European Union identity today. It also shows how current debates on European Union foreign policy and on European identity tend to be kept separated as if the process of identity formation had only an internal dimension or it was not related to the external behaviour of an international actor.

This new book examines the values and principles that inform EU foreign policy in order to achieve a better understanding of the EU as an international actor and to explore implications of these values and principles on the process of the construction of the European Union identity. Conceiving EU foreign policy in its broadest context, as a set of political actions that are regarded by external actors as 'EU' actions, the contributors focus on both Pillar I and Pillar II policies, involving EU and member state actions, and material political actions and less material ones such as speech acts.

Adopting a multidisciplinary perspective and drawing on political science, political economy, sociology, environmental science and women's studies this book will be of great interest to students and scholars of European studies and politics.

Sonia Lucarelli is a Senior Lecturer at University of Bologna, Forlì, Italy; and Director of Research, Forum on the Problems of Peace and War, Florence, Italy. Her research interests include IR theory, European security, EU foreign policy. Her publications include: *Europe and the Breakup of Yugoslavia: A Political Failure in Search of a Scholarly Explanation*; and *Mobilising Politics and Society? The EU Convention's Impact on Southern Europe*.

Ian Manners is a Senior Lecturer in Political Science at Malmö University, Sweeden. His research interests include European integration theory and the European Union's external actions. His publications include *Substance and Symbolism: an Anatomy of Cooperation in the New Europe*; and with Richard Whitman (eds) *The Foreign Policies of European Union Member States*. His article 'Normative Power Europe: a Contradiction in Terms?' won the prize for the best article in the *Journal of Common Market Studies* for 2002.

Routledge Advances in European Politics

Values and Principles in European Union Foreign Policy

**Edited by Sonia Lucarelli
and Ian Manners**

Routledge
Taylor & Francis Group

LONDON AND NEW YORK

First published 2006
by Routledge
2 Park Square, Milton Park, Abingdon, Oxon, OX14 4RN

Simultaneously published in the USA and Canada
by Routledge
270 Madison Ave, New York NY 10016

Routledge is an imprint of the Taylor & Francis Group, an informa business

Transferred to Digital Printing 2007

Typeset in Baskerville by Taylor & Francis Books

British Library Cataloguing in Publication Data
A catalogue record for this book is available from the British Library

Library of Congress Cataloging in Publication Data
A catalog record for this book has been applied for

ISBN10: 0-415-37136-8 (hbk)
ISBN10: 0-415-46002-6 (pbk)

ISBN13: 978-0-415-37136-0 (hbk)
ISBN13: 978-0-415-46002-6 (pbk)

Contents

Illustrations

Figures

Tables

Contributors

Susan Baker, Professor, Cardiff University, Wales

Rosa Balfour, Researcher, Centre for the Study of International Politics (CeSPI), Rome, Italy

Federico Bonaglia, Economist, OECD Development Centre, Paris, France

Andrea Goldstein, Senior Economist, OECD Development Centre, Paris, France

Knud Erik Jørgensen, Professor, Aarhus University, Denmark

Sonia Lucarelli, Senior Lecturer at University of Bologna, Forlì, Italy; and Director of Research, Forum on the Problems of Peace and War, Florence, Italy

Ian Manners, Senior Lecturer, Malmö University, Sweden

Roberto Menotti, Senior Researcher, Aspen Institute Italia, Italy

Stefania Panebianco, Associate Professor, University of Catania, Italy

Fabio Petito, Visiting Assistant Professor, ESCP-EAP, Paris and University L'Orientale in Naples, Italy

Andrea Pető, Associate Professor, University of Miskolc, Hungary

Adrian van den Hoven, Trade Policy Adviser, External Relations Department of the Union of Industries of the European Community (UNICE); Brussels, Belgium

Ian Welsh, Senior Lecturer, Cardiff University, Wales

Acknowledgements

In the five-year evolution of this project we have all profited greatly from the contributions of many who discussed the project with us, as well as from the logistic and financial support of a number of institutions.

In the first place, we are indebted to the people who discussed the papers and project with us in various research workshops, particularly Luciano Bardi, Ana Becerro, Andrei Belyi, Annika Björkdahl, Kathrin Blanck, Marcello Buiatti, Tom R. Burns, Irina Busygina, Furio Cerutti, Chad Damro, Dimitri D'Andrea, Dirk De Bièvre, Andreas Dür, Magnus Ekengren, Miriam Gomes Saraiva, Sebastien Guigner, Stefano Guzzini, Ulla Holm, Anna Home, Pertti Joenniemi, Bart Kerremans, Catarina Kinnvall, Ulrich Krotz, Margarita León, Francesca Longo, Anna Loretoni, José Magone, Susan Millns, Carla Monteleone, Jan Orbie, Luigi Pellizzoni, Jess Pilegaard, Sara Poli, Ulrich Sedelmeier, Orla Sheehy, Helene Sjursen, Karen Smith, Catharina Sørensen, Debora Spini, Emma Stewart, Rodolfo Ragionieri, Vincenzo Randazzo, Angela Wigger, Kataryna Wolczuk, and Alasdair Young.

We are equally indebted to Ole Elgström and Michael Smith for giving us the opportunity to present our work in their workshop at the 2004 ECPR Joint Sessions of Workshops (Uppsala, April 2004) and at their panel at the Second Pan-European Conference on EU Politics (Bologna, June 2004).

As for institutions, we wish to thank the Forum on the Problems of Peace and War, Florence for hosting the research project that led to this publication and the Italian Ministry of University and Scientific Research for financial support. We also wish to thank the European University Institute for hosting one of our workshops. We are especially grateful to Matteo Bardelli, Giacomo Guatteri and Giuseppe Sorgente for editorial assistance. Finally, we wish to thank our fellow contributors for fruitful suggestions, sincere effort, and much patience.

July 2005
Sonia Lucarelli
Ian Manners

Abbreviations

ACP	Africa, the Caribbean, and the Pacific Countries
AEBC	Agriculture and Environment Biotechnology Commission
APEC	Asia-Pacific Economic Cooperation
BSE	Bovine Spongiform Encephalopathy
CARDS	Community Assistance for Reconstruction, Development and Stabilisation
CBA	Cost Benefit Analysis
CEC	Commission for the European Communities
CEE	Central and Eastern Europe
CEEC	Central and Eastern Europe Countries
CET	Common External Tariff
CFSP	Common Foreign and Security Policy
CMLR	Centre for Mined Land Rehabilitation
COM	Communication from the European Commission
COMECOM	Council for Mutual Economic Assistance
CoP	Conference of the Parties (UN Framework Convention on Climate Change)
CSCE	Conference on Security and Cooperation in Europe
CSDP	Common European Security and Defence Policy
DAC	Development Assistance Committee
DCP	Development Cooperation Policy
DDA	Doha Development Agenda
DG	Directorate-General
DSB	Dispute Settlement Body
EAPs	Environmental Action Programmes
EC	European Community
ECHO	European Community Humanitarian Office
ECHR	European Convention for the Protection of Human Rights and Fundamental Freedoms
ECJ	European Court of Justice
ECSC	European Coal and Steel Community
EDF	European Development Fund
EEA	European Environmental Agency

EEC	European Economic Community
EGE	European Group on Ethics
EIDHR	European Initiative for Democracy and Human Rights
EMP	Euro-Mediterranean Partnership
ENP	European Neighbourhood Policy
EP	European Parliament
EPA	Environmental Protection Agency
EPAs	Economic Partnership Agreements
EPC	European Political Cooperation
ESS	European Security Strategy
EU	European Union
EU FP	European Union Foreign Policy
FRY	Former Republic of Yugoslavia
FYROM	Former Yugoslavia Republic of Macedonia
GATT	General Agreement on Tariffs and Trade
GDP	Gross Domestic Product
GM	Genetically Modified
GMO	Genetically Modified Organism
GSP	Generalised System of Preferences
HAP	Health, AIDS and Population
HRD	Human Rights and Democracy
ICB	International Commission on the Balkans
ICPD	International Conference on Population and Development
IGO	International Governmental Organisation
ILO	International Labour Organization
IMF	International Monetary Fund
IPCC	Intergovernmental Panel on Climate Change
IR	International Relations
LDCs	Least Developed Countries
LICs	Low-income Countries
MDGs	Millennium Development Goals
MEA	Multilateral Environmental Agreement
MEDA	Mesures d'ajustement
MEP	Member of the European Parliament
MICs	Middle-income Countries
MP	Member of Parliament
MSF	Médecins Sans Frontières
NATO	North Atlantic Treaty Organization
NBAC	National Bioethics Advisory Commission
NGO	Non-governmental Organisation
NIS	Newly Independent States
NSS	National Security Strategy
OBNOVA	Community Assistance for Bosnia-Herzegovina, Croatia, Federal Republic of Yugoslavia and FYROM
ODA	Official Development Assistance

OECD	Organization for Economic Cooperation and Development
OSCE	Organization for Security and Co-operation in Europe
PCSD	President's Council on Sustainable Development
PHARE	Pologne et Hungrie: Actions pour la Reconversion Économique
PR	Proportional Representation
RN-DI	Recipient Needs-Donor Interests
SAA	Stabilisation and Association Agreements
SAP	Stabilisation and Association Process
SEA	Single European Act
SEE	Southeastern Europe
SHAPE	Supreme Headquarters Allied Powers Europe
SME	Small and Medium Size Enterprises
SSK	Sociology of Scientific Knowledge
STABEX	System for the Stabilisation of Export Earnings
SYSMIN	System for Promotion of Mineral Production and Exports
TACIS	Technical Assistance to the Commonwealth of Independent States
TEC	Treaty establishing the European Community
TEU	Treaty on the European Union
TRIPs	Trade Related Intellectual Property Rights
UK	United Kingdom
UN	United Nations
UN FCCC	Framework Convention on Climate Change
UNHDR	Human Development Report
UNICE	Union of Industrial and Employers' Confederations of Europe
UNPF	Population Fund
US	United States
USAID	Agency for International Development
USEU	United States Mission to the European Union
USTR	United States Trade Representative
VIP	Values, Images and Principles
WEU	Western European Union
WID	Women in Development
WMD	Weapons of Mass Destruction
WTO	World Trade Organization
WWF	World Wide Fund for Nature

1 Introduction

Values, principles, identity and European Union foreign policy

Sonia Lucarelli

What are we for, what do we believe, what are we prepared to do? Does
Europe really have any collective sense of how it can and should stand up
for the principles and ideas that (with US help) shaped our current destiny?
Do we have in Europe any remaining value-driven vision of the world?

(Patten 1998)

Introduction

The analysis of European Union (EU)[1] foreign policy has long put much more
emphasis on its 'hardware' dimensions (including institutional infrastructure,
personnel, and military equipment) rather than on its 'software' dimensions
(including visions, aspirations, worldviews, principles, norms, and beliefs). For
the first five decades of the life of the EU, in all its guises, the vast majority of
discussions regarding its relations with the rest of the world focused on politics,
policies, and practicalities. The study of the EU's common commercial policy,
association agreements, development policy, external relations, and political
cooperation, for example, was primarily concerned with 'what were the policies?' rather than 'what did the policies tell us about the EU?' Since the end of
the Cold War, and particularly since the agreement of the Treaty on European
Union (TEU), discussions of the EU's relations with the rest of the world have
changed. An increasing emphasis is placed on understanding, conceptualising,
and thinking more broadly about the EU as a political entity which participates
in world politics, and is partially constituted by that participation.

This book is an attempt to move into a generation of scholarship which goes
beyond the phases described above, and tries to think thoroughly about the way
in which the EU is constituted as a political entity by the values, images and
principles (VIPs) which shape the discourse and practice of the EU's relations
with the rest of the world. This endeavour is by no means unique in this respect:
the volume undoubtedly stands on the shoulders of scholars who have benefited
from the liberating effects of the post-Cold War academic environment to think
in new ways about the ontological qualities of the EU, the way in which its
policies shape our understandings of the EU, and the way in which the EU is a

political and social agent embedded in, and employing, political and social institutions.

We argue that EU foreign policy should tell us far more about the EU as a political and social system than it has so far told us. It should be able to tell us more about the dynamic nature of the EU – the process whereby the Europeans construct their political identity – and about the relationship between values, principles, and foreign policy. To summarise, the book has two basic aims:

1   to analyse the EU as an international polity, intending specifically to high-light the values, principles, and images of the world it represents, voluntarily or not, in its international conduct; and
2   to investigate the implications for the process of identity formation of such a principles-embedded behaviour. What EU international identity and what identity for Europeans?[2]

In other words, we seek to investigate what type of relationship exists between the values and the principles that are embedded in EU external political behaviour.

The troublesome questions that we are dealing with pose many conceptual and empirical difficulties for the researcher. The very definitions of the terms employed are subject to debate, as are the theoretical relationships between the concepts. Moreover, empirical research on issues such as values and principles poses great methodological problems. The rest of this introduction deals with some of these problems. It first deals with the way that key actors in EU foreign policy, as well as academic observers, frequently refer to values, images of the world and principles that characterise the EU and (should) provide the basis for its role in world politics. It then analyses the fundamental concepts employed in the research project and presents our claim regarding the relationships among them, before turning to the theoretical and methodological research framework. The chapter closes with a presentation of the rest of the volume.

Values and principles in European Union foreign policy

The EU is increasingly presented as an international actor with a principled behaviour in foreign policy. Both key policy actors and academic commentators point to a distinctive role of the EU in world politics that derives from its par-ticular nature. Furthermore, this image is reinforced by examples of foreign policy that seem to point in the direction of a novel international actor that behaves according to a set of dynamic, yet identifiable values, principles, and images of the world. All this is located in a literature that depicts the EU as a novel type of international actor, as we shall consider here.

The EU's self-representation

Key actors in EU foreign policy frequently refer to values, images of the world, and principles that characterise the EU and that should provide the basis for its role in world politics. During moments of crisis, and during debates on the future of Europe, references to European values and how they should guide EU foreign policy are common. Equally frequent are references to the 'historic *responsibility* [of the EU] in the world' (Ciampi 2002, emphasis added). In the Laeken Declaration that paved the way for the debate on the future of Europe and the European Convention we read:

> Does Europe not, now that is finally unified, have a leading role to play in a new world order, that of a power able both to play a stabilising role worldwide and to point the way ahead for many countries and peoples? Europe as the continent of humane values, the Magna Carta, the Bill of Rights, the French Revolution and the fall of the Berlin Wall, the continent of liberty, solidarity and above all diversity, meaning respect for others' languages, cultures and traditions. ... Europe needs to shoulder its responsibilities in the governance of globalisation.
>
> (European Council 2001)

Even in the *European Security Strategy* (European Council 2003) we read:

> Europe should be ready to share in the responsibility for global security and in building a better world. ... The development of a stronger international society, well functioning international institutions and a rule-based international order is our objective. ... Spreading good governance, supporting social and political reform, dealing with corruption and abuse of power, establishing the rule of law and protecting human rights are the best means of strengthening the international order.

These and many other declarations and speeches delineate an international actor that has two characteristics rarely assigned to a traditional state actor:

1 a stabilising effect in contemporary world politics that Europe derives from its history and its historically-developed and formed values and principles;
2 external relations inspired by an 'ethics of responsibility' towards others.

Does this mean that key European actors regard the EU as an example and a motor of a changing paradigm in world politics? Are we actually living in a world of 'goodness'? What type of political animal is the EU that it deems it necessary to refer to itself with Laeken-like type of terminology? Most importantly of all, can we dismiss all this as 'simply rhetorical discourse'?

What we can claim from the start, even before presenting our research results, is that the self-representation of the Union cannot be dismissed as simply 'rhetorical'. As the arrival of Giddens' structuration theory (Giddens 1979) in International Relations has shown, in world politics, as in any social context, discourse and rhetoric matter in the discursive construction of interests, rather than being simply the product of underlying interests. Interests and identities cannot exist in isolation with respect to the context in which agents and structures interact. Rhetoric is a performative act which might respond to actors' interests in any given structural context, but which shapes collective understandings of that context and the identities of the actors involved. Put differently, not only can rhetorical discourse become a 'trap' which limits the space for manoeuvre of those who use it (as in the case of EU enlargement, Schimmelfennig 2003), but it can even change their very interests and self-perception, as we will explore in the conclusion.

Thus, even if references to values and principles remain exclusively discursive, they would undoubtedly be worth studying in order to better understand both the EU and its relations with the world that contribute to shaping its self-representation. However, as we will argue, this is not the case as the actual performance of EU foreign policy demonstrates recurring patterns of guiding values and principles.

The EU's principled foreign policy

At various points, the EU and its member states have actively challenged the principles adopted by other international actors that are considered cornerstones of foreign policy in the realist tradition, still predominant in most diplomatic circles. At international negotiations on climate change, for instance, in Kyoto (1997), Bonn (2001) and later in Johannesburg (2002), the EU has showed an attitude towards environmental protection and towards the possibility of turning to alternative sources of energy that distanced it from that of the main other power in world economy – the US (see Baker in chapter five). Differences with the US also emerged at the Doha summit of the World Trade Organization (WTO) in November 2001 as in various other occasions of trade negotiations (see van den Hoven in chapter eleven). The EU's role in the creation of an International Criminal Court, including building the momentum that carried along its more 'reluctant governments' – Britain and France – (Human Rights Watch 1999) – is a further example of activism and faith in the development of international norms and cosmopolitan institutions which seem to distance the EU from the major state powers.

A different attitude has also been deployed as far as food protection and research on genetically modified organisms (GMOs) is concerned. The latter case in particular seems to point in the direction of a constitutive difference in European and US conceptions of the relationship between science, technology and nature (see Welsh in chapter four) and of individual 'freedom', which is a shared value in the Western world and a cornerstone of modernity. In Europe, most voices call for a compromise between individual freedom and the right to protect present and future generations from the potentially negative consequences of manipulations to the DNA of nature.

Moreover, the EU is at the forefront of the fight against landmines, with more than 60 million mines lying hidden and a stockpile estimated at some 250 million. In terms of development aid, the EU followed the lead of the Jubilee 2000 movement in its demands to drop the debt for the world's poorest countries and to revise the highly indebted poor countries initiative. This has resulted in the everything-but-arms commitment by the EU to systematically open up its markets to these countries for tariff-free trade in all areas except arms.

In the area of democratisation, the EU has been an active agent in the provision of election assistance and observation and has developed guidelines that go beyond simple observation and towards the principles of good governance. In the area of human rights, the EU has developed a pro-active policy of being at the vanguard of the abolitionist movement against capital punishment (Manners 2000a, 2002). Particularly striking in the aftermath of the end of the Cold War is the way in which the EU has led the way in broadening understandings of security by linking military security directly to the development of democratic institutions and economic development in third countries. This rediscovered emphasis on the links between democracy, peace, and security in post-Cold War Europe is not limited to the EU. In an apparent rediscovery of Kantian democratic peace, all the institutions of the European security architecture (including the US) have dedicated a substantial part of their redefined roles in the post-bipolar world to democratisation. Overall, this is resulting in the gradual development of a 'system of liberal-democratic security communities' characterised by different degrees of maturity and tightness, but with a common sense of 'us' – liberal democracy (see Lucarelli 2002a, 2002b).

Problems arise when peace is shattered. When the use of force is required in order to support a value or principle previously affirmed, the EU often fails to maintain consistency (see Lucarelli and Menotti in chapter nine). Agreement on a lower common denominator or paralysis due to disagreement among the member states still tends to be the rule in the 'hard cases' such as Yugoslavia 1991–95 and Iraq 2003. Is it possible that the EU is value-led in some spheres (namely those in which decisions are 'communitarised') and not in others (namely where the member states have the main say)? Is it a question of institutional structure and sovereignty, a question of unwillingness to pay high costs, or something that has to do with a power which is 'civilian' in the narrow sense of refusing to use military force?

Representations of EU 'gentle power'

Either as a result of wishful thinking or prescriptive argumentation, or as a result of a particular reading of examples of EU foreign policy, there has been a certain tendency to describe the EU as an international actor with a principled behaviour in the international sphere. François Duchêne's well-known image of the EU (then EC) as a *civilian power* (1972; 1973) was not just the description of an economic giant with little political power, but the representation of an international actor that spreads civilian and democratic standards of governance on the basis of an 'ethics of responsibility' which is usually associated with home affairs (Duchêne 1973). A recent evolution of this line of thought is Jürgen Habermas's idea of *Weltinnenpolitik* – domestic politics of the world as the disappearance of barriers between internal and international politics make any political decision-maker responsible before all those affected by their decisions, despite a formal belonging to a political community (Habermas 1998; Bonanate 2001; Badie 1999). The civilian power EU would be better equipped than others to assume such a responsibility.

Focusing more on the normative content of the EU foreign policy is Göran Therborn's image of Europe (and particularly the EU) as 'normative area' – a loosely coupled system of regulatory norms, which developed through historical experiences (basically the 'isms' of European history), and 'a certain legacy of social norms, reflecting European experiences of class and gender' (Therborn 2001: 85). The role that Europe (and the EU within it) can have in tomorrow's world, affirms Therborn, is directly linked to this 'normative' nature and its economic institutional model – exerting 'influence' (rather than 'power') by providing an economic model – 'of market unification and supra-state economic organisation' or/and (the two possibilities are not incompatible) a normative model 'of human rights, citizenship, gender and generation relations, of supra-national norms and institutions.' (Therborn 2001: 92).

Attention to norms then becomes central, in Ian Manners' representation of the Union as a 'normative power' (Manners 2000a, 2002):

> The concept of normative power is an attempt to suggest that not only is the EU constructed on a normative basis, but importantly that this pre-disposes it to act in a normative way in world politics. It is built on the crucial, and usually overlooked observation, that the most important factor shaping the international role of the EU is not what it does or what it says, but what it is.
>
> (Manners 2002: 252)

Identity and foreign policy are here strictly interconnected. The construction of the Union, its specific constitution is what characterises it most as an international actor (also Manners and Whitman 2003).

More specifically focused on the characteristics of EU foreign policies is Stephan Keukeleire's concept of 'structural foreign policy' (Keukeleire 2000, 2002). A 'structural foreign policy', as opposed to a 'traditional foreign policy', is one which 'aims at influencing in an enduring and sustainable way the relatively permanent frameworks within which states relate to each other, relate to people, or relate to corporate enterprises or other actors, through the influence of the choice of the game as well as the rules of the game' (Keukeleire 2002: 14).

Building on Keukeleire's work (Telò 2001b: 264), Mario Telò argues that the Union's structural foreign policy aims at affecting 'particularly the economic and social structures of partners (states, regions, economic actors, international organisations, etc.), it is implemented through pacific and original means (diplomatic relations, agreements, sanctions and so on), and its scope is not conjunctural but rather in the middle and long range' (Telò 2001b: 264; Telò 2003; see also

Padoa-Schioppa's concept of 'gentle power Europe', 2001). These and other representations of the nature of the international identity all point to the idea that the EU is a different type of international actor as it has a different type of foreign policy (see Manners and Whitman 1998, 2003 on international identity).

Before we discuss the hypotheses that can explain 'EU difference', a clarification is necessary. Our discussion of the EU's self-representation, including examples of principled foreign policy and scholarly attempts to describe the EU, might easily lead to a misunderstanding. A VIPs-informed foreign policy is not necessarily a benign or soft one. As Knud Erik Jørgensen argues in chapter three, 'values, images and principles are completely agnostic along the dichotomies of benign/malign and soft/hard. Indeed, some of the worst foreign policy practices are based on strong values, deeply held images and principles etched in stone'. What is of interest for us is not to demonstrate that the EU is a realm of goodness that exports goodness, but to gain insights into the EU as a political and social polity from the analysis of the VIPs in its foreign policy.

A constitutive identity?

The most common response to the argument that the EU tends to adopt a structural foreign policy (to use one of the labels we have just introduced) is that there is nothing else it can do. To put it simply, this would be a 'necessary virtue', given the fact that the EU lacks traditional foreign policy capacity (the CFSP branch of EU foreign policy), while it has developed instruments and decisional capacity of a non-military, non-diplomatic nature (namely, the external relations branch of EU foreign policy). This argument can be taken to an extreme by concluding that developing a military capacity (typical of traditional foreign policy) would put civilian power Europe at risk (K. Smith 2000).

This explanation, although not easily dismissible, is by no means satisfactory. Even recognising that the unbalanced sovereignty and decision-making capacity of the Union in Pillar I (external relations) and Pillar II (CFSP) is such that the Union is better equipped to perform a structural rather than a traditional foreign policy, this does not explain the value and emphasis placed on democratisation and respect for human rights as a means to construct a safer international environment. Furthermore, on issues such as global warming, despite having similar economic concerns to those of the United States, the Union has assumed a different attitude, constructing a legitimising discourse for its position that refers to principles other than those held by the US.

The second type of explanation, that builds on and enlarges the first one, has to do with the 'incomplete' character of the Union. The fact that the Union is at the same time an *actor*, a *process* and a *project* makes it behave differently in comparison to traditional actors in world politics. In any foreign policy decision, the involved agencies also tend to evaluate the decision for its implications on the next step of European integration (see Lucarelli 2003). Where integration is already more consolidated, such as in Pillar I, there are less implications and decisions are easier to take, despite any potential financial costs for the member states (as in the case of climate change). Moreover, the existence of the 'EU as a process' influences the self-representation of the Union made by relevant European figures such as the presidents of the institutions. Thus the 'EU project' and 'EU self' are intertwined and compounded in the self-representations of the Union that we have discussed.

However, reading the Union as 'incomplete' misses the point of what the Union actually represents in contemporary world politics – a post-national political system. States and regions continue to exist and be relevant within the Union, but the Union as such is the first ever post-national polity. It is both a *laboratory* and a *motor* of the political changes brought about by, and expressed in, the processes of globalisation. The claimed effects of globalisation on the transformation of politics, such as 'post-sovereign governance' (Scholte 1997; Holton 1998), are clearer in the case of the Union. Expectations that the Union will one day be 'complete' are probably wishes that underestimate the deep transformations of politics that are more consonant with uneasy EU 'governance' rather than with the notions of traditional 'government'. If EU foreign policy is structural because the EU is incomplete, then we can expect the Union to continue to perform structural policy for a very long time.

It seems to me that although each of the previous lines of reasoning have some strength, it is not possible to understand the values and principles that guide and permeate EU foreign policy if we do not look at the historically constituted character of these practices. The integration process started as a semi-idealistic project of peace through cooperation amongst former enemies, economic development, and democratic consolidation (if not transition) of the member states. Although the Union's *telos* is not as strong and visible as it was at the outset (as Joseph Weiler 2001 has denounced; see also Habermas 2001), the founding values of the Union were never abandoned in the political system and continue to be visible in its foreign policy performance. To those founding values of peace, liberty and democracy, others have been added over time. If we look carefully at the values and principles of specific EU foreign policies, we see values that have constituted the Union since the beginning and others that have achieved political consensus later. We can see differing interpretations or contending priorities concerning values and/or principles among the various actors involved in EU foreign policy making. We can see inconsistency both over time and across cases, but we are always left with the impression that we are dealing with constitutive elements of the EU's political identity. Before I come back more explicitly on the link between foreign policy and European political identity (below) some terminological and conceptual clarifications are needed.

Contested concepts in European Union foreign policy

Each of the concepts employed in this book is or has been the object of a debate in the literature. For this reason, it is fundamental that a common set of definitions is provided so that misunderstandings may be avoided.

European Union foreign policy

Given the particular nature of the EU, the conceptualisation of EU foreign policy is more complicated than is the definition of foreign policy in a state context. For clarification, we can point to three branches of literature that provide differing understandings of the term.

Under the label of CFSP/CSDP (Common European Security and Defence Policy) studies are those works that deal solely with Pillar II issues. This branch of studies focus on the *CFSP institutional machinery* (for example, Eliassen 1998). Attention is also devoted to EU crisis management (Jørgensen 1997) and to the development of a defence component to the CFSP (Missiroli 2000; Howorth 2001).

Unlike the previous focus on CFSP/CSDP, the second branch of literature deals primarily with *member states' foreign policy*. This used to be the predominant approach when the EU's own foreign policy was not developed and cooperation in the foreign policy field was limited to European Political Cooperation (Hill 1983; Ifestos 1987; Pijpers *et al.* 1988; Holland 1991; Nuttall 1992). Since then, despite the creation of a CFSP and more recently of a CSDP, member states' foreign policies continue to exist and play a significant role in the definition of a European foreign policy stance (as the 2003 transatlantic rift on the Iraqi war showed all too clearly). Inevitably, many studies of EU foreign policy deal, more or less exclusively, with EU member states' foreign policies (Manners and Whitman 2000; Lucarelli 2000).

A third branch of literature focuses attention more specifically on the *external relations of the EC* – Pillar I – or specific policies within it (international trade; economic cooperation, development aid, etc.). Even when dealing with the EU as an international actor at large, these studies refer more to the EU's external economic relations than to its CFSP capacities (Piening 1997; Dent 1997; Lister 1997, 1998a; M. Smith 1998).

These branches of literature illuminate three aspects of the complex area of EU foreign policy that we claim here should not be separated. What all the contributors adopt here is an inclusive definition of EU foreign policy which encompasses all three aspects discussed above, although putting more emphasis on the EU as a political system rather than on its member states. In other words, we are looking at *EU foreign policy as the political actions that are regarded by external actors as 'EU' actions and that can be considered the output of the Union's multilevel system of governance in foreign policy* – EU FP (see White 1999; also Peterson and Sjursen 1998; K. Smith 1999; Bretherton and Vogler 2006; H. Smith 2002).

Values, images of the world, and principles

The other key terms employed here are by no means less controversial than 'EU FP'. The controversial character of these terms is extensively discussed in Knud Erik Jørgensen's chapter three; what I want to do here is to formulate some working definitions that will be used in the book's case studies.

Values – starting with the more abstract of the three terms, we define 'values' as notions laden with an absolute (i.e. non-instrumental) positive significance for the overall order and meaning we try to give to our world. General examples of values include, for instance, 'freedom', whether as a moral or a political concept. Further examples are summarised in the titles of the Charter of Fundamental Rights – dignity, liberty, equality, solidarity, justice. It should be stated that values are not necessarily of a moral type and that almost any notion can be claimed to be of value within a given community. An understanding of the relationship between different values, the interpretation which is given to them and their actual translation into principles of action, is crucial to the analysis of common identifications around a certain set of values.

Images of the world – or worldviews (*weltbild*) are the pictures we have, based on our experiences and cultural traditions of the relationships between the physical and social worlds. For example, a Copernican or Ptolemaic view of the solar system; whether the (astrological) stars, gods, or bacteria and viruses are the causes of disease; whether individuals or groups are the base elements of human agency and the ultimate bearers of human dignity. Images of the world provide the cognitive frame within which values are defined and translated into principles and political action. They are thus sensitive to changes in their political context.

Principles – are normative propositions that translate values into general 'constitutional' standards for policy action. The mode of translation depends on how values are interpreted according to a particular worldview and the underlying cultural traditions – freedom has a very different meaning according to an individualistic-liberal or communitarian-collectivistic view of the social world. Our focus on principles allows us to understand how constructed EU values are turned into principles of action. In terms of the actions that we are seeking to explain, our focus on principles allows us to encompass loosely constituted ideals and potentially instrumentalist policies.

Relations among values, images and principles – values are not automatically translated into principles, or principles into policies. In examining a political and social system such as found in the EU, attention is given to how far this 'translation' has succeeded, or shared values and principles have failed to influence legislation and behaviour. These circumstances are an additional reason (beside the definitions given above) for not looking at these terms as synonyms.

Furthermore, our focus on 'values' as well as on 'principles' and 'images' gives us a tool of comparison between the EU and other international actors that might help us understand more about the nature of the EU. For example, we could run into a universally acclaimed value that is translated by the EU into a principle, but by other international actors into another, even opposite, principle with significant policy implications. Thus, within the EU Charter of Fundamental Rights, 'dignity' is recognised as a value on the basis of which it is affirmed that 'everyone has the right to life' (chapter 1, article 2.1) and 'no one shall be condemned to the death penalty, or executed' (chapter 1, article 2.1). This implies that the 'right to life' (as an expression of the value of dignity) is prior to any other value and should be read together with an interpretation of the value of 'justice', where justice does not translate into a directly proportional punishment for the offence. This is clearly not the case in the non-European states where the death penalty, amongst other cruel and unusual punishments, is applied.

Particularly interesting is the case of the different interpretations on the two sides of the Atlantic given to the value of 'liberty' in the context of *freedom of speech*. While in the US blasphemy and racist speech are treated in the same manner (there is a right to both on the basis of a right to free speech), in the EU blasphemy is legal because it is an attack on ideas, while racist speech is illegal because it is considered as an attack on a person (Haarscher 2001: 98–101).

Finally, focusing on all values, principles and images offers us a better tool to learn more about the processes of European integration. If and when we find values that do not translate into principles, the effort to understand why and how this uneven translation takes place will shed some light on the nature of the Union and its transformation.

Political identity

If references to the political identity of the EU are frequent in the official documents and the political speeches of EU leaders, as we saw at the beginning of this chapter, there is also a growing academic attention to this issue. As happens with most concepts, the term assumes different meanings according to the theoretical approach taken. In the first place, it should be specified that in this book we deal with *political* identity, which we keep separated from a *cultural* identity.

Views in the literature about relationship between cultural and political identity diverge significantly. If we look at the variety of positions regarding EU *political* identity, a set of ideal-type positions can be suggested:

1 Political identity is/should be based on cultural identity:

> *'Neo-nationalists'* – in the case of political identity conceived as possible only in nation-like communities, the possibility of EU political identity is regarded sceptically, if not denied (A. Smith 1992). Political loyalty, in these conceptions, is linked to a cultural similarity that is missing in multinational political systems such as the EU. Thus, this position is regarded as 'essentialist' (Delanty 1995; Calhoun 2001; Manners and Whitman 2003) in that identity represents the 'essence' of a nation which is pre-given with little possibility of constructing an EU political identity over time.

> *'European culturalists'* – if the requirements for cultural identity are less stringent and go beyond elements such as a common language, to look at

common cultural heritage of classicism, humanism, renaissance, Christianity etc., then common cultural roots may be found and a political identity can be developed with the recognition of these historical-culturally shaped similarities. Here political identity is not pre-given; it is 'constructed' predominantly through shared cultural experiences (Cerutti and Rudolph 2001b). Calls for the introduction of references to Europe's Christian roots in the preamble of the EU Constitutional Treaty pointed in this direction. However, despite the claimed differences, references to the enlightenment or romanticism also respond to the same logic of the malleability of European cultural heritage.

'Civilisationalists' – in contrast, if cultural identity is predetermined by civilisational fault-lines, then European cultural identity might be regarded as a sub-set of Western civilisation and an EU political identity might follow the same lines – political identity *does follow* cultural identity according to Huntington (1996).

Most of the above studies however, with the exception of the 'neo-nationalists', do not theorise the precise relationship between cultural and political identity and how a common culture creates the basis for a common political identity. This, on the contrary, is done by those who focus attention on *political* identity in the first place.

2 Political identity is/should be a 'constructed' phenomenon that does not indispensably need the recognition of common cultural roots. These 'post-nationalists' can be put into two groups (although very close to one another):

'Communicative' – an EU political identity should be engendered through a process of public communication among citizens. The creation and development of an EU public sphere (which does not deny national public spheres) is the indispensable condition for the gradual affirmation of a European *demos* with a shared political identity. This is the position of Jürgen Habermas (2001) who regarded the debate on a European constitution to be crucial in the creation of an EU public sphere, the definition of broad objectives for the integration process and the definition of a common constitutional asset. From this perspective, the elements around which a political identity is created have to do with a process of communication among EU citizens about what political actor they want to create and with what purpose. Communication and 'politics' are the key words. Elements of a common culture are present but not particularly relevant.

'Functionalists' – for this group of scholars, political identity is a construct that is not, and should not be, derived directly from a common culture (although they do not deny the importance of a common culture). The main idea is

that all 'politics', 'policies' and common historical experiences matter for the construction of an EU political identity (Cerutti 2001a, 2003, 2005).

In this book, we share a post-nationalist perspective and we define political identity as the set of social and political values and principles that Europeans recognise as theirs and give sense to their feeling of belonging to the same political entity. Such values and principles do not by themselves shape the identity – they need to be interpreted. Culture, history, legal practices and institutions are the frameworks within which political values are interpreted and, thereby assume meaning. In this perspective, identity is not a 'given' but part of processes of self-identification by the individuals in a group, in which foreign policy is particularly important. The way we conceive our international role (Holsti 1970; S. Walker 1987; Aggestam 1999) is functional to the way in which we conceive ourselves; at the same time, the way we 'perform' our role feeds back into our political identity. A credibility crisis (if not a true form of democratic deficit) can take place when the political entity of reference (a state, the EU) does not perform the foreign policy its citizens expect it to perform. However, the degree of impact on political identity of foreign policy – and the group's concern for such impact – is different in groups characterised by a different self-esteem of the maturity of their political identity. In the case of a political identity in-the-making, like the EU, the processes of self-identification are particularly sensitive to the image that the political group demands of itself through its politics and policy, including foreign policy. In particular, through EU foreign policy, EU citizens:

1   experience the proclaimed common values and principles applied;
2   experience a certain type of international actor developing;
3   have the opportunity to debate core political values (e.g. use of force, role of international law, the role of solidarity and justice in world politics);
4   see the image of Europe that the rest of the world sees, through which communities recognise themselves both for the similarities and the differences with respect to significant 'others'.

Through EU foreign policy, the *existence* of an EU political community – with its values and principles – is made clearer to EU citizens and to the rest of the world.

Research framework

A common set of questions

So far we have provided some working definitions of the concepts employed and a discussion of relationships that exist between values and principles, foreign policy and identity. The common research approach employed in this book requires that we now develop a common set of questions to be addressed in the case studies.

Empirical research on values in foreign policy involving multidisciplinary research presents a number of difficulties for comparative analysis. In order to overcome these difficulties, we agreed on a set of common questions that guide each chapter, and can be summarised in four questions:

1   What are the values and principles that shape EU external behaviour? Furthermore, to what extent is the EU building an international role for itself on the basis of these values and principles? To what degree is the EU prepared to engage in political conflict in order to safeguard these values and principles?
2   Where do these values and principles originate?
3   Are EU values and principles specifically European, Western (with a European interpretation), or universally recognised values and principles?
4   What role does the external projection of values and principles play in the EU identity formation process? How does this process contribute to the construction of an identity that differentiates the EU from significant 'others' (e.g. the US, Russia, China)?

Methodology

How can we study VIPs in foreign policy? What should we look at? Are we looking for VIPs as the 'real causes' of foreign policy? And how would we detect the presence of VIPs in EU foreign policy? These are some of the difficult questions that this book has to confront. In providing collective guidelines, we set out a firm methodological approach based on the four questions discussed above, together with a shared interpretivist approach.

As we have seen, we share an understanding of VIPs as inevitably present in a political process but this does not mean that they are the only causal factor behind action. As the literature suggests, VIPs might be present in a number of ways. They may provide road maps that help to select among a set of preferred courses of action (Goldstein and Keohane 1993). They can represent the objective/final aim of a foreign policy, for example, the expansion of democracy as an aim in itself, with the only other aim to construct 'a better world order'. VIPs may simply help in the selection of instruments to pursue an aim, for example, the exportation of democratisation in order to achieve security. Finally, VIPs may provide the basis for a legitimising discourse (rhetorical argumentation). The contributors were encouraged to examine various forms of VIPs in EU FP, but stress was placed on not looking for unrealistic links between VIPs and political decisions. Thus, all the contributors to the book were clear in the shared questions and the interpretivist methodological approach used in the comparative analysis of EU foreign policy. By interpretivist, we mean an emphasis on the understanding of the EU policy process as socially situated, with an emphasis on the analysis of the self-understandings of those involved in these processes (Winch 1994). This methodology involves the analysis of both primary and secondary sources (of a predominantly qualitative nature), with the understanding that we are attempting to interpret these sources within the context in which they are bound (Geertz 1973).

Organisation of the book

In the rest of the book we look at EU values and principles from three slightly different perspectives with an emphasis on theory (chapters 2 and 3); specific VIPs (chapters 6 to 9); and specific foreign policy areas (chapters 4, 5, 10 and 11). These three perspectives allow us to trace the relationships between EU VIPs and EU foreign policy in both directions – i.e. from political theory, through broad political values, to policy outcomes, and in the other direction by deconstructing how foreign policy outcomes are informed by VIPs.

In chapter two, Ian Manners examines the constitutive nature of values, images and principles in the EU. The VIPs present in the Union's international conduct, affirms Manners, are not simply idealistic symbolism in the pursuit of EU material gains, but they are the defining elements of a polity which is constructed differently to pre-existing political forms, and that this particular difference pre-disposes it to act in a normative way. The chapter documents the historical evolution of EU values, images and principles and shows how they permeate contemporary EU foreign policy. The chapter also looks at the way in which the EU's VIPs are seen by actors outside of the Union, before finally reflecting on the way in which self-perceptions and external perceptions, together with policy practices co-constitute the international identity of the EU.

In chapter three, Knud Erik Jørgensen provides an analysis of the ways major IR theoretical traditions – Liberalism, Realism and the English School – have conceptualised VIPs, and an understanding of the ways contending conceptions of VIPs play a role (or not) in theories of foreign policy. Jørgensen shows that the controversial nature of these terms is confirmed by the different meanings they assume in different theoretical traditions. As for the relationship between VIPs and foreign policy, Jørgensen warns that VIPs cannot provide a valid guide for policy as contending principles are frequently present. In this context, choice of principles is ultimately made by decision-makers. Jørgensen is clearly critical of unreflexive research projects, but his chapter reinforces the importance of the rest of the book. Contesting principles and values are always present in the EU, thus the fact that certain VIPs are chosen, keep re-emerging and are even endorsed through legal and political practices tells us something very important about the EU political system and its foreign policy.

Chapter four starts the series of case studies with Ian Welsh's analysis of the role of VIPs in science within the EU. It makes a comparison between the EU and the US and between older 'big science' projects (nuclear fusion and space exploration) and 'emergent' domains such as biotechnology where EU policy is still in a process of contested consolidation. It is argued that the EU can *potentially* articulate a set of value-based science stances distinguishing it from the US in a range of areas with significant environmental and social implications that simultaneously have implications for the external image of the EU. This potential can only be realised if ways can be found of securing consensus between member states on a science agenda consistent with the centrality of the citizen within EU primary legislation.

Specific EU principles are shown to be at work in the case of EU global environmental policy. In chapter five, Susan Baker looks at the EU's and US's climate change policies, reaching the conclusion that transatlantic divergences on this issue are driven by marked differences in how the environmental *problematic* is understood, as well as the relative weight given to environmental and to economic values on the two sides of the Atlantic. Despite differences among the EU member states, there is a general consensus in Europe that environmental protection cannot be left to market forces. This consensus is endorsed through a set of clearly defined and articulated environmental principles, primarily shaped by the concern for sustainable development.

In chapter six, Andrea Pető and Ian Manners analyse gender protection by the EU with reference to enlargement and development policy. Pető and Manners show how the value of equality has been slowly transposed into EU legal principles through employment law in the 1970s and 80s, leading to the development of 'gender mainstreaming' in the 1990s. They juxtapose the steady development of gender equality values and principles within the EU with those encountered in the accession states and through development cooperation. The process of eastern enlargement has involved encounters and negotiations between the different understandings of gender equality found in the EU's 'liberal feminism' and Eastern Europe's 'statist feminism'. The parallel, yet radically different processes of development cooperation have involved the gradual mainstreaming of gender issues into relations with ACP countries in particular since 2001. Pető and Manners argue that gender equality is one of the most distinctive, yet highly problematic, principles in EU FP (as enlargement and development clearly demonstrate).

Chapters seven and eight deal specifically with two of the most well-known values of the EU – democracy and human rights. In chapter seven, Rosa Balfour analyses three EU regional strategies – enlargement to Central and Eastern Europe, stabilisation strategy in the Western Balkans, and the Euro-Mediterranean Partnership – in order to trace the development of the EU's norms and instruments in support of democracy and human rights. The analysis shows that the EU, more than any other international actor, has matched its commitments by developing a legal basis for promoting human rights and democracy promotion, and has equipped itself with sets of tools for this purpose. However, this idealistic image is counterbalanced by the chapter's critical approach that demonstrates not only a 'flexible adherence to principles' (i.e. inconsistency), but also that the main driving force behind the EU's push towards democratisation and respect of human rights in CEEC and SEE is security concerns, by contrast with the Southern Mediterranean where security and human rights are tied together only rhetorically.

The analysis of EU democracy and human rights promotion continues with Stefania Panebianco's analysis of EU relations with Russia and China in chapter eight. In this informative chapter, Panebianco is critical about reading the EU's policy as exclusively value guided and stresses the security concerns that guide EU policy in these areas. It shows the inconsistencies of such a policy and the difficulties that the EU encounters when trying to export a culturally bound concept of human rights that is by no means as 'universal' as it might appear. The author also engages in an interesting discussion of the way in which EU democracy and human rights promotion with Russia and China serves as an important element in the construction of EU identity as distinct from that of other actors who are also building relations with these countries, such as the US, WTO, and APEC.

In chapter nine Roberto Menotti and I deal with the troublesome area of the EU's use of force. The chapter starts by acknowledging that the prevailing security discourse in the EU regarding coercion and force are only rarely conceivable. Indeed, the 'structural' nature of the EU's external action confronts a serious challenge when facing the dilemmas of coercion. One of the cases in which the EU has conceived the use of force is when human rights are at risk, namely in the case of *humanitarian intervention*. Menotti and I claim that a distinctive political dynamic – manifested during the 1990s and not yet fully crystallised – has led the EU to read all cases of crisis management in the 1990s as cases of humanitarian intervention. This has turned into a specific approach to the use of force that is now pushing the EU toward gradually accepting a wider notion of intervention (as the 2003 EU intervention in the Congo demonstrated), for which, however, it is not ready in terms of capabilities nor in terms of conception of its overall international role.

Shifting policy area, in chapter ten Federico Bonaglia, Andrea Goldstein and Fabio Petito analyse the VIPs in the EU's Development Cooperation Policy (DCP). By making a comparison between the VIPs informing the EU's documents in the DCP field and EU actual policy in sub-Saharan Africa, the authors reach a number of interesting conclusions. First, textual analysis reveals that the promotion of sustainable development, social justice, democracy and human rights are the fundamental principles of the EU's DCP, whose overarching objective is the eradication of poverty. However, this is at odds with the second point that aid is not necessarily directed towards the poorest countries as commercial interests, the recipient government's stance, and the behaviour of other donors all influence the EC's aid giving. Third, although it is difficult to claim that the VIPs in the EU's DCP are unique, the way in which they are implemented is. For instance, the greater emphasis on people-oriented development, poverty reduction, gender equality and sustainable development can be traced back to EU VIPs.

In his chapter eleven study on the EU's policy in multilateral trade negotiations, Adrian van den Hoven examines a specific EU worldview of globalisation – one that requires the establishment of common rules for the world market – labelling it 'regulatory capitalism'. In particular, the chapter analyses EU, US, and Canada's views of the WTO and then analyses the EU position in some specific problem areas – agriculture, textiles, services, investment, intellectual property rights, environment, consumer rights, social standards, competition rules, development. In each area, van den Hoven seeks to determine the extent to which the EU's position is primarily a reflection of interests or values. The overall conclusion is that EU values have some impact on its trade policy in the WTO – although we cannot claim that these values are interest free, there is evidence that in certain cases, values take precedence over interests in trade policy.

In chapter twelve, Ian Manners and I summarise our results through a discussion of the values, images and principles in EU foreign policy that have been analysed throughout the book. The conclusion provides an opportunity to bring together the comparative findings of our study by reflecting on the project as a whole, the values and principles of EU foreign policy, the way in which these principles are implemented, as well as some of the theoretical insights into the EU and Europeans' identities. What is clear is that we have seen evidence of several identifiable ways in which principles are put into practice in EU foreign policy. These include the institutionalisation of principles, the role of regulation, use of structural prevention, inclusion of civil society, working through partnership, the problems of consistency, and concerns for double standards. In the conclusion, we argue that the EU values principles in the conduct of foreign policy, but equally importantly, that the conduct of these policies plays a significant role in shaping both policy and EU identity.

Notes

1 For brevity I will generally refer to the EU despite legal distinctions between the European Community (EC) and the EU.
2 The two are distinct although correlated concepts, as the first refers to the way in which 'the EU is constituted, constructed and represented internationally' (Manners and Whitman 2003: 383), while the second refers to Europeans' sense of belonging to the same political and social entity.

2 The constitutive nature of values, images and principles in the European Union

Ian Manners

> Europe needs to project its model of society into the wider world. We are
> not simply here to defend our own interests: we have a unique historic
> experience to offer. The experience of liberating people from poverty, war,
> oppression and intolerance. We have forged a model of development and
> continental integration based on the principles of democracy, freedom and
> solidarity – and it is a model that works. A model of a consensual pooling
> of sovereignty in which every one of us accepts to belong to a minority.
>
> (Romano Prodi 2000: 3)

The quote from Romano Prodi serves several purposes in this chapter – first
and foremost it illustrates the extent to which the President of the European
Commission's understanding of the EU was clearly located in the notion of a
European model, rather than the naked pursuit of European interests. But it
also tells us something about the nature of Prodi, his speechwriters, and the
shared self-understandings of the Commissioners and their cabinets. The speech
talks not of the EU, but of Europe; it talks not of 'own interests', but of being
here to share interests; it talks not of utopia, but of horrendous experiences; it
talks not of expediency, but of principles; and finally it talks not of majoritarian
politics, but of a consensual model. So for those behind the speech, the European model is spoken of as part of a European understanding of self, history,
principles, and politics.

Whether this is hyperbole, rhetoric, contested discourse, or simply a speech,
what is important is that the EU's relations with the 'wider world' are self-evi-
dently informed by a series of values, images and principles (VIPs) which are not
unimportant. What I wish to do in the rest of this chapter is to follow Sonia
Lucarelli's conceptual introduction with a more conceptual discussion of the
values and principles which constitute the EU as a 'hybrid polity' (Manners
2002: 240). My more constitutive discussions of European values and the principles within the EU will serve as a useful foundation for Knud Erik Jørgensen's
following chapter on theorising VIPs in foreign policy. My chapter will first
engage in a multiperspectival discussion of constructions of 'Europeanness' from
the five perspectives of economics, society, the environment, conflict, and politics. Second, I will describe what I have observed to be nine constitutive values

and principles within the EU, ranging from the liberal democratic (such as peace, liberty and democracy) to the social democratic (such as equality, solidarity and sustainable development). Finally I will discuss the ways in which these values and principles constitute the EU as a hybrid polity and contribute to co-existing and competitive EU self-images.

Ultimately it may be that any claims to the uniqueness (and potential superiority) of European values run the risk of ending up as vacuous and meaningless as the 'Asian values' debate. During the debate many argued that respect for authority and an emphasis on community were responsible for the Asian economic boom of the 1980s and 90s (see discussions in M. Thompson 2001; Dittmer 2002; and Wiessala 2002). In contrast, 'Western values' of moral decay and excessive individualism (including democracy and human rights) were argued to be responsible for relative Western economic decline during the same period. Some even went as far as to argue that it is possible to contrast the 'European way of thinking' as Cartesian with the 'Asian way of thinking' as holistic (Servaes 2000: 58–59). However, it is quite clear that these sorts of arguments based on elite discourses are used by some Asian governments as 'pretexts for resisting calls for democracy and human rights' and that we must look at 'who has the power to determine such values and definitions' (Kyi Aung 1995: 11–12). Hence, as Catarina Kinnvall argues, we need to understand both the issues of culture and context in order to make sense of 'the message of authoritarian leaders concerning so-called "Asian values"' (Kinnvall 2002: 9).

European perspectives

After five hundred years of internationalising trade patterns, fifty years of superpower domination, and at least thirty years of globalising sociocultural practices, are there any distinctively European perspectives on life? In this first section, I will attempt to identify what I consider socially constituted shared European perspectives that provide the cultural context in which a discussion of the EU must sit.

With the cautionary tale of 'Asian values' foremost in our minds, we can now turn to the question of considering five general European perspectives without falling into the trap of allowing elite discourses to subvert universal rights and values (such as democracy and human rights in Asia). The obvious difficulties of differentiating between supposed Western perspectives and those of Europe make this a difficult task. The countries of the developed world, in particular members of the Organization for Economic Cooperation and Development (OECD), share far more than they disagree on. However, I believe it is possible to make an argument for European perspectives that are capable of differentiating Europe from countries such as the USA, Canada, Australia, and New Zealand. In order to do so, I will compare and contrast Europe and the world from the five perspectives of economics, society, the environment, conflict, and politics (see Buzan 1991; Manners 2000b and 2006). As part of this comparison, Figures

2.1–2.7 compare aggregate data from the EU 25 states, weighted by population, with the 10 most populous countries in the world (plus Canada, Australia and New Zealand). Only the 13 most populous EU states are illustrated in the figures.

Economic perspective

European economic perspectives are generally characterised by reference to 'solidarity' – the belief in a social market economy characterised by income redistribution, government intervention, and stakeholder capitalism (Hutton 2002: 343). Many observers argue that the European economy is focused on 'socially-regulated economic governance' (Burgoon 2001: 62). This European capitalism is built on 'a sounder foundation of social acceptability. ... [in which] income transfers and guarantees of European social security systems can be defended as a politically necessary insurance against discontent and social instability' (Strange 1998: 111–112). European economic solidarity involves government intervention and expenditure, rather than simple regulation. It also involves a commitment to tackling economic inequalities, including those caused by regional disparities and structural economic change.

As Figure 2.1 illustrates, average levels of economic solidarity, measured in terms of inequality and poverty, reflect this European social market economy. While average GDP per capita in the EU remains among the highest in the world (with Luxembourg having the highest), Figure 2.1 suggests that European economic solidarity is reflected in relatively low levels of inequality and poverty. Among the developed world, average EU inequality is higher than that of Japan and Canada, but lower than the US, New Zealand, and Australia. In comparison, average EU relative poverty levels are the lowest in the developed world.

Clearly there is considerable divergence between EU states, in particular between the relatively wealthy small European trading states (Luxembourg, Ireland, Denmark, and the Netherlands), and the relatively impoverished new EU member states (Latvia, Lithuania, Poland, and Estonia). However, such simple dichotomies do not explain the differences in European economic solidarity. The degree of relative inequality is largely determined by the difficulties in coming to terms with the new European economy. Hence Europe's most equal states are those that have adapted most readily to the new economic realities of post-Cold War Europe (Hungary, Denmark, Sweden, and Belgium). In comparison, Europe's most iniquitous states are those that have faced tremendous economic challenges in post-Cold War Europe (Portugal, Estonia, Italy, and the UK). In contrast, the level of relative poverty is more clearly determined by the socio-economic structures of the country. Hence, higher levels of relative poverty are to be found in those states with greater structural imbalances (Italy, the UK, Estonia, and Ireland), than those with more fair socio-economic structures (Czech Republic, Finland, Luxembourg, and Sweden).

However, the argument that Europeans share a socially constituted economic perspective is still valid – Europeans relate their high levels of development to the achievement of economic solidarity; they value their low levels of inequality because they believe them *integral* to their high levels of development; and as a result Europeans cherish the lowest relative poverty levels in the developed world. This sharing of beliefs about development, equality and relative wealth contributes to Europe seeming *fairly* different to much of the world.

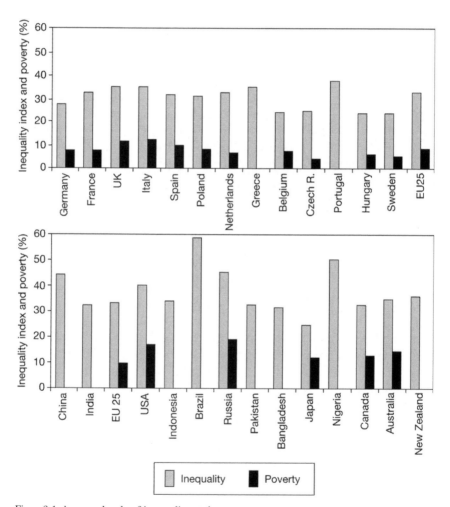

Figure 2.1 Average levels of inequality and poverty
   Note: Inequality index – Gini index measuring inequality over the entire distribution of income or consumption. A higher number indicates greater inequality.
   Relative poverty – percentage of population living below 50% of median income.

Source: UNHDR: 150–151; 188–191

Social perspective

European social perspectives are also characterised by reference to 'solidarity' – the belief in a European social model encompassing social legislation, social welfare and social infrastructure investment. Although most authors agree that there is no one 'European social model' there is a strong argument that high levels of spending, broad social programmes and considerable employment protection are found across Europe (Kleinman 2002: 57–58; and Gough 1998: 90). Additionally, 'a solidaristic wage policy', 'detailed social security provisions', and 'good social investment in human and social infrastructure capital' are all seen to be part of these European social models (Schulten 2002: 173; CMLR 1993: 445; and Gough 1998: 90). European social perspectives are located in 'a certain normative core of social liberalism [which] still provides a formative background for social solidarity' (Habermas 2003a: 10). These observations lead to the argument that 'social legislation is one of the few fields in which Europe is a real world leader' (CMLR 1993: 445).

As Figure 2.2 illustrates, average levels of social solidarity, measured in terms of percentage of GDP spent by the government on education, health and the public sector reflect this European social welfare commitment. Figure 2.2 suggests that average EU public expenditure on social welfare is the highest in the world. European social solidarity is reflected in high levels of public-sector education, health, and welfare provision. Among the developed world, average EU public expenditure on education and health is below that of New Zealand, Canada, and the US, and broadly comparable to that of Australia and Japan.

There appears to be considerable divergence between EU states, in particular between the relatively developed welfare states of Northern and North-Western Europe (Denmark, Sweden, France, Belgium, Austria, Germany, and Finland), and the developing states of Eastern Europe (Latvia, Lithuania, and Slovenia). Although relatively high levels of public expenditure in Poland and Greece, and relatively low levels of public spending in Ireland, suggest that geographical differences are not so very important in this respect.

Although there are differences, the argument that Europeans share socially-constituted social perspectives is still valid – Europeans believe in high levels of public sector expenditure *because* of the importance they give to social solidarity; they value some of most extensive public education and health systems in the world (shared with other industrialised countries) because they deem them *integral* to their commitment to social solidarity and development; and as a result Europeans cherish some of the highest literacy rates and longest life expectancies in the world (UNHDR 2004: 139). This sharing of beliefs about education, health and social welfare contributes to Europe seeming *noticeably* different to much of the world.

Environmental perspective

European environmental perspectives are characterised by a commitment to a more 'sustainable development' – an attempt to reconcile economic growth with protection of the environment in both the short and long term (Baker 1997: 91). European environmental sustainability includes the mainstreaming of environmental issues into economic, development, and social policies, as well as legal commitments to the 'precautionary principle' (Baker 1997; Bäckstrand 2001; Usui 2003). Such progressive legalisation has extended to including environmental protection in the European Convention on Human Rights, the Charter of Fundamental Rights of the European Union, as well as extraterritorial environmental measures by the EC (Desgagné 1995; Hedemann-Robinson 2000).

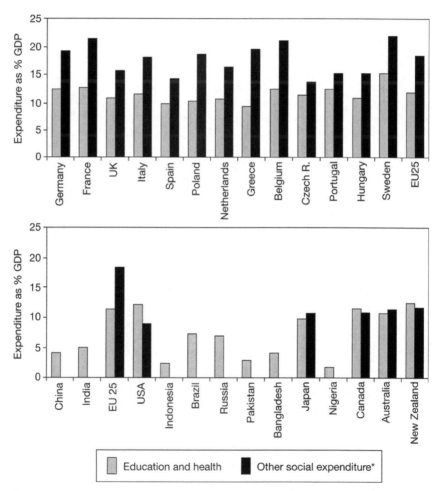

Figure 2.2 Average levels of education, health and other social expenditure

Note: *OECD members only for 'Other social expenditure'

Sources: UN Human Development Report 2004: 202–205; and OECD Social Expenditure Database 2004

As Figure 2.3 illustrates, average levels of environmental sustainability, measured in terms of GDP per unit of energy use, ecological footprint, and CO_2 emissions reflect this European commitment to sustainable development: Figure 2.3 suggests that average EU levels of energy use are among the more efficient in the world. Amongst the ten largest countries in the world, Bangladesh, Brazil and Japan have higher levels of GDP per unit of energy use. As expected, the

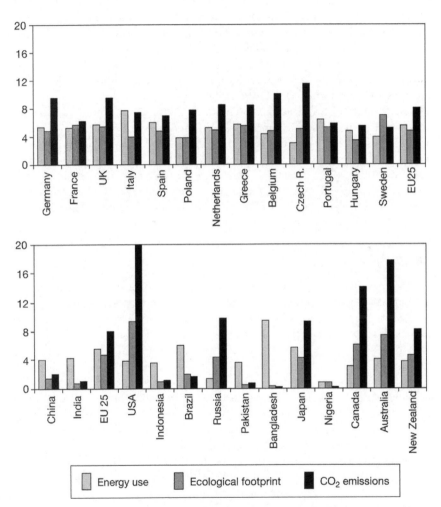

Figure 2.3 Average levels of energy use, ecological footprint and CO_2 emissions
   Note: Energy use – GDP per unit of energy use (PPP US$ per kg of oil equivalent). A higher figure indicates a more efficient use of energy in the economic activity of the economy (UN Human Development Programme 2004: 207–210).
   Ecological footprint – the total area required to produce the food and fibres consumed, sustain energy consumption, and provide space for infrastructure (1 hectare of average biological productivity per person). A higher figure indicates a larger footprint, and thus a less sustainable lifestyle (WWF 2004: 24–31).

average EU ecological footprint and CO_2 emissions are higher than those of the developing world, but are lower than those of the US, Australia, Canada, New Zealand, Japan, and the emissions of Russia.

Again, there is significant divergence between EU states, largely dependent on a combination of relative level of development, urbanisation, and latitude (i.e. mean air temperatures). Thus relatively developed member states, such as Italy, Denmark and Ireland, have higher levels of GDP per unit of energy use, whereas relatively developing member states, such as Estonia, Slovakia, and the Czech Republic have lower levels of GDP per unit of energy use. Urbanised Luxembourg and rapidly developing economies such as Estonia and Ireland have the largest ecological footprints and the highest levels of CO_2 emissions, compared to rural and less energy-dependent Latvia and Lithuania which have smaller footprints and lower CO_2 emissions.

Despite these divergences, it is still the case that Europeans share socially-constituted environmental perspectives – Europeans value more efficient levels of energy use *because* of their history of industrialisation and urbanisation; they believe in lowering their ecological impact and CO_2 emissions because this is *integral* to their ideas about achieving more sustainable lifestyles in densely populated Europe. This sharing of beliefs about energy use of sustainability, together with relative ecological impact and CO_2 emissions, contributes to Europe seeming *sustainably* different to much of the world.

Conflict perspective

European conflict perspectives are characterised by a commitment to a more 'sustainable peace' – resolving both the structural causes and violent symptoms of conflict (Manners 2005). European sustainable peace involves addressing the structural causes of conflict through extensive development aid policies and support for bottom-up, local development programmes that tackled the roots of inequality such as health, education, and infrastructure. In contrast, European states also contribute significant amounts of resources to military research, technology and forces, in particular through participation in the North Atlantic Treaty Organisation (NATO). This uneasy compromise between peaceful development policies and interventionist military capabilities is further compli-cated through long standing European participation in United Nations (UN) peacekeeping missions. This compromise has been demonstrated in the com-plexities of the three most visible military interventions involving European forces in the former Yugoslavia, Afghanistan and Iraq.

As Figure 2.4 illustrates, average levels of military expenditure and UN peacekeeping forces reflect this European commitment to sustainable peace. Figure 2.4 suggests that the average EU military expenditure is above that of most of the world, but significantly below that of the five militarised states of Pakistan, Russia, the USA, China, and India. The average contributions by EU member states to UN peacekeeping operations is significantly smaller than those of Nigeria, Bangladesh, Australia, and Pakistan, but greater than those of most of the developing world, in particular the insignificant contributions of China and the USA.

As expected, there is considerable divergence between the EU states, depending on historical experiences and recent security concerns. The level of military expenditure is largely determined by historical experiences such as colonial empires providing the foundations of large forces for UN Security Council members France and the UK, or neutrality ensuring small forces in Ireland, Austria and Malta. More recent security concerns in Greece ensure

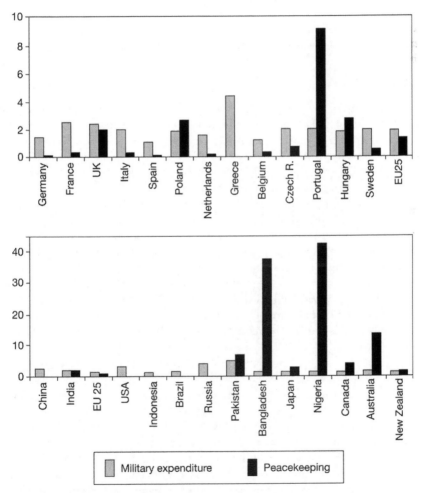

Figure 2.4 Average levels of military expenditure and UN peacekeeping forces
    Note: Military expenditure – 2002 public spending on military resources as a percentage of GDP (UN Human Development Programme 2004: 202–205).
    Peacekeeping – 2003 UN peacekeeping forces per 1,000 military personnel (Kaldor *et al* 2004: 286–290).

that it has the highest level of military expenditure in the developed world. In contrast, the contributions to UN peacekeeping forces are determined by a mixture of factors, including neutral internationalism (Ireland and Austria), NATO-driven capabilities (Slovakia, Poland and Hungary), and more liberal internationalism (Portugal and the UK).

Once more, the argument that Europeans share socially-constituted conflict perspectives is still valid – Europeans believe in contributing to extensive development aid programmes and maintaining relatively high levels of military preparedness at the same time *because* of historical experiences of addressing the structural causes and violent symptoms of conflict; they value participating in UN peacekeeping missions as *integral* to their internationalist commitment. This sharing of beliefs about contributions, capabilities, and commitments contributes to Europe seeming *principally* different to much of the world.

Political perspective

European political perspectives are characterised by 'cosmopolitical supranationality' – the belief in multilayered politics shaped by a vibrant international civil society, more equal rights for women, the pooling of sovereignty, and supranational law. European cosmopolitical supranationality involves the recognition that domestic politics and international politics are deeply interdependent. It also reflects the post-war birth of cosmopolitan Europe as a reaction to the modern Europe of nation-states (Beck 2003; Habermas 2003a). The pooling of sovereignty within Europe has made all European states, and especially EU members, far more accepting of post-national politics in the 21st century (Rabkin 2000; Ward 2003). The cosmopolitical perspective reflects this interplay between the solidarist activities of civil groups and the supranational legal structures above the state, or as Pascal Lamy put it, 'the notion of cosmopolitics describes a new world that is coming into being. ... More generally, cosmopolitics may simply be about thinking globally and acting locally' (Lamy 2004a: 13 and 20; see also Cheah and Robbins 1998; and Archibugi 2003).

As Figures 2.5–2.7 illustrate, average levels of cosmopolitical supranationality, measured in terms of density of international civil society, the empowerment of women and participation in cosmopolitan international law reflect these European political perspectives. As Figures 2.5–2.7 suggest average EU cosmopolitical activity is among the highest in the world. The average density of European international civil society is greater than most of the world, with only Australia, Canada and New Zealand close. The average level of women's empowerment is higher in Australia, Canada, New Zealand and the US than in the EU, although five EU states have higher averages than Australia (Sweden, Denmark, Finland, the Netherlands, and Belgium). The average number of significant international laws ratified by EU member states is the highest in the world, with only New Zealand, Australia, and Brazil relatively close.

Clearly there is considerable divergence between EU states, depending on the level of development, and entry into international society. The density of international civil society is largely determined by the entry and participation in international society, with recently independent states having the lowest density (Poland, Lithuania, and Slovakia for example) and internationalist states such as Belgium, Luxembourg, and Netherlands having the highest density (although the presence of EU institutions in Belgium and Luxembourg has a huge impact). The degree of women's empowerment is largely determined by level of development, but in addition the Northern European states have achieved the highest levels in the world (for example, Sweden). In comparison, less developed states such as Malta, Cyprus, Lithuania, and even Greece have lower levels of women's empowerment. Finally, the number of ratified cosmopolitan international laws is determined by the entry and participation in international society, led by 13 European internationalist states with 31 ratifications, traced by the

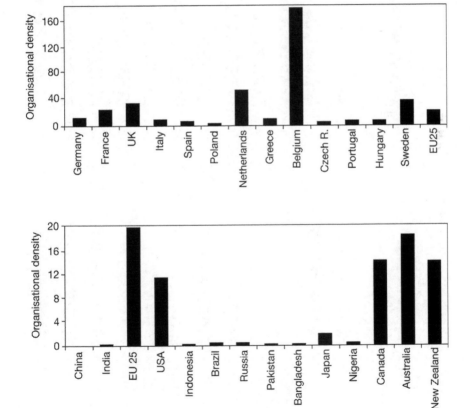

Figure 2.5 Average density of international civil society

Note: International civil society organisational density is the number of internationally-oriented non-governmental organisations (in 2003) per million population (Kaldor *et al* 2004: 297–302)

more recently independent states of Latvia (26), Estonia (27), Czech Republic (28), and Poland (28).

However, the argument that Europeans share socially-constituted political perspectives is still valid – Europeans enjoy dense and active international civil societies partially *because* of their relatively internationalised public spheres; they value higher levels of women's empowerment *integral* to their higher levels of development (particularly in Northern Europe); and they believe in actively

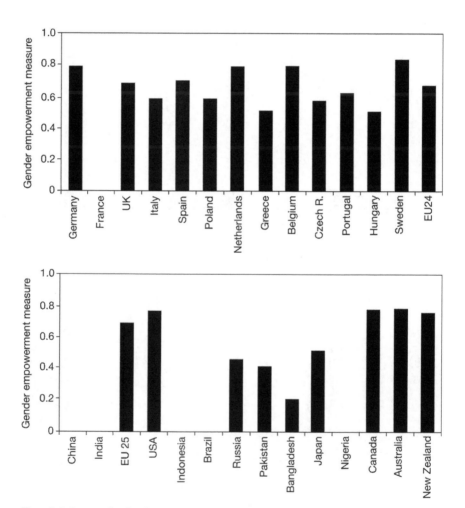

Figure 2.6 Average levels of women's empowerment

> *Note:* UNDP Gender Empowerment Measure based on women's participation in politics and professional employment, and female income ratio (UN Development Programme 2004: 221–224).

participating in cosmopolitan international law in ways which make Europe seem *significantly* different to much of the world.

This combination of five European perspectives constitute the cultural context within which EU relations with the rest of the world are conducted. It is important to note that statistical data *proves* nothing but might *illustrate* something. Figure 2.8 illustrates how this interface between the 'star' of Europe and the 'circle' of the world could be represented.

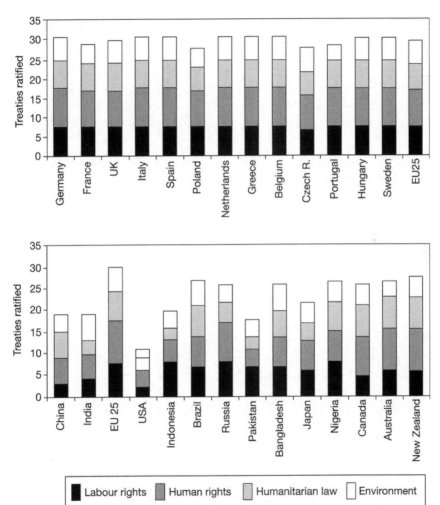

Figure 2.7 Average number of international law treaties ratified
  Note: International law treaties ratified include eight ILO labour rights conventions, ten human rights instruments, seven humanitarian laws, and six environmental treaties. The highest number possible is 31.

Sources: UN Human Development Report 2004: 207–210, 238–245; and Kaldor *et al.* 2004: 264–269.

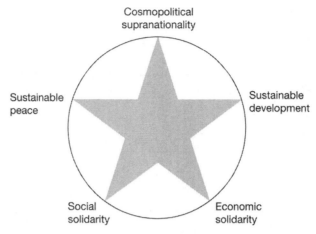

Figure 2.8 European perspectives

European Union values and principles

Article I-2: The Union's values

> The Union is founded on the values of respect for human dignity, free-
> dom, democracy, equality, the rule of law and respect for human rights,
> including the rights of persons belonging to minorities. These values are
> common to the Member States in a society in which pluralism, non-dis-
> crimination, tolerance, justice, solidarity, and the principle of equality
> between women and men prevail.

Article I-3: The Union's objectives

> 4. In its relations with the wider world, the Union shall uphold and pro-
> mote its values and interests. It shall contribute to peace, security, the
> sustainable development of the earth, solidarity and mutual respect among
> peoples, free and fair trade, eradication of poverty and protection of
> human rights, in particular the rights of the child, as well as to strict
> observance and development of international law, including respect for the
> principles of the United Nations Charter.

As Articles I-2 and I-3 of the Constitution for Europe illustrated, over the past
fifty years the EU has developed a series of constitutive values and wider
objectives in the world. I have elsewhere identified nine norms that, I will now
argue, are constitutive of the EU as a hybrid polity and as part of its international identity in world politics (Manners 2000a: 32–34; 2002: 242–243;
Manners and Whitman 2003). Clearly, as the values identified in Article I-2 are
shared with the world's liberal democracies, I will clarify particular EU interpretations of these constitutive values. In contrast, the wider objectives

promoted in Article I-3 are more specific to the way progressive social democracy is constitutive of the EU. In both cases I shall suggest how values are
translated into principles guiding EU policies.

Sustainable peace

The first EU value is peace – Robert Schuman's opening words on 9th May
1950 provided the historical *raison d'être* for European integration; 'world
peace cannot be safeguarded without the making of creative efforts propor-
tionate to the dangers which threaten it'. Reiterated again in the preambles of
the European Coal and Steel Community (ECSC), the Treaty establishing the
European Community (TEC), and the Treaty on European Union, Article I-3
of the Constitution for Europe was to establish peace as the EU's primary
objective: '1. The Union's aim is to promote peace, its values and the well-being
of its peoples.'

The particular EU interpretation of this value is the principle of *sustainable*
peace (see Manners 2005). As discussed under European conflict values above,
the EU approach to conflict prevention emphasises addressing the roots or
causes of conflict, mirroring the European experience of ensuring that war
'becomes not merely unthinkable, but materially impossible'. The EU policy
emphasis is placed on development aid, trade, interregional cooperation, political dialogue, and enlargement as part of a more holistic approach to conflict
prevention. However, the EU's growing civil and military operational capacity
also has a *sustainable* peace mission with its focus on 'peace-keeping, conflict
prevention and strengthening international security in accordance with the
principles of the United Nations Charter' (Article I-41, Constitution for Europe).

Social liberty

The second EU value is liberty – freedom within a social context. Liberty,
similar to the principles of democracy, rule of law and human rights, was codified as a founding principle by the revised article 6 of the consolidated Treaty on
European Union after the Amsterdam summit in 1997. The Charter of fundamental rights of the European Union adopted at the Nice European Council in
December 2000, and incorporated into the Constitution for Europe, develops
the EU understanding of liberty. Title II of the Charter sets out 19 freedoms,
starting with Article II-6: 'Everyone has the right to liberty and security of
person.'

The particular EU interpretation of this value is the principle of *social* liberty.
Liberty within the EU operates within a distinctive socio-legal context. Thus,
liberty is always just one of several rights held alongside other, equally important, values such as democracy, rule of law and human rights. Therefore, within
the EU *social* liberty is circumscribed by the need to ensure that other values are
not compromised by unwarranted freedoms, such as anti-social behaviour, hate
crimes, inflammatory speech, and pornography. The wider implications of EU

social liberty are significant, not least in references to 'protection of children's rights' as a foreign policy objective, as EU extraterritorial legislation on 'sex tourism' illustrates.

Consensual democracy

The third EU value is democracy – the promotion of a particular form, organisation and philosophy of political life. The participation and requirements of democracy have been a constitutive value of the EU since its birth, with Schuman arguing in the French National Assembly in 1948 that 'we intend to prepare for its [Germany's] admission to a peaceful, democratic organisation of European nations'. Thus, from the inception of the ECSC until 1970, democracy was the membership condition of the EC. This value was clarified in the 1970 Luxembourg Report which stated that a 'united Europe … must assemble democratic states with freely elected parliaments'. Following the end of the Cold War and the 1990 Charter of Paris for a new Europe, the EU was far more explicit in the promotion and requirements of democracy for membership (Copenhagen Criteria 1993), for development aid (Resolution on Human Rights, Democracy and Development 1991; conditionality clauses 1995), and in its foreign policy provisions.

The particular EU interpretation of this value is the principle of *consensual* democracy. *Consensual* democracy is the operating principle within the majority of EU member states and includes proportional representation electoral systems, coalition governments, and power sharing amongst parties. Similarly, the EU itself is a consensual form of polity, with PR and power sharing in the European Parliament, non-majoritarian voting in the Council (either Qualified Majority Voting or unanimity), and power sharing amongst all the member states. The EU has helped to spread *consensual* democracy into Central and Eastern Europe as part of the transition and accession processes.

Associative human rights

The fourth EU value is human rights – one of the most visible and promoted values of the post-Cold War era. Alongside democracy and the rule of law, respect for human rights was made explicit in the December 1973 Copenhagen Declaration on 'European Identity' (Manners and Whitman 1998: 236). Within Europe, human rights law had been progressively developed through the European Convention on Human Rights, and the interpretations of the European Court of Justice during the 1960s and 70s, culminating in the 1977 joint declaration recognising human rights as general principles of law. The 1980s saw the European Parliament being particularly proactive in advocating human rights, while the renegotiations of the Lomé Conventions provided the first examples of human rights promotion, finally enshrined in the 1989 Lomé IV Convention. By the 1990s, similar to democracy, human rights were given prominence in the Treaty on European Union (first through article F, then article 6) and are now promoted through conditionality clauses in enlargement and development policies.

The particular EU interpretation of this value is the principle of *associative* human rights. *Associative* human rights include both individual human rights and collective human rights. These are *associative* because they emphasise the interdependence between individual rights such as freedom of expression and collective rights such as the right of association. The associative nature of EU human rights has developed since 1973 through the 1986 Declaration of Foreign Ministers of the Community on Human Rights and the 1991 Resolution of the Council on Human Rights, Democracy and Development. All of these documents emphasise the universality and indivisibility of these *associative* human rights with *consensual* democracy, *supranational* rule of law, and *social* solidarity (see also Article III-292, External Action general provision, Constitution for Europe).

Supranational rule of law

The fifth EU value is the rule of law – the political foundations provided by just legal systems and equal protection for all. The rule of law is seen to be essential for ensuring the stability and success of the other liberal-democratic values of liberty, democracy, and human rights. Hence, these four values are to be found promoted through development aid, CFSP, and the Copenhagen membership criteria, amongst others. The Constitution for Europe sought to ensure that the rule of law continued to be promoted in external action and international relations, but with additional references to 'the strict observance and the development of international law, including respect for the principles of the United Nations Charter' (Article I-4).

The particular EU interpretation of this value is the principle of *supranational* rule of law. As suggested under European political perspectives above, the EU principle of the rule of law is supranational in three senses – communitarian, international, and cosmopolitan. First, the EU principle of communitarian law promotes the pooling of sovereignty through the *acquis communautaire* – the supranational rule of law within the EU. Second, the EU principle of international law encourages participation by the EU and its member states in supranational law above and beyond the EU (Manners and Whitman 2003: 399). Third, the EU principle of cosmopolitan law advances the development and participation of the EU and its member states in humanitarian law and rights applicable to individuals (Manners 2002: 241).

Inclusive equality

The sixth EU value is equality – the legal prohibition of discrimination together with proactive policies to promote equality. Equality has recently become one of the most promoted constitutive values discussed here, moving from a relatively narrow focus on preventing discrimination based on nationality to the far broader and prominent value of equality in Article I-2 of the Constitution for Europe. In the 1990s, the focus of equality expanded beyond nationality to include equality between men and women (TEC article 2), protection of minorities (Copenhagen Criteria), and 'action to combat discrimination based on sex, racial or ethnic origin, religion or belief, disability, age or sexual orientation' (TEC article 13).

The particular EU interpretation of this value is the principle of a more *inclusive*, open ended and uninhibited understanding of which groups are particularly subject to discrimination. Hence, the Constitution for Europe included references to the prohibition of discrimination 'based on *any ground* such as sex, race, colour, ethnic or social origin, genetic features, language, religion or belief, political or any other opinion, membership of a national minority, property, birth, disability, age or sexual orientation' in Article II-81 (Charter of Fundamental Rights of the Union, emphasis added). One weakness with the implementation of this principle is the extent to which discrimination based on nationality is still widespread in a majority of member states. This is particularly true of employment practices in consensual societies that promote homosociality (Roper 1996).

Social solidarity

The seventh EU value is solidarity – the promotion of the social economy, the social partnership, and social justice within the EU, and in relations with the developing world. Alongside the values of democracy, rule of law and respect for human rights, *social* solidarity has been emphasised as a value in the 1973 Copenhagen Declaration, 1986 Foreign Ministers Declaration, 1991 Council Resolution, 2000 Charter of Fundamental Rights of the Union, and the Constitution for Europe. The Charter of Fundamental Rights makes these principles explicit with its Title IV on solidarity, including workers', family, health and social security rights.

The particular EU interpretation of this value is the principle of *social* solidarity. The extensive understanding of *social* solidarity became clear as the objectives of Article I-3 of the Constitution for Europe referred to 'balanced economic growth, [and] a social market economy, aiming at full employment and social progress', combating 'social exclusion', as well as promoting 'social justice and protection', inter-generational solidarity, and social solidarity among (and between) member states. The principle of *social* solidarity goes beyond inner-EU relations to inform and shape EU development and trade policies as Article I-3 also illustrates when it refers to the Union's contribution to 'solidarity and mutual respect among peoples, free and fair trade, eradication of poverty'.

Sustainable development

The eighth EU value is sustainable development – a commitment to 'development which meets the needs of the present without compromising the ability of future generations to meet their own needs' (Brundtland 1987: 5). This commitment, and the difficulties of reconciling economic and environmental interests, has evolved slowly since the initial 1972 declaration by heads of member states on Europe's environment (Baker 1997: 92). The December 1988 Declaration on the Environment, the June 1990 Declaration on the Environmental Imperative, and the Treaty on European Union all contributed to the codification of the value of sustainable development in the Fifth Action Programme on the Environment and Sustainable Development (Manners 2000b: 77).

The particular EU interpretation of this value involves an emphasis on the dual problems of balance and integration. The EU principle of sustainable development is intended to provide a balance between uninhibited economic growth and biocentric ecological crisis: 'it seeks to promote balanced and sustainable development' (preamble to the Charter of Fundamental Rights) and 'shall work for the sustainable development of Europe based on balanced economic growth' (Article I-3 of the Constitution for Europe). In parallel, the principle also involves the integration, or mainstreaming, of sustainable development into the policies and activities of the Union (Articles II-97 and III-119 of the Constitution for Europe). The EU seeks to promote these principles of sustainable development beyond Europe through its enlargement, development, trade, environmental and foreign policies (Articles I-3 and III-292 of the Constitution for Europe).

Good governance

The ninth EU value is good governance – the provision of open, participatory and democratic governance without creating hierarchical, exclusionary and centralised government. Good governance is the most recent value to develop within the EU, specifically reflecting its external promotion through enlargement and development policies, and the concerns of internal accountability and democracy within the EU. The value has its origins in the dual concerns for encouraging stable institutions through the accession process (1993 Copenhagen Criteria) and the international spread of human rights, democracy and development through good governance (1991 Council Resolution).

The particular EU interpretation of this value emphasises equality, representation, participation, social partnership, transparency and accountability in 'the democratic life of the Union' (Constitution for Europe). The EU principle of good governance has two distinctive elements that have both significant internal and external consequences – the participation of civil society and the strengthening of multilateral cooperation. Since the Commission Presidency of Romano Prodi, 1999–2004, significant emphasis has been placed on the promotion of good governance through the participation of civil society in order to encourage openness and transparency, as well as to facilitate democratic participation (Articles I-47 and I-50 of the Constitution for Europe). In parallel, the unilateral invasion of Iraq has ensured that member states have strengthened their commitments to the promotion of 'an international system based on stronger multilateral cooperation and good global governance' (Article III-292 of the Constitution for Europe).

The complex interaction of these nine values and principles is constitutive of the EU's relations with the rest of the world. Figure 2.9 illustrates the pyramid of the EU values and principles motivating and mediating the Union's external actions.

European Union self-images

To conclude the chapter I would like to reflect on three views that help to characterise the complex and often contradictory European Union self-images, as constituted by the five European perspectives and nine EU values and principles. I think it is important to note the extent to which these three views reflect European 'co-integration' (a mixture of intergovernmental cooperation and supranational integration) through which 'the EU has evolved into a hybrid of supranational and international forms of governance which transcends Westphalian norms' (Manners 2000b: 28; 2002: 240). The first article of the Constitution for Europe, Article I-1 'Establishment of the Union', reflected this intertwining of cosmopolitan politics (a union of citizens), supranational politics (a union of states) and state politics (member states confer competence) thus:

> Reflecting the will of the citizens and States of Europe to build a common future, this Constitution establishes the European Union, on which the Member States confer competences to attain objectives they have in common.

Figure 2.9 European Union values and principles

In order to capture this hybridity I will call these three views *state* Europe, *supranational* Europe, and *cosmopolitan* Europe. *State* Europe is a self-image of the EU as being constructed from liberal-democratic member states who choose to confer competence on the Union. Taking a positive view, the self-image of state Europe is one where member states are the bearers of Kantian civil constitutions and thus democracy, as well as French republican values of *liberté*, *égalité*, and *fraternité*. However, taking a negative view, the self-image of state Europe is one where the EU is viewed as being responsible for 'the decline of European nation-states as principles of economic and political organisation':

> The project of European unification has in fact triggered a wave of reactions that are simultaneously anti-European and racist. As Stuart Hall put it, the great resistance against European union, as well as American suspicion of it, is a defensive response to a process of effective overcoming of the very idea and reality of European nation-states.
>
> (Griffin and Braidotti 2002: 11)

Supranational Europe is a self-image of the EU as a union of states representing the Kantian pacific federation (*foedus pacificum*), as well as the supranational incarnation of European identity:

> A complex set of deeply historical values issuing from the Greco-Latin synthesis, a constellation of ideas about the rights and obligations of human beings that emerged from the Renaissance, and a set of politico-moral principles that served as the motor for the American and French Revolutions.
>
> (Burgess 2002: 467)

Zygmunt Bauman refers to supranational Europe as being driven by the 'logic of local retrenchment' in which the EU 'stems the tide' of globalisation by 'reconstructing at the Union level the legal-institutional web which in the past held together the "national economy" within the boundaries of a nation-state's territorial sovereignty – but no longer does' (Bauman 2004: 136).

Cosmopolitan Europe is a self-image of the EU as a union of people promoting the Kantian cosmopolitan rights of hospitality to strangers, common rights to the earth's surface, and universal community (Kant 1991: 105–106). In this respect the cosmopolitan self-image is one in which the EU constitutes a decisive break with all previous political and legal history:

> Cosmopolitan Europe was consciously conceived and launched after the Second World War as the political antithesis to a nationalistic Europe and the physical and moral devastation that had emerged from it. Cosmopolitan Europe was founded as something that struggles morally, politically, historically, and economically for reconciliation.
>
> (Beck 2003: 33–34)

In contrast to the logic of local retrenchment in supranational Europe, Bauman describes cosmopolitan Europe as being driven by the 'logic of global responsibility' in which the EU seeks 'lasting and truly effective solutions to the planet-wide problems ... through the renegotiation and reform of the web of global interdependencies and interactions' (Bauman 2004: 137).

Figure 2.10 illustrates these three self-images, and the political beliefs which differentiate them. European Union self-images lie somewhere among the views identified above. *State* Europe has a tendency to promote a state-centric world-view often characterised by pluralist approaches towards the rest of the world. As Knud Erik Jørgensen explains in the next chapter, pluralists believe that a diversity of states constitute international society. The relationships between Europe and the UN are a good example of state European self-images – a desire to develop international society sometimes hindered by 'national interests'. *Supranational* Europe has a tendency to promote regional integration as a worldview sometimes characterised by the prioritisation of European concerns in relations with the rest of the world. The debates and concerns over the creation of a 'fortress Europe' serve as a good example of the complexities of a supranational European self-image. *Cosmopolitan* Europe has a tendency to promote globalism as a worldview that may be characterised by 'the role of the European Union as a promoter of norms which displace the state as the centre of concern' (Manners 2002: 235–236). This globalist outlook towards 'solidarism' (an emphasis on universalist rights) is sometimes weakened by the international legal framework which tends to be dominated by 'pluralism' (an emphasis on particularist rights, usually held with respect to the state). The role of Europe in negotiating international legal instruments such as the WTO, the Kyoto Protocol and the International Criminal Court all serve as examples of a cosmopolitan self-image.

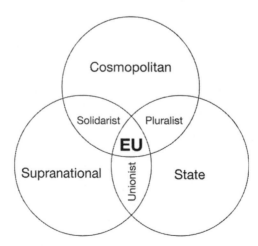

Figure 2.10 European Union self-images

All five European perspectives, and nine EU values and principles, can be discerned as playing a constitutive role in shaping the EU as a hybrid polity, as well as EU self-images and EU relations with the rest of the world. Hence, EU values and principles such as democracy, liberty, and equality are to be found in the common practices of the EU member states. EU values and principles such as peace are to be found in the supranational practices of the Union itself. EU values and principles such as human rights, sustainable development, and social solidarity are to be found in the cosmopolitan practices of the EU hybrid polity in world politics. Finally, EU values and principles such as the rule of law and good governance are to be found in the combination and interaction of these three EU self-images – state, supranational and cosmopolitan.

Finally, I will end with a simple but critical warning – any and all of the values and principles discussed in this chapter are not uniquely European, and neither is Europe. Claims I have made about relative EU attachment to a particular combination of values and principles largely reflect fairly recent (post-World War, post-Cold War) practices and constructions that can be undone as quickly as they have been achieved. Furthermore, as Edward Said and Shirin Ebadi have spent their lives reminding us, all human beings share universal values such as human rights, justice, and dignity, as participants in the building of the perpetual peace of humanity, something we should never forget (Triggs 2003, UNHDR 2004: 23).

3 Theoretical perspectives on the role of values, images and principles in foreign policy

Knud Erik Jørgensen

Introduction

Do values, images and principles belong to the 'soft' benign dimension of foreign policy? Do values, images and principles belong to the stuff that makes high politics, or, to the repertoire of window dressing? Are we dealing with 'luxury goods' that will most likely be abandoned if national or European interests are at stake? How does an ethical dimension of foreign policy relate to other dimensions? These and similar questions invite further reflection. Hence, the contemporary research agenda on the promotion of democracy, human rights, ethics, normative power, values, and principled behaviour. Consequently, a particularly good reason to make sense of key concepts such as values, images and principles (VIPs).

Research on conceptions of VIPs involves at least five analytical problems. First, the terms belong to the class of essentially contested concepts, making it a major task to account for their different meanings. We should, thus, expect that theorists conceptualise VIPs differently – rather than expect some kind of neutral, shared language. Even translations between theoretical languages may pose problems. Because there is no shared language, it obviously makes little sense *a priori* to thoroughly describe the 'precise' or true meaning of each term or possible linkages between them and, in turn, compare the 'correct' meaning to conceptualisation within the theoretical traditions.

The second problem emerges when we ask whether it is self-evident that VIPs are playing in the same league, and, if they are, how they are related? One solution would be to perceive images as related to issues of identity and worldviews, to regard values and principles as constituting part of normative superstructures. Policy belongs to a sphere of its own, related to but not determined by normative superstructures. Following this line of thinking would imply that three loosely connected spheres are created and the terms structured.

Third, there is the problem of conceptual 'relatives', i.e. notions that are synonyms or next-door conceptual neighbours. Thus, some would argue that principles are closely connected to but not identical with norms and rules, perhaps suggesting a distinction between political, moral and legal principles.

It is part of the conceptual game to specify the connection and argue for the distinction. In the context of the present chapter, it is useful to make a distinction between systemic and foreign policy principles. Hence, some regard principles as the grand organising principles of international society: capitalism and the free market, human rights and secular liberal democracy, and the nation-state framework of international relations (Fuller 1995). Others have a profound interest in principles guiding actors in the exercise of prudent statecraft (Kennan 1995). Turning to images, the notion seems to be a broader term than both 'values' and 'principles'. In other words, images belong to the cluster of phenomena where we also find issues of identity, recognition and worldviews. John Garnett offers a broad view on conceptual connections, writing about, 'an internal coherence of the facts, rules, ideas, concepts, values which, taken together, make up images of reality relevant to an understanding of international politics' (1984: 21). Though Garnett does not include principles, 'images' appear to subsume both values and principles. Finally, several authors distinguish between particularistic and universal values. In the case of particularistic values, they can be either country-specific or regional: American, Asian or European (Payne 1995; M. Thompson 2001). But does it make sense to speak about distinctly European values and principles? Generally, foreign policy actors may wish to project images of their country internationally (Coles 2000). In this context, the notion of value promotion gains relevance. Values can also be connected to principles, as in Kenneth Thompson's characterisation of a moralist, 'The moralist inflates the place of values by sanctifying short term and parochial interests, absolutising higher goals into rigid principles that obstruct the political process, and raising moral formulations to the level of irrelevance' (1992: 135).

The fourth problem is that the notions are employed in both discourses of foreign policy practice and in discourses of theory, i.e. employed both by policy makers and policy analysts. The precise relationship between these discourses is contested. Some reject the distinction, arguing that discourses of foreign policy constitute just one single realm: practice is theory – theory is practice. Though the argument carries some weight, I will nevertheless make an analytical distinction and throughout focus on discourses of theory.[1]

The final problem concerns the precise relationship between VIPs and the conduct of foreign policy. Which role should we expect VIPs to play when explaining foreign policy? Should it be the role of an independent variable, an intervening variable or some third role? In the case of the European Union (EU), this problem is even squared because we have foreign policy at both Union and member states level.

The purpose of the chapter is to provide an analytic review of the ways major International Relations' (IR) theoretical traditions have conceptualised VIPs, and to seek an understanding of the ways contending conceptions of VIPs play a role (or not) in theories of foreign policy. Luigi Bonanate defines in a most useful way tradition as, 'a corpus of centuries of research, characterized by classics, schools of thought, original proposals and a specialized debate' (1992: ix). Thus, the notion of 'tradition' connotes something quite loose but at the same time sufficiently coherent to qualify as a body of knowledge. Needless to say, endless debates can be conducted about what it takes to be a 'tradition', about the nature of traditions and about the relative importance of various schools and currents. The prime reason for taking the point of departure in traditions is that such a perspective enables a structured account of the role values, images and principles play – according to major theories. If, by contrast, only specific theories had been accounted for, it would have been very difficult to examine dialectics between general and specific lines of reasoning.

The chapter will focus on three major traditions: liberalism, realism and the English School. Realism is often said to be a tradition reaching back to Thucydides or Machiavelli. In this respect, the English School is more modest, only claiming Grotius as the originating philosopher. Liberalists in turn often quote Kant, Locke or Montesquieu as those who launched the liberal tradition. Each of the traditions includes 'branches' or currents of thought. In the case of realism, a distinction will be made between classical realism, neorealism and post-neorealism. Concerning the English School, I adopt the conventional distinction between pluralists and solidarists. Finally, liberalism will be subdivided into weak and strong liberalism. Each of the traditions and currents contains several substantive schools and theories. While these theories include more or less explicit claims about foreign policy in general and the role of VIPs specifically, they do not necessarily have an identical nature. Indeed, the term theory often refers to different kinds of theory, serving different functions and asking different kinds of questions (Myers 1990; Brown 1997; Jackson 2000). This fact makes comparison difficult and sometimes even nonsensical.

Liberalism

Liberalism is a rich tradition of thought, drawing on a wide range of philosophical and political ideas. It is one of the major traditions in international relations theory. Indeed, liberalism plays a unique role in the history of IR. In the early twentieth century, it was *part of the liberal project* to establish an academic discipline on international relations, specifically in order to improve our understanding of such relations. In short, IR was originally *founded by* liberal thinkers and therefore created in the *image* of key liberal ideas. Since then, liberalism has developed through several phases. Being a tradition, liberalism has many intellectual sources. Some of these sources are directly related to values, images and principles; including the idea that human nature is basically good, provided that human beings have the right conditions for their development. One of the purposes of politics should therefore be to provide for such 'right conditions'. In general, the twentieth century has not been friendly to liberalism, developing in the shadow of three systemic wars: the First World War (1914–18), the Second World War (1939–45) and the Cold War (1947–91), and significantly being marked by these wars.

Main strands of contemporary liberal theory

Contemporary liberalism can be divided into two major groups with distinct natures: weak and strong liberalism. Weak liberalism is 'weak' because it accepts many of the premises of realism. Strong liberalism is 'strong' because its representatives are less inclined to 'give in' to criticism informed by realism or other traditions. Let us have a look at each current in turn.

Robert Keohane is among the main representatives of weak liberalism. One should note that weak liberalism belongs to the liberal tradition because some of the basic liberal assumptions remain in place. Thus, Keohane professes that, 'I am a child of the Enlightenment – a chastened child, to be sure, but nevertheless a believer in the *possibility* of progress, though by no means in its inevitability' (1989: 21). For a while, in the early 1980s, Keohane flirted with game theory and formal models but then concluded, 'that it was unlikely that greater formalization derived from game theory would provide a clear structure for precise and insightful investigation of world politics' (1989: 29). Instead he created neoliberal institutionalism, a perspective on world politics, *not* a theory as such. The perspective focuses partly on international institutions and their functions and, partly on state interests. According to Keohane,

> Neoliberal institutionalism is not a single logically connected deductive theory, any more than is liberalism or neorealism; each is a school of thought that provides a perspective on world politics. Each perspective incorporates a set of distinctive questions and assumptions about the basic units and forces in world politics. Neoliberal institutionalism asks questions about the impact of institutions on state action and about the causes of institutional change; it assumes that states are key actors and examines both the material forces of world politics and the subjective self-understanding of human beings.
>
> (Keohane 1989: 2)

His view on cooperation is important for understanding his conception of the role of VIPs:

> International cooperation does not necessarily depend on altruism, idealism, personal honor, common purposes, intellectual norm, or a shared belief in a set of values embedded in a culture. At various times and places any of these features of human motivation may indeed play an important role in processes of international cooperation; but cooperation can be understood without reference to any of them.
>
> (Keohane 1989: 159)

In other words, Keohane's version of liberalism does not depend on many of the factors characterising other strands of liberalism. Instead he strikes a balance between 'material forces' and 'subjective self-understandings'.

Neoliberal institutionalism is a perspective operating at the international system level, focusing on the interplay between states and international institutions and asking questions about state behaviour – rather than questions about state identity. To the degree subjective factors are included, it is the self-understandings and beliefs of human beings that are prioritised, rather than inter-subjective understandings or images. In other words, the perspective does not ask questions about social or ideational structures and their impact on state identity or behaviour (Goldstein and Keohane 1993). While Keohane has devoted much attention to neoliberal institutionalism, termed a systemic perspective, he has been less engaged in research on foreign policy. The volume *Ideas and Foreign Policy* (co-edited with Judith Goldstein 1993) makes an exception. Though VIPs do not figure prominently as such, attention is given to the role of 'individual' ideas and beliefs. In response, Wendt (1994) points out that including subjective factors does not equal an inclusion of social factors. Consequently, factoring in the 'beliefs or ideas' of *individuals* does not make Goldstein and Keohane part of the constructivist turn in IR.

Keohane deliberately distances himself from two other liberal schools of thought:

> my arguments diverge from those of much liberal international political theory. Liberalism in international relations is often thought of exclusively in terms of what I have elsewhere called *republican* and *commercial* liberalism. Republican liberalism argues that republics are more peacefully inclined than despotisms. In its naïve version, commercial liberalism argues that commerce leads necessarily to peace.
>
> (Keohane 1989: 11)

In other words, Keohane subscribes to neither the 'strong liberal' democratic peace argument nor to 'naïve' versions of commercial liberalism. In research on the EU, weak liberalism is best represented by Andrew Moravcsik's (1998) liberal intergovernmentalism. Similarly to Keohane's neoliberal institutionalism, Moravcsik creates his theoretical framework on a rationalist, material platform, thereby defining the role of VIPs out of his research agenda.

Strong liberalism

Unlike weak liberalism, strong liberalists do not begin with the basic assumptions of realism. According to Wendt, they do not adopt an exclusively behavioural approach, according to which, 'process and institutions may change behaviour but not identities and interests' (Wendt 1992). Furthermore, strong liberals do not assume states to be the dominant actors in the system and, finally, they do not define security exclusively in 'self-interested terms'. Strong liberals want more. The 'more' they want differs, meaning that also strong liberalism comes in different varieties.

First, the democratic peace proposition: democracies are more peaceful than non-democracies. In other words, Kant was right (Doyle 1983). The proposition – that domestic forms of governance *do* have effects on international relations – tends to be verified regarding relations among democracies which rarely fight each other. This conclusion is very significant. The logical follow-up argument is that if democracies do not fight each other, well, then we had better promote democracy worldwide. However, principles for doing so vary. Some states emphasise the power of playing role model. Other states engage in missionary like activities – actively promoting democracy, so to speak. Still other states engage in crusades – directing their non-pacific energies towards non-democracies. In fact, some liberals are so fond of democracy and individual freedom and rights that they are ready to promote such values by almost all means. Therefore it is not entirely unjust to talk about liberal interventionism, even the label 'B52 liberals' has been employed.

The second version of strong liberalism attempts to keep a prudent course in the difficult waters between pacifism and bellicism. Some cultivate the doctrines or principles of 'just war', for instance Richard Falk at Princeton University, arguing that by all means states should avoid war but if they do engage in war, they should adhere to just war principles. In other words, war is not regarded as merely a naked exchange of power but as a social institution embodying numerous rules, norms and principles.

Alexander Wendt (1999) represents a third version of strong liberalism, having created a constructivist liberal theory of international cooperation. According to Suganami (2000), 'when all its theoretical décor is stripped, the architectural substance of his *Social Theory of International Politics* turns out to be a structurationist/symbolic interactionist answer to Robert Axelrod's earlier path-breaking work on the evolution of cooperation'. On the one hand, it is telling that the book is entitled strikingly similar to the main work of Kenneth Waltz (1979). This similarity signifies that Wendt's theoretical ambition is to build a systemic theory, yet emphasising social rather than material structures. Furthermore, Wendt's theory is 'robust' in the sense that it can deal with a significant number of key questions. Yet such a theory does not please the more 'pure' schools of thought. Why then categorise Wendt within strong liberalism? Primarily because he emphasises a process-perspective which, in fact, somewhat dilutes his state-centrism. In his view, constructivists and strong liberals share a lot

> with respect to the substance of international relations (...) both modern and postmodern constructivists are interested in how knowledgeable practices constitute subjects, which is not far from the strong liberal interest in how institutions transform interests. They share a cognitive, intersubjective conception of process in which identities and interests are endogenous to interaction, rather than a rationalist behavioral one in which they are exogenous.
>
> (Wendt 1992)

Essentially, he criticises his fellow strong liberals for not working with social theories matching their interest in the substance of social ontology. It seems to me that Wendt's theory is too abstract to be directly applicable in research on foreign policy. It should, however, be possible to derive a theory of foreign policy. His notions of identity and interest can be linked to images, just as his focus on social and ideational factors could be linked with values and principles. It remains to be seen if such expectations can be met.

Debates between weak and strong liberals have dealt with a number of issues. One of these issues concerns the specific role of VIPs in foreign policy. The literature on international regimes is highly relevant here because the so-called consensus definition includes as elements 'sets of implicit or explicit principles' [...] understood as 'beliefs of fact, causation and rectitude' (Krasner 1982). In general, Krasner's definition brings principles together with norms, rules and procedures. Given the purpose of the chapter, there is no reason to go into regime analysis as such. What is important, however, is to understand that in drawing the analytical consequences of this definition, we find one of the sources of 'the great divide' between constructivist and rationalist approaches to the study of international institutions (Kratochwil and Ruggie 1986; Keohane 1989).[2] Hence, a matrix combining the dimensions of approach (constructivism and rationalism) and level of analysis (systemic and state level) defines the potential growth area of liberal conceptions of the role of VIPs.

Realism

Realism cannot be described as anything else but a well-established theoretical tradition; sometimes it plays the role as theoretical hegemon, at other times it is among the prime revisionist powers; thus it always plays at centre court of our multipolar discipline. However, realism is widely perceived as having nothing to offer studies of ethics and identity, indeed realism is often presented as antithetical to such issues. For many critics, realism's *raison d'être* is to be there in order to have something to blame or criticise. Therefore realism often plays the humiliating role of a straw man. Alternatively, the tradition is simply ignored, 'because the realist view is fairly well known' (Smith and Light 2001: 4–5). By contrast, Chris Brown (2001) and others claim that this image of the realist tradition is 'pop-realism' in the sense that it is both widespread *and* largely unfounded. Crucially, he points out that pop-realism is, on the whole, unfounded in both theory and state practice. Brown adds that, 'the notion that action can only be described as ethical if motives are absolutely pure and untainted by self-interest is bizarre, and, as suggested above, unsupported by any plausible moral philosophy' (Brown 2002: 182).[3] Such contending views on realism and ethics explain why realism should be one of the three selected theoretical traditions. Contending views simply invite an account for realism's take on the role of VIPs in foreign policy. During the twentieth century, realism has developed within three distinct currents: classical realism, neorealism and post-neorealism. Each current has its own distinct conception of the study of foreign policy in general and of the role of values, images and principles specifically.

Classical realism

Classical realism comprises a large number of theorists and can only be described as a very rich current, thriving before social science techniques were developed. Classical realism is foremost a blend of political theory, IR theory and historical analysis. The space available does not allow for an exhaustive analysis of classical realism. Instead Hans Morgenthau, Inis Claude and George Kennan will be presented as illustrative examples.[4]

Morgenthau's strong emphasis on politics, power and the national interest is unsurprising, particularly if one takes into consideration that he has been deeply influenced by Carl Schmitt's conception of politics and that he wrote a PhD thesis at the University of Munich in 1929 on the limits of international law vis-à-vis international politics. Similar to Michel Foucault, Morgenthau thinks power is ubiquitous, implying that it is naïve, at times dangerously naïve, to believe in 'power-free' zones. Furthermore, there is a direct link between power and politics, indeed power is regarded as the essence of politics. Finally, by means of foreign policy instruments, states (and their representatives) will always do their utmost to further what is perceived to be in their national interest. Thus far, everything described is set for creating contradictions like interests vs ethics – or realists vs normative theorists. Even a superficial reading of *Truth and Tragedy* (Thompson and Myers 1984) or the annual *Ethics and International Affairs* suggests that such contradictions are false. In general, founders of realism such as Reinhold Niebuhr, Hans Morgenthau and Martin Wight developed a strong linkage between religion, politics and realism. It is thus hardly surprising they shared a profound interest in morality and ethics and, thus, in values and principles.

Tension between principle and pragmatism is so commonplace that it has attracted intense scholarly interest. To Inis Claude, the master proposition is, 'that states do not, but certainly should, consistently engage in principled behaviour in the international setting' (Claude 1993: 215). He points out that calls for (more) principled behaviour flow from three sources: from moral disapproval of states unguided by principles, from alarm about the consequences of such behaviour and from moral aspiration for a better world order. Furthermore, he outlines the historical tradition of appealing to adherence to principles, ranging from the launch of international law in the sixteenth century to the 'turn to institutions' in the early twentieth century. In Claude's words, international law and organisation constitute the reform movement in international relations. The purpose of his article, however, is not to join these appeals and this movement but to make a plea for pragmatism, that is, flexible adherence to principles. The prime reason for making flexibility a deed is, according to Claude, the very diverse nature of states and the lack of uniformity in the international system. He rejects the view that pragmatists necessarily are immoral actors and instead talks about the moral value of adapting policy to fit special circumstances.[5] Jack Donnelly reaches a similar conclusion, 'There need be no real inconsistency in treating similar violations differently. [...] A blind demand that violation x produces response y is simplistic and silly' (cited from K. Smith 2001: 198).

Concerning operational foreign policy principles, George Kennan (1995) provides a particularly apt definition, highly relevant for our understanding of the role of principles in foreign policy. According to Kennan, 'a principle is a general rule of conduct by which a given country chooses to abide in the conduct of its relations with other countries'. He further specifies the main features of a principle. The first feature concerns the delicate relationship between rule and exception. Because a principle is a general rule of conduct, it is, 'designed to cover the entirety of possible or presumptive situations. It merely defines certain limits, positive or negative, within which policy, when those situations present themselves, ought to operate.' In other words, there may well be exceptions where the principle in question cannot or should not apply, but generally it should. Otherwise, it ceases to be a principle and degenerates into empty rhetoric or window-dressing. The second feature is, according to Kennan, that principles are self-engendered, declared by political leaders and, thus, not the outcome of some interactive process involving other international actors. If some interactive aspect of principles is present, it is on the internal side. In Kennan's words:

> the principle finds its reality, if it finds it at all, in the degree of acceptance, tacit or otherwise, that the proclamation ultimately receives from the remainder of the political establishment and from the populace at large. If that acceptance and support is not forthcoming in sufficient degree, a principle ceases to have reality.
>
> (Kennan 1995)

In Kennan's view, principles cannot possibly be the outcome of a democratic process – 'you would never get agreement on it'. Consequently, 'defining a principle must be seen not just as a privilege, but also a duty of political leadership'. Finally, Kennan points out that principles can have both negative and positive aspects, that is, they can guide actors to limit action and, they can prescribe certain actions. Finally, Kennan connects principles and images the following way:

> a country, too, can have a predominant collective sense of itself – what sort of a country it conceives itself or would like itself to be – and what sort of behaviour would fit that concept. The place where this self-image finds its most natural reflection is in the principles that a country chooses to adopt and, to the extent possible, to follow.
>
> (Kennan 1995)

Though only briefly presented, the examples presented above suggest that classical realism has more to offer than commonly assumed. It seems to me that the current of thinking is less well known than often claimed.

Neorealism

A systemic, material IR theory like neorealism, insisting on not being a theory of foreign policy (Waltz 1979; 1996), seems to have little to offer on questions concerning the role of VIPs in foreign policy. In this perspective, focusing on VIPs is close to a waste of time, and focusing on the role of VIPs in the foreign policy of a non-state actor like the EU is irrational research practice *par excellence.* Furthermore, neorealists characterise actors *a priori* (and therefore deliberately ignore real actor characteristics), identify a few prime players in the international system (great powers) and, on this basis, structurally deduct the likely behaviour of these prime players in changing structural settings (varying polarities). Finally, neorealists are content to explain a few but important things, and are happy to leave what they regard as nitty-gritty analysis of VIPs to those who care about such things.

However, neorealism may have more to offer than intuition suggests. First, though Waltz has insisted on neorealism not being a theory of foreign policy, the aim of his systemic theory is to explain state behaviour (Fearon 1998). Thus neorealism explains different kinds of state behaviour such as balancing, bandwagoning, seeking relative or absolute gains, etc. No matter which kind of behaviour, it will always be explained by systemic structural factors, i.e. strategically by polarity and, tactically or operationally, by balance of power theory.

This is where systemic principles, for instance sovereignty, non-intervention etc., could come in. Jackson (2000: 63–64) argues that Waltz's neorealism is more normative than it is widely perceived to be. In Jackson's words, 'even a cursory review indicates that normative concepts and categories are intrinsic to his argument, not at its extremities but at its foundations' (2000: 63). Thus, values and norms play a key role in the theory, though there are very few references to such phenomena. Furthermore, the international system may well be a system constituted by the kind of political entities we call states but more importantly, these entities count as states because they have been *recognised* as such by other states. It seems safe to predict that these processes of recognition are closely related to images, whether self-images or images of others. In summary, values and norms play a role *in* the theory and as part of Waltz's constitutive explanation, yet in the causal explanatory framework of neorealism, VIPs are at best regarded as weak intervening variables not having an impact on systemic structures.

Post-neorealism

The evolving realist tradition did not stop with the publication of Waltz's *Theory of International Politics* (1979).[6] While some continued as 'appliers', others took different paths. New groupings like 'defensive' and 'offensive' – and 'neoclassical' and 'postclassical' – realists have emerged. Whether these developments are best regarded as the degeneration of a paradigm or as the potentially innovative dynamics of a tradition (Wivel 2002), will not be assessed in the present context.

Instead I stick to my focus, i.e. to ask whether these contemporary currents of realism, be they neoclassical or postclassical realism, have conceptualised or considered the role of VIPs in foreign policy? On the whole, they have not. Instead, they have been shuffling and reshuffling a limited number of rather traditional variables. Heated debates between defensive and offensive realists may have triggered innovative theoretical developments but have not really produced value-added knowledge about the role of VIPs in foreign policy. This meagre outcome is possibly because VIPs are regarded as less important factors, thus continuing the tradition from neorealism; possibly because post-neorealists remain steeped in the parameters of material theories or feel uncomfortable in dealing with the kind of theory that would be adequate to apply when handling issues of ethics, images and identity.

Exceptions to this broad-brush painting of post-neorealism should be noted. Stephen Walt (1987) coined the concept of balances of threat – and it is difficult to conceive of balances of threats without some kind of role for images or perceptions, perhaps particularly images and perceptions of others. Generally, Walt is less materialistic than Waltz, and by incorporating social factors he has significantly modified neorealism. Furthermore some, particularly post-classical, realists have cultivated a pronounced interest in various intervening variables operating between international structures and the conduct of foreign policy. As a result of this interest, they have engaged in studies of foreign policy, focusing on both non-material and domestic factors (Snyder 1991; Elman 1996). Because such diverse phenomena as ideational, social and cultural factors qualify as non-material, it will take a long haul engagement to sort out precisely how one can square realism and non-material factors. Samuel Huntington (1993) and Henry Nau (2002) have demonstrated that realism and 'the cultural factor' are far from antithetical, and Walt and Snyder have demonstrated that political elites risk being caught by their own political rhetoric. This said, what so far have been brought forward by post-neorealists on VIPs constitutes a modest beginning. Potentially, realist key notions like 'interest' and 'power' could be reconsidered and related to both 'ethics' and 'identity'. Reconsiderations along this line would presumably result in a kind of realism similar to Hans Morgenthau's classical realism.

The English School

The English School, also called the international society tradition, represents a tradition of thought reaching back to Hugo Grotius (Bull 1966; Wight 1991). However, though some early signs of a distinct school can be traced back to the 1950s, it was only during the 1960s that the English School emerged as a fairly coherent approach – and it was as late as the early 1980s that the school was explicitly *recognised* as a school (Jones 1981; Dunne 1999). At the end of the 1990s, an attempt has been made to 'reconvene' the school (Buzan 2001). The English School represents a *via media* perspective on international relations. As such it is much more balanced than extreme perspectives, yet also always forced to argue for its distinct nature, i.e. being more than just a blend or a diluted version of more coherent extremes. Among the most important characteristics is the school's notion of international society – its defining feature – i.e. avoidance of making order dependent on hierarchy. In other words, international society is regarded as anarchical, yet this does not exclude order. The issue of justice in such an orderly international society is a different but related matter. This section on the school's conceptualisations of VIPs takes its point of departure in a crucial distinction between two particularly discernible currents of thought within the school: pluralist and solidarist conceptions of international society (Bull 1968). Both currents are closely related to issues of order and justice.

Pluralist conceptions of values, images and principles

Scholars adhering to pluralism strongly emphasise the pluralist nature of international society, i.e. that states constitute international society. Yet each state cultivates its own conception of the 'good life', implying that international society consists of different value systems (value pluralism). Pluralists do not necessarily value order more than justice but they argue that order is a more basic value than justice. In their view, it would make little sense to promote justice in a non-orderly society of states. To the degree order has been achieved, they argue, we can begin contemplating putting issues of justice on the agenda, provided that order is not put at risk. Among leading pluralist members of the English School, I primarily draw on Hedley Bull and Robert Jackson.

Hedley Bull (1968: 73) famously concluded that the solidarist conception of international society had proved 'premature'. What was his argument? First that it had been difficult to find much evidence supporting the solidarist conception of an international society – that is, an enhanced commitment to justice – and, second, that what he saw he did not like. Basically, he was questioning whether the consequences of well-intended action were counter-productive for the maintenance of international order. Whether or not this fruitless search had been due to one of the few examples of personal values entering Bull's analysis, it is a fact that he devoted most of his work to the pluralist conception. Most of his classic work, *The Anarchical Society* (1977), applies pluralist conceptions and the title of the book clearly connotes this emphasis of his. He had serious doubts about collective enforcement of international law, argued against the conception of a right of individual states to humanitarian intervention, and found limited space for individual human beings in the society of states.

Jackson's *The Global Covenant* (2000) is an eminent re-statement of the pluralist conception of international society. It deals with the world of states and statespeople as well as how we can or should be studying this world. Jackson has a powerful argument for taking values and principles seriously. They matter, indeed they are of utmost importance. The book is one long argument about the crucial importance of the normative superstructure of international society, a fabric woven by threads such as norms, doctrines, rules, principles and values. However, Jackson's employment of these terms is not always entirely clear or consistent. Having a strong distaste for scholasticism of any sort, he is not the kind of scholar who delves for too long into conceptual explication. Concerning the role of values, he makes a plea for 'bringing values back into view' (chapter 3, section 3). However, he does not really point out which values he has in mind or the role values play in foreign policy. Rather, he is primarily concerned with two issues. First, he points out that seemingly value-free classics like Kenneth Waltz's *Theory of International Politics* (1979) and Thomas Schelling's *The Strategy of Conflict* (1980) are based on specific normative foundations without, however, realising or recognising that this is the case. Second, in responding to the so-called window-dressing critique, i.e. the criticism claiming that values and norms are merely window-dressing or empty rhetoric, which hides other more important moti-vating factors, Jackson points out that these other seemingly value and norm-free factors – e.g. national interest – are not and cannot be value or norm free.

This said, Jackson does exemplify values by pointing to the values of equal sovereignty of states, territorial integrity and non-intervention (2000: 178), and to personal as well as national security (2000: 65; 185–188). Furthermore, he elaborates on the notion of value pluralism, explaining that it refers to diversity and plurality of states, which each cultivate and is free to cultivate its set of domestic values, 'there are many groups in world politics, each with different values, or different versions of the same value, which are distinctive to themselves' (2000: 179). Finally, he insists that we, as academics, should be sceptical about not only 'prevailing values' but also of 'reforming values', for instance ambitious ideas about reforming international society (2000: 81). His argument is that despite the value of democracy, actors should not be missionary or crusading in their conduct of foreign policy. All this said, one should not forget that the entire book has been written to argue that diplomacy and foreign policy cannot be conceived without taking the role of values into account. This is the prime reason for his criticism of Waltz and Schelling, who do not recognise the role of values, including the values and normative structure present in their own classics.

In Bull's (1968) critique of the Grotian conception of international society, he shows a preference for notions such as doctrine, rights and rules. He only infrequently employs the term principle, referring to (a) 'the principle that the justice of the case, defined in relation to the purposes of international society as a whole, must override partial alliances' (1968: 63); (b) 'if an individual believes the cause of the war in which he is ordered to bear arms to be unjust, he should refuse' (1968: 64); and (c) 'Grotian principles' (1968: 70) in the sense of defining features of the Grotian conception of international society, including their pos-sible 'detrimental' influence on international order (1968: 70–1). Recalling Jackson's claim that world politics cannot be understood without exploring the normative superstructure, it is worthwhile knowing that he rarely employs the term principle, as he clearly has a preference for the notion 'norm'. Concerning norms, he makes an important distinction between two different vocabularies: on basic procedural norms and basic prudential norms, respectively. Basic prudential norms concern the ethics of statecraft.[7] In his discussion of responsibilities in independent statecraft, he makes a distinction between national, international and humanitarian responsibility, and he does not try to hide the fact that he considers national responsibility to be primary. Jackson (2000) is very keen on the importance of 'the situational ethics of independent statecraft', i.e. the outcome of meetings between actor, circumstance and standards of conduct. Realists tend to emphasise circumstance and denigrate standards of conduct (but see Kennan 1995). Idealists do the opposite. Members of the English School 'exercise judgement' based on endogenous standards. Jackson strongly insists that imposing exogenous standards is as irrelevant and misleading as it possibly can be. Robert Jackson's contribution to the international society tradition is both distinct and comprehensive. He has much to say about international society, considerably less about foreign policy. However, because he focuses on the important role of prudent judgement by states-people, his IR theory has more relevance for foreign policy analysis than most other general IR theories.

Solidarist conceptions of values, images and principles

Compared to pluralists, solidarists are much less reluctant to push for justice in international society; indeed they do not accept the state-centric approach of pluralists. Instead, solidarists cultivate the notion of a world society constituted by individuals, each entitled to enjoy human rights. Suppressors of human rights should not be able to hide behind state borders. It is the responsibility, for some solidarists even a duty, of individuals and states to protect and promote human rights, also beyond state borders. Furthermore, solidarists strongly believe in the potential of collective enforcement of international law (including legal principles) – and collective management of international order and international affairs more generally (global governance). Finally, according to the solidarist conception, sovereignty is qualified in the sense that sovereignty can be nullified if rulers do not adhere to the principles of human rights. The solidarist current of thought has been less widespread than pluralism. For a time it was mainly represented by John Vincent (1986). However, during the 1990s it has been gaining ground. Among contemporary solidarists, I draw on Nicholas Wheeler and Tonny Brems Knudsen.

Solidarist arguments have been put forward by numerous scholars, some belonging to the English School. The solidarist research agenda began with issues related to the enforcement of international law. Due to the lack of a global law enforcement agency, responsibility concerning enforcement would necessarily rest with states. To which degree would they enforce law? How solidarist would they behave? Contemporary solidarists within the English School have primarily worked on humanitarian intervention (Knudsen 1999; Wheeler 2000). The conclusion is that there is or ought to be exceptions to the rule that intervention is illegitimate. In cases of gross violations of human rights, it should be possible to relax the principle of non-intervention, particularly if intervention is conducted collectively and preferably authorised by the United Nations Security Council. In short, in certain circumstances and with certain provisos humanitarian intervention should be considered legitimate.

Some claim states have a right to humanitarian intervention (Knudsen 1999; Wheeler 2000), even if this is incompatible with the principle of non-intervention or with the basic ordering principle of state sovereignty. Such questions are closely related to international deontological ethics, i.e. to issues concerning not the rights but the *duties* of states in international society. Though there has been a tradition of thought on such issues since Grotius, it has lately experienced a renaissance, cf. writings by Michael Walzer and Luigi Bonanate (for a brief introduction, see Hardin 1995; Donaldson 1995). Within the English School, primarily Vincent (1986) and Wheeler (2000) have contemplated issues of duty.

Do solidarists contribute to an understanding of the role of values, images and principles in foreign policy? To some degree they do. Wheeler's broad interest is with humanitarian intervention, the principle of non-intervention and the value of human rights, i.e. a foreign policy practice that, since the end of the Cold War, has been fairly high on the agenda of world politics. His solidarist theory of legitimate humanitarian interventions is an attempt to identify the criteria or requirements that are compulsory for an intervention to be legitimate. In other words, he lists the foreign policy principles applicable within the field of practice we call humanitarian intervention. This is somewhat similar to Inis Claude's reflections on relations between principle and pragmatism. Principles should not be regarded as etched in stone. The difference is that both Wheeler and Knudsen find it necessary to have explicit principles for exceptions to the rule. The *raison d'être* of such criteria is that they contribute to reduce the risk of abusing the right to intervention; they provide legitimacy, shape common expectations and enable collective action.

As the reader may have noticed, there is a considerable overlap between the solidarist and strong liberal currents. To a considerable degree, they share motivations, concerns, and normative agendas. It is therefore likely that both currents would benefit from an intensified dialogue. Pushing the frontiers of each current in order to overcome some of their limits could be accomplished by further specifying the role of values, images and principles in foreign policy.

Conclusion and perspectives

The key concepts – values, images and principles – have been explicated and connections between them explored. As we have seen, values and principles belong to the normative dimension of politics, whereas images belong to the subjective or inter-subjective dimension. But, crucially, the key terms assume different meanings in different theoretical traditions. Even within specific traditions, we have seen that we are dealing with contested concepts, as the significant contrast between classical realism and neorealism illustrates. Therefore, it is only after having comprehended the meaningful substance of these terms that we can begin studying the role values, images and principles play in international society.

The second conclusion is that we should not expect VIPs to be able to do too much for us. For instance, we should not expect a causal relationship, i.e. trying to explain foreign policy behaviour by means of VIPs or, generally, expect direct relations between VIPs and policy. A related reason for principles being unable to serve directly as determinants for foreign policy action is that in numerous situations several contending principles are available, so to speak. Thus, they are a poor guide for political choice and action. Instead, actors are left with the imperative of prudent statecraft, choosing among principles. In each case moralists – celebrating a certain principle – have a free hand to criticise the choice made.

A third conclusion concerns linkages between, on the one hand, values, images and principles, and, on the other hand, benign, soft, well-intended foreign policy. Many seem to believe that this is the right connection between VIPs and a foreign policy of goodness. Joris Voorhoeve writes about the 'idealistic, well-informed, and active groups which would like to turn foreign policy mainly into advocacy of values, give less emphasis to defence of interests, and often neglect practical considerations of effectiveness' (1979: 308). Yet no conceptual logic links values, images and principles to benign, soft, well-intended foreign policy. In contrast to a common (mis)understanding, values, images and principles are completely agnostic along the dichotomies of benign/malign and soft/hard. Indeed, some of the worst foreign policy practices are based on strong values, deeply held images and principles etched in stone.

Though the chapter has focused on VIPs, it has also included reflections on non-VIP aspects of foreign policy. The distinction between VIPs and non-VIPs is crucial for a proper understanding of the particular role VIPs play in the conduct of EU foreign policy. However, the distinction is more difficult to handle than should be expected. What seems clear is that scholars leaning towards material factors tend to dismiss the role of VIPs altogether, or, alternatively, to explain away the role of VIPs by referring to other more real factors like 'security', or 'interests' such as trade. The number of foreign policy specialists, conceiving of themselves as the 'knowers of things as they really are', is far from small. They are prone first to denigrate possible mixed motives situations, second to make a distinction between values and interests, pointing out that values and principles do not count, there are other (often hidden) true motives of foreign policy action.

Research on the role of VIPs has suffered from a certain fear of touching normative issues. Research has been a quest for not only value-free research of politics but also for research on politics without values and principles. In Steve Smith's (1992) words, it has been, 'a forty years detour'. The effects of this detour have been devastating for achieving an understanding of the role of values and principles in foreign policy (Jackson 2000). However, at least some international relations scholars and foreign policy analysts have had an enduring interest in issues of ethics and identity. Hence, it is a classic theme, though a theme which has experienced its ups and downs. Lately, there has been a pronounced renewed interest in the field of values, principles, ethics, identity and related issues.[8] For this reason, scholars with an interest in the role of VIPs in EU foreign policy have a unique window of opportunity to integrate insights from (international) political theory into studies of the EU's international conduct. Such studies – for instance reflections on power and morality in the European foreign policy tradition – may even benefit policy making, which in the case of the EU tends to be unrelated to public philosophies, or exist in the limited form of free-floating administrative programmes.

Notes

1 Joris Voorhoeve (1979), the scholar, has analysed the role of principles in Dutch foreign policy, while Voorhoeve as a policy maker (Dutch minister of defence), has been involved in the ethics of statecraft, for instance during the Bosnia crisis, including the 1995 Srebenica genocide.
2 Contemporary research on multilateralism (Ruggie (ed.) 1993) is closely related to these debates.
3 Brown's analysis corresponds well with Friedrich Kratochwil's (1982) explication of the notion of interest. Only in extreme cases are states not at all other-regarding, i.e. states seldom cultivate a very narrow, purely egoistic, short term conception of national interest.
4 On classical realism, see Stefano Guzzini (1998) or read Hans Morgenthau, John Herz, Arnold Wolfers or George Kennan.
5 Ruggie (1991), K. Thompson (1992) and Kennan (1995) have similar perspectives on the tension between principle and pragmatism.
6 I am grateful to Anders Wivel for commenting on a previous version of this chapter.
7 In this context, it is worth remembering that Jackson regards International Relations as a craft discipline, i.e., not as a scientific enterprise. Statecraft is like an art and our role, as scholars, is similar to the one played by art critics.
8 See the works of Chris Brown, Mervyn Frost, Furio Cerutti, Luigi Bonanate and Klaus-Gerd Giesen, among others.

4 Values, science and the European Union

Biotechnology and transatlantic relations

Ian Welsh

Introduction

Values assumed renewed prominence within political discourse following the demise of Soviet Communism and the post-11th September challenge of stateless network actors. Fukuyama's 'end of history' thesis based on the ascendancy of liberalism has also been challenged by movements contesting neo-liberal economics and techno-science. To McMurty these are *Value Wars* (2002) structured by the global extension of Western technocratic order.

The Treaty of Rome creating the European Communities coincided with the assumption that science would banish all forms of irrationality divorcing 'the world of value and the world of facts.' (Koyre 1957: 2). Scientific and technological cooperation from space exploration to microbiology is now central to an expanded European Union (EU), emphasising distinctive European values prioritising the citizen. The pursuit of progress through science within the EU has taken place with little public and political scrutiny contributing to concerns over technocratic dominance (Ellul 1964) through increasingly 'autonomous technology' (Winner 1978). The attempt to forge a united Europe around a common science and value base makes the EU a strategic global competitor and constitutes a contested public domain in the context of multilayered governance. The public sphere becomes a site where issues of social and economic justice, moral order, values and technical progress meet and are represented via increasingly diverse media.

These underlying value debates made the introduction of genetically modified (GM) crops controversial within the EU despite their apparently uncontroversial acceptance in the US. The ensuing EU moratorium on further GM crops resulted in US legal action for violating the primary values of free trade and objective science. Biotech controversy intensified with the sequencing of the human genome particularly within Christian religious traditions (Bauer and Gaskell 2002) with stem cell research featuring prominently in the 2004 US Presidential elections. The principles and values associated with biotechnology and wider science policy assume a prominence within politics and international relations unequalled since the advent of nuclear weapons.

Decisions about GM crops and genomics have raised intense technical debates between proponents of competing techniques and the public consequences associated with their adoption. These debates reflect a number of value domains *within* scientific, economic, political, regulatory institutions and publics making the technical resolution of difference an *irrational* goal. Addressing the value commitments associated with science assumes a position of central importance in terms of both the internal and external image of the EU. The dominance of 'risk' and 'sound science' within regulatory approaches in the EU and US have assumed technocratic forms neglecting the moral implications of scientifically colonising the future (Beck 1992; Giddens 1990, 1991). As an emergent techno-science, risk assessments of biotechnology proceed in the face of incomplete scientific knowledge which can take at least 50 years to yield reliable standards (Collins and Pinch 1996) for regulatory purposes.

The absence of certainty makes social and political decisions about science unavoidable or even preferable as a durable basis for societal judgements in the face of unresolved and irresolvable moral dimensions (Habermas 2003b). Para-doxically, advances in complexity theory raise the prospect of parallel universes with different and incompatible laws of physics problematising notions of uni-versal laws and predictive knowledge (Eve *et al.* 1997; Chesters and Welsh 2005). Biotechnology embraces both determinacy and complexity, simultaneously emphasising control through the manipulation of specific genetic traits and indeterminacy due to the role of proteins, environmental and 'lifestyle' factors in shaping genetic expression (Wynne 2005).

Science and the 'rational values' consolidated within enlightenment thought are central to contemporary debates about governance and 'bio-citizenship', individual and collective identity precisely because science offers both negative and positive genetic selection. 'Negative' attributes can be screened out whilst 'positive' attributes may be enhanced raising the prospect of 'a liberal eugenics regulated by supply and demand' (Habermas 2003b: vii). The power to shape the future anatomy of commercial crops and human populations raises issues of inter-generational equity not amenable to resolution via technical debate. Both the EU and US responded by establishing bioethics advisory groups, the Eur-opean Group on Ethics (EGE) and the National Bioethics Advisory Commission (NBAC), respectively. Whilst the EGE deals with values across the interrelated fields (Salter and Jones 2002) determining the development of any 'big science' (Galison and Hevly 1992), the NBAC was established to provide advice on stem cell work. Biotechnology thus reflects the increasing prominence of moral issues associated with war, wealth, human rights and attitudes towards the state within international relations (Halliday 1998: 16–19). It is in this context that the EU's strategic and regulatory science stances assume a position of centrality in terms of values, images and principles both internally and externally.

Science, politics and identity

Techno-science is fundamental to the production of material culture embodying and expressing underlying social aspirations through the pursuit of images, principles and values. Science has been central to fundamental elements of modernity with notions of democracy and progress assuming renewed prominence after World War II. Competition between nation states within the international order extends to the frontiers of scientific advance regarded as crucial to economic and military security (Luard 1986). Political and economic commitment to a trajectory occurs before a robust scientific consensus (certainty) has been achieved being legitimated by the articulation of elements of an established national identity with the 'promise' associated with a particular 'advance'.[1]

The EU is at once distinctive, lacking an historically constituted 'national identity' or 'imagined community' (Cederman 2001, Anderson 1991) which can be evoked to legitimate particular scientific ambitions. Further, the existence within the EU of several prominent nationally-based scientific communities, each with its own institutions, customs and practices increases the tendency for conflict within the EU over the direction of science policy, its technical anatomy and the location of particular projects (e.g. Green and Griffith-Jones 1984).[2] Confronted by 'big science' projects with long lead times the EU, like other geo-political actors, also faces problems associated with significant value shifts, a process often exacerbated by the simultaneous emergence of issues either previously omitted or downplayed within the public sphere.[3]

Irrespective of these novel features the dominant external image of the EU is that of competitor in American eyes (Ancarani 1995). The importance attached to attracting venture capital, sustaining viable scientific cadres and skilled workers within a knowledge economy indicate the continued importance attached to competitive positioning within the EU (see Commission 2002e). Manners (2002) considers that the EU is an actor with the potential to reconfigure the global normative domain through the pursuit of a particularly European view of civilisation. Part of this vision entails international co-operation at the frontiers of theoretical and applied science, an area where the EU is experience rich and increasingly able to exercise world leadership.

Despite such high profile collaborations, value differences play a significant role in the non-alignment of the EU and US over biotechnology which is explored here primarily through a consideration of GM crops. Throughout this treatment there is an attempt to separate value domains structured around economics, science and citizenship as sites constitutive of value debates which operate with different temporal dimensions. Established accounts (Bauer and Gaskell 2002; Bowring 2003; Toke 2004 and Vogel 2001) focus upon competing and conflicting orientations towards risk, regulation and the discursive representation of such differences with little attention to the underlying value domains framing these orientations.

Founding values, initial conditions and images of nature

Hutton (2002, chaps 1 and 2) provides one of the clearest comparisons of the evolution of European and American value systems as they impact upon relations between state, science, property, economy, religion and the individual. Hutton argues that Conservative US administrations pursue a form of American exceptionalism based on a unique set of values prioritising economic liberty resulting in a 'particular capitalism'.[4] This historic specificity is traced to the absolute property rights arising from the universal availability of landed property enjoyed by the Protestant settlers and extended through popular shareholding. Legislatively the American state upholds property rights diminishing the capacity for intervention in pursuit of a common good or interest, let alone redistributive aims. Hutton argues (via Locke) that the Protestant belief in a direct relationship with God is reflected in the constitutional equivalent of an American 'divine right' to prosper. Protestantism thus underpins economic and citizenship values prioritising individual liberty and freedom to own property and to profit.

Despite the diverse traditions constituting the EU, Hutton identifies four key areas where European civilisation is united by common values – property, equality, social solidarity and the public realm (Hutton 2002: 50). European property relations entail reciprocal obligations arising from the influence of Catholicism and the transformation of feudal rights and commitments to redistributive justice. Economic and citizenship values recognise rights to property but also duty towards a social collective making a regulatory, even interventionist, state credible. These differing traditions have implications for the prioritisation of value stances relating to biotechnology but before addressing these it is important to deal with the relationship between religion and science.

Religion, science and identity

The prominence of the religious right within American politics has rendered more tangible a fundamental difference between the US and the EU which exists irrespective of the presiding US administration. In Europe declining participation in Christianity has been accompanied by significant increases in non-traditional religious affiliation. In America around 40 per cent of citizens regularly attend a weekly church service. In both cases the assumption that scientific rationality would displace religious belief as the basis for social behaviour is problematic.

European polytheism sits uncomfortably with Western science's historical appropriation of a Christian 'God' as an aid in revealing the 'laws' of nature evident in the work of central figures such as Descartes, Spinoza and Newton, who 'referred to the "laws" of physics because he thought the laws of God had been revealed to him' (Raju 2003: 142). These philosophical roles underline the historically significant relationship between science and Christianity widely regarded as transforming humanity from spectator to 'owner and master of nature' (Koyre 1957: vii). This interpretation of the Judeo-Christian ethic forms part of a historically persistent ecological critique of modernity (Bratton 1984; Wall 1994) with competing interpretations alternately depicting 'man' as master or steward of nature. Feminist arguments about the dual domination of women and nature (Merchant 1983) add further to the dominance hypothesis associated with 'god moves' (Haraway 1995) by male scientists.

Gender and religion are but two examples of the centrality of 'difference' to biotechnology controversies that potentially affects all members of genetically differentiated groups in societies. The control of external nature familiar within eco-theological debates extends to control over human 'nature'. The perception of external nature and human nature play central roles in the attribution of social meaning to the environment (MacNaghten and Urry 1998) and ontological status to the embryonic individual (Romeo-Casabona 2002; Wertz 2002). Whilst European identity as a science-based civilisation has developed an accommodation with its Christian heritage, US science has an antagonistic relationship with Christian fundamentalist influences blocking federal stem cell work.

Values, ethics and science in contemporary EU debates

Contemporary discussions of EU science policy tends to emphasise that 'Greco-Latin and Judeo-Christian traditions' are constitutive of 'European values ... which ordains the respect of all individuals, including those of a non-European background' (EGE 2000: 3). It is argued that 'science and technology must increase – and not decrease – freedom and choice for everyone' in the context of a European civilisation where any replacement of 'nature or tradition' by scientific or technological means must depend on the capacity 'to show more active generosity than nature or tradition show' (EGE 2000: 3).

Discussions of biotechnology typically note that 'the EU is not merely an economic area, but also an area of shared fundamental values based on respect for human dignity' (European Parliament 2002b: 6). Here respect includes commitments to freedom of access to information, active public involvement, protection against genetic surveillance or discrimination and the maintenance of a collective 'safety net' (ibid: 4–6). Whilst there are considerable tensions between these ideals and their implementation they constitute a 'portal of access' (Giddens 1990) through which a diverse range of interests and standpoints can engage in debate over the 'moral trajectory' of scientific futures.

'External' nature and genetically modified organisms

Contemporary accounts of 'nature' argue that the binary division of social/natural is better understood as co-causative, a position which questions the binary opposition of man/nature and nature/society (MacNaghten and Urry 1998). Public response to the new genetics in Europe shows greater scepticism over agricultural uses of biotechnology and greater acceptance of therapeutic medical techniques (Bauer and Gaskell 2002; Hampel *et al.* 2000). Polling data gathered during a period of techno-scientific emergence is not necessarily a reliable indicator of future public acceptability after 'virtual' promise is realised as concrete application. This is important given the very long time frames associated with macro-level policy transformations through value shifts (Lane and Ersson 2002, esp. chap. 10). Public reticence towards GM crops reflects values relating to the exercise of choice and control over food consumed, which in Europe has centuries of cumulative cultural codes codified in 'consumer protection' legislation. Other significant elements include urban publics' relation to the 'natural environment' in terms of landscape, flora and fauna. Here there are some significant differences between Europe and America.

The relationship between 'man' [sic] and nature was central to liberal enlightenment thought with 'state of nature' theories being particularly influential. In liberal theory the state is axiomatic to social order and the construction of an abstract and universal individual. Coherent philosophical universalism is challenged by other disciplines with anthropologists noting the diversity of socially organised perceptions of, and relationships with, the 'natural' order (Strathern 1992). Similarly sociologists identify a range of contested natures (MacNaghten and Urry 1998) which social historians identify as a key constituent of national identity (Schama 1995).

In terms of such identity issues America and Europe have fundamentally different orientations towards nature. In America the availability of land in an 'unsettled' country granted a primacy to ownership and an expansionist frontier mentality pursued by 'pioneers' (Zinn 2002). By contrast European civilisation colonised the majority of desirable available space over centuries establishing a wide range of both exploitative and reciprocal relations. To Hutton, the US preoccupation with ownership rights developed with no equivalent of these reciprocal relations. Relations with 'nature' in Europe were in effect more intimate and pervasive as the environment as a whole was and is central to the sustenance, recreational activities and well being of people.

The development of conservation ethics and national parks policies illustrate this divide with America orientated towards the 'protection of wilderness – pristine nature' whilst national parks in countries such as the UK coincide with some of the most heavily husbanded and intensively visited regions. The contiguous nature of Europe also means that transboundary concerns are a norm forcing member states to confront issues in a context that transcends, however inconveniently, narrowly defined 'national' interests. Further, the renegotiation of EU agricultural subsidies included measures to enhance ecological stewardship through diversification.

A focus on the preservation of wilderness leaves the rest of the environment available for intensive farming under due regulatory conditions. Two important spheres where value considerations are relevant to US and EU stances in relation to genetically modified organisms (GMOs) arise from this. First, there are sets of value considerations influencing what is regulated, why it is regulated and to some degree how it is regulated. Second, there are significant value-related elements that shape if not determine levels of public acceptability of GMO products. The institutional anatomy of regulatory provision represents the 'common ground' where these domains intersect and around which issues of political legitimation revolve. The existence of differing regulatory cultures and institutional structures is well established within the sociology of science and technology and has been widely applied (Jasanoff 1993; Nelkin 1995).

There are some well established arguments here that are worth rehearsing briefly before elaborating the future trajectories associated with these debates in terms of VIPs and science policy. In institutional terms American acceptance of GMOs is widely attributed to the overarching rigour of the federal Food and Drugs Administration. The adoption of 'benchmark' standards applied to risk regulation, particularly cancer risks, in the US is widely seen as establishing a firm basis of public trust (Russell and Vogler 2000; Vogel 2001). Whether such trust is the product of 'realist' standards or the effective presentation and public management of information (Hilgartner 2000), America definitely benefits from a set of integrated federal institutions with uniform regulatory reach and high public confidence compared to the EU.

Differences in US and EU responses to GM foods are commonly ascribed to significant regulatory failure in EU member states, such as BSE, which are seen as undermining public confidence in a unique manner. The high profile use of 'species barrier' arguments by politicians to reassure publics in the BSE case contributed to a fundamental questioning of regulatory assumptions, standards and competences across the European public sphere.[5] This debacle reinforced the standing of the precautionary principle within the EU intensifying tensions between member states with a significant biotechnology base, such as the UK, and the wider union.

Perhaps the most fundamental difference between the US and EU in terms of 'external nature' lies in Americans' unambiguous subordination of the organic realm to the pursuit of what Hutton termed 'US exceptionalism'. President George W. Bush's contribution to the Department of Agriculture website considers that it is 'in our national security interests that we have a strong farm economy. And the farmers of America contribute to the values of our nation' (Bush 2001). The US Undersecretary of State for Agriculture publicly asserted that 'US Foreign Policy is devoted to a longer term struggle to gain world acceptance of agricultural biotechnology' (BBC, *Seeds of Strife*, Radio 4, 7 January 2003).

US agricultural policy thus melds domestic and foreign policy domains in the global pursuit of economic liberty and the freedom of business to pursue profit originating in the seventeenth century (Hutton 2002; Wertz 2002). The primacy of economic value contrasts markedly with the EU emphasis on the place of the citizen and citizenship rights within declaratory positions, something which becomes apparent through a consideration of the relationship between science, GMOs and genetic resources.

Strategic science, GMOs and genetic resources

The European Commission identified biotechnology as an area of strategic science simultaneously with other major world players including the US and Japan. One of the dominant images associated with this new science within the public sphere was of a second 'green revolution' which would 'feed the world'. Like the 'atoms for peace' initiative of the 1950s, Western science would breathe hope into developing nations confronted by famine and starvation through the concentration on crops with significant Western markets (Welsh 1999). Like the peaceful uses of atomic energy, biotechnology was promoted through the auspices of the United Nations, eventually leading to the Universal Declaration on the Human Genome and Human Rights (Rothman 2000).

Between 1970 and the mid-1990s growing corporate involvement in biotechnology in both Europe and America was accompanied by a rapid decline in the number of seed supply firms as a result of aggressive takeover policies pursued by companies such as Monsanto. Simultaneously, the translation of the General Agreement on Tariffs and Trade (GATT) into the World Trade Organization (WTO) coincided with the formalisation of a Trade Related Intellectual Property Rights (TRIPs) regime covering seeds (see Purdue 2000). This regime established the primacy of knowledge claims to products gained through laboratory manipulation irrespective of whether the active component had already been identified and selectively enhanced by 'traditional' techniques. Science and the application of laboratory-bench techniques were thus elevated to a position of primacy over established techniques practised in both developed and developing nations. This marked a significant transformation of both labour processes and plant husbandry practices with control moving from farmer to corporation. In developing nations this resulted in widespread direct action against multinationals, scenes which EU nations remained relatively insulated from (Walton and Seddon 1994).

TRIPs arrangements and patenting more generally generated concerns within the science community as corporate actors filed patents on significant strings of genetic material on the basis of a single application derived from one genetic component. The granting of such patents precluded other scientists from working on the entire genetic sequence covered by the patent, infringing the scientific value of freedom of publication and open access to information in the pursuit of knowledge. The more aggressive use of patent law, often on the basis of the casting vote of one Supreme Court judge, has been American, increasing the importance of well qualified scientific scrutiny within patent offices and arguably equal expertise in a range of ethical concerns related to patenting (EGE 2002).

The extension of patent control from plant to cellular organisms, to animal and human life forms commodifies the human in ways that make respect for human dignity problematic (Danish Council of Ethics 2004, www.etiskraad.dk). Experience with GMOs suggests that the commercial application of such genetic knowledge elevates underlying value commitments to a position of prominence. The associated stakes were sharpened considerably by the US decision to pursue the EU through the WTO in June 2003 over its *de facto* ban on licensing further GMO products. The principal argument being that the EU embargo on precautionary grounds lacks scientific rigour and represents an unfair impediment to free trade, condemning the developing world to continued hunger by 'blighting' the spread of beneficial technology. In effect the EU was charged with unscientific behaviour and reasoning – of standing in the way of 'rational' progress for ideological reasons, charges rehearsed within GM labelling debates in the US (Klintman and Boström 2004).

US positions remain tied to a classical risk analysis approach emphasising 'sound science' which points to the absence of any proven adverse human health effects after decades of exposure to GM, which is present in 80 per cent of commercially available US processed foods. The adage 'absence of evidence is not evidence of absence' is an effective way of summarising *elements* of EU concern calling for a precise scientific approach.[6] This would entail detailed, longitudinal monitoring and investigation of volunteer groups exposed to a variety of dietary regimes. Similar longitudinal scientific work is regarded as essential to assess arguments that GM crops are not detrimental to biodiversity. Here, the cross pollination of GM and non-GM strains and impacts on wildlife are particularly important issues.

GM regulation and values in Europe and America

Any consideration of the regulation of GM products in Europe and America must recognise that uncertainty is a central feature of both the science and the associated moral and value trajectories. In the case of biotechnology, Levidow and Carr (1999) and Levidow *et al.* (2000) argue that uncertainty is constitutive of risk controversy that becomes structured around a range of value conflicts. They emphasise that such value conflicts extend far beyond the 'value' attached to competing expert statements about degrees of risk or confidence in regulatory measures, extending to wider registers of individual security, worth and influence. Faced with complexity individuals adopt 'frames' which enable sufficient sense making to constitute them as ontologically secure actors confronted by complex issues (Chesters and Welsh 2005). Importantly, this means that within the public sphere the ethical, moral, political and economic implications of new scientific and technological developments are inseparable from narrower technical issues and thus cannot be reduced to public fluency in technical knowledge. The trajectory of GM issues through the EU illustrates how this entire gamut of 'values' have been institutionally addressed resulting, ultimately, in the realisation of the WTO 'trade war'.

According to Barling (2000: 240–241) the consolidation of industrial lobbyists, government departments and scientists in the US diverted attention away from moral, ethical and environmental issues associated with GMOs by the late 1980s through the assertion of 'substantial equivalence'. Substantial equivalence exempted GM crops from pre-market risk evaluations subjecting them to existing regulatory standards and procedures, precluding the need to label GM food. The US regulatory system focuses upon the end product regarding it as unexceptional whilst the EU's regulatory stance includes the process of genetic modification itself. This exposes the entire GM production process to regulatory scrutiny with implications for the predominantly American multinational corporations heavily engaged in agricultural biotechnology. Demanding regulatory regimes also act as a barrier to entry for small and medium size enterprises where much of the 'potential' of the biotechnology sector is thought to lie (European Parliament 2002b).

The successful establishment of a technocratic discourse coalition was initially reproduced within the EU whilst the Commission maintained dominance (Patterson 2000) in the face of demands for an increased role for the European Parliament arising from 'democratic deficit' arguments. Patterson's account emphasises the centrality of DG XI in producing the primary drafts of key EU regulatory Directives 90/219 and 90/220 as *chef de file*. The resultant emphasis on the protection of the environment and human health subordinated internal and external market factors that became the focus of subsequent amendments. The necessary process of conciliation between Commission, Council and Parliament was completed and the resultant Directive put before the Parliament where it was voted down. One institutional account emphasises the recently elected status of many members of the Parliament, their unfamiliarity with foregoing debates and the desire to use new powers. However, other factors relating to the vitality of the European public sphere were also operating. Qualitative sociological accounts reveal the importance of social movement actors representing diverse sets of socially organised expressions of the ethical and moral stakes associated with the global application of biotechnology (Purdue 2000).

Within this process core EU values (such as human dignity) with universal implications acted as crucial discursive hinges facilitating the articulation of particular interpretations of key principles – such as precaution and sustainability. These principles reflect core values emphasising the sanctity of the citizen and presenting the EU as 'not merely an economic area, but [is] also an area of shared fundamental values based on respect for human dignity' (European Parliament 2002b: 6). The ambition to apply respect for human dignity on a global stage extends the reach of such values through incorporation into principles that apply to all individuals 'irrespective of their stage of development' (European Parliament 2002b: 12). This respect for a universal individual is implicitly extended to national actors where co-operation in pursuing biotechnology is presented as a process which cannot be advanced simply by the 'transfer of European ideas on foreign ground.' (European Parliament 2002b: 15).

The implications of these values and principles are profoundly amplified by the overlapping nature of genetic techniques. For example, the production of GM crops to yield pharmaceutical products complicates industry and political ambitions to develop 'one stop', 'single letterbox' regulatory regimes to enhance an efficient transition to market. The closure achieved in the face of such complexity by the notion of 'substantive equivalence' in the US has not been evident within the EU, amplifying tensions between universal values, economic competitiveness and efficiency.

Civil society actors and biotechnology in the EU and US

Patent regimes are fundamentally important to the biotechnology sector as effective markets and profit streams cannot be protected without them. The development of intellectual property rights regimes is a complex arena spanning national, supranational and global arenas with profound implications for pre-existing distributions of rights and power over associated labour processes. The rejection of the European Commission's initial proposals in this area by the European Parliament reflected these tensions. Purdue details how the EU commitment to the 'dignity of man' could not be easily reconciled with genetic processes such as reproductive cloning or the patenting of human genes. Purdue also details the sophisticated understanding of EU procedures by civil society actors. Knowing that a bad compromise would be easier to overturn within the EU conciliation process the NGO sector left MEPs to their own devices before engaging in any significant lobbying. Their subsequent campaign included an emphasis on 'the human gene issue' which mobilised 'the churches and medical lobbies' crucial to the fall of the legislation in 1995 (Purdue 2000: 32). Another example of civil society actor influence, this time from engaged academic commentators, was the adoption of Levidow and Tait's definitions of 'precautionary' and 'preventative' (Patterson 2000: 325).

An EU patenting directive 98/44 was not passed until 1998 but remains an area of considerable debate and tension where, for example, errors with ethical implications were detected by Greenpeace rather than internal procedures (European Parliament 2002b: 9). The directive was unsuccessfully challenged in the European Court of Justice and awaited implementation in seven of the fifteen member states in May 2004. Internally then, the commitment of the EU to advance a set of European common values which can be embodied within science policy remains an ambition rather than an actuality in the biotech sector. Eurobarometer surveys reveal continuing ambivalence and scepticism which, despite some national variance, demonstrate a continuing gulf between public perceptions and the technocratic vision of Europe as a significant global player in biotechnology. One significant EU response mode reintroduces the deficit model of public understanding of science which assumes, amongst other things, that better public knowledge will automatically result in both understanding and acceptability vis-à-vis biotechnology (Wynne 1995, 2005). The emphasis upon public education and interventions within educational curricula orientated towards a biotech 'knowledge economy' (European Parliament 2002b) co-exist with exhortations for the 'rational' application of the precautionary principle based on sound science in the face of public doubts about a new technology 'some of which are not really rational' (European Parliament 2002b: 8).

For present purposes two important consequences for the EU flow from this. The recourse to a simplistic view of science as a disciplinary enterprise underpinned by certainty generating a reliable substantive rationality reproduces sets of social relationships inimical to public trust in institutions. Secondly there is a marked emphasis on transparency through the provision of information and public involvement and consultation. The combination of these factors results in an institutional interpretation of the ethical dimension where the moral obligation to pursue 'progress' through scientific and technical advance is juxtaposed with 'other' forms of ethical concern such as those arising from 'individual' religious beliefs for example.[7]

In terms of the external image of the EU, the US WTO action included charges of failure to fulfil the ethical obligation to produce secure food supplies for developing nations following the rejection of US food aid in the form of GM crops by African nations. EU scepticism over GM crops was seen as prompting this refusal. EU responses to the US action have in effect reiterated the right of nation states to refuse GM products, lifted the moratorium on further licence applications and maintained the commitment to clear labelling of foods containing GM products.

Whilst the US remains committed to its WTO action in the face of this labelling initiative US citizens campaigning for compulsory food labelling considered the EU strategy as an example of good practice, calling for 'tougher regulation than the EU' in their proposed legislation known as Measure 27 (BBC Radio 4, *Seeds of Trouble*, 7 January 2003). Measure 27 was defeated following a $5 million campaign emphasising that implementation would cost $100m in taxes. Monsanto contributed $1.5m to this campaign arguing that 'the European approach is label absolutely everything. If you took your approach to its logical conclusion the label would be the size of a telephone book' (ibid.). This sensitivity to labelling is perhaps underpinned by the implications for market share. US research evidence showed declining sales of GM products in states adopting voluntary labelling schemes (Buttel 2000) with some reporting that 60 per cent of US consumers would not buy foods labelled to show GM content (Pollack and Shaffer 2000: 49). In the UK, supermarket chains reacted to consumer concerns by securing non-GM supply chains for their own brand labels and show no inclination to abandon this stance. In this sense the GM food component of the biotech revolution identified by the US, Japan, the then USSR and EC in the 1970s is acknowledged to be running the risk of consumer rejection within the market place through the attempt to impose a 'supply orientated concept'.

American fears of a domestic backlash against genetically modified crops have been compounded by the electoral success of candidates standing on explicitly anti-GM platforms in key states such Montana. These victories are underpinned by the difficulty of securing sales for GM crops in the world market combined with the appearance of persistent transgenic strains from previous years' planting underlining the potential for unforeseen GM contamination of crop and weed species.[8]

EU responses to US challenges and internal image

Emergent EU responses to the regulatory challenges of biotechnology attempt to produce a degree of uniform regulatory reach across the member states by introducing a range of regulatory protocols and procedures. The Commission's clear focus on restarting the stalled GM industry dominates key texts which articulate regulatory strategies and structures for 'stakeholder' dialogue. Wider ethical issues and citizen rights, in stark contrast, remain under-specified and are predominantly addressed as if they can be resolved *within* the process of reorientating the biotech sector under a 'global governance' approach. The implicit and explicit use of public deficit models of public understanding of science evident within these documents is indicative of the continued presence of top-down technocratic decision-making and associated democratic deficits. Commentaries on biotechnology within the EU have frequently rehearsed the tension between organic and biotech agricultural sectors and the importance of detailed epidemiological studies of GM foods.

These issues are absent from the Commission's approach to the labelling of GM products, which relies upon laboratory procedures to prescribe a level of GM contamination below which a product can be marketed as organic. The setting of an organic food standard based on an 'acceptable' level of GM contamination in effect heralds the end of 'authentic', 'pure' organic food production. Within publics where organic preference leads to one of the fastest growing markets this is a form of alien 'world making' far from the aspirational political ideals expressed around science policy. Irrespective of the technical considerations surrounding residual contamination, the imposition of *some* degree of contamination of organic food across Europe undermines the expression of individual free choice by imposing, on the grounds of an assumed collective economic interest, a science-based technology that does not enjoy a clear consensus. The Commission and member states will face continued public disquiet and antagonistic engagement in the face of this attempt at technocratic closure.

The centrality of the citizen and the right to difference within EU legislation cannot easily be collapsed into neo-liberal market ethics in the face of technological developments which require a profound rethinking of ethics to reinstate issues of collective interests (Glasner and Rothman 2001). The dominance of ethical concerns such as individual rights, compensation, insurance and informed consent do not engage with wider ethical questions relating to public and environmental health for example. These concerns continue to be articulated by DG XII and contain the basis for ethical stances which place human and environmental health at the centre of complex relationships which now extend from the laboratory to food, air, water, and land quality. In the context of complex risk controversy involving a wide range of interactions occurring at molecular and cellular levels with known and yet to be identified vectors, the residual degree of scientific uncertainty remains high with the prospect of continuing and intensifying expert conflict. Post-normal science (Functowicz and Ravetz 1993) operating in 'open systems' in effect operates upon a terrain where complexity and uncertainty are key features increasing both the prominence and contested nature of values.

Within regulatory regimes there is a tendency for scientific and technological risks and the associated moral trajectories to be translated into economic risks. This involves a shift in the temporal frame applied to the controversy with attention being directed away from long-term 'up stream' issues towards the 'immediate' economic risk of not pursuing the trajectory in question. Such economic risk discourses appear more tangible and concrete leading to clear and apparently unambiguous imperatives to guide policy action. The GM example is yet another case where the economic promise has proved less rosy than predicted.

In relation to GM the initial strategies of the US and EU were not fundamentally different with both deploying technocratic decisional fora which insulated debate from wider value-based questions. The decisive divergence arose from the presence of more engaged actors within civil society in the EU, supported by a range of critical scientists (for example, the International Network of Engineers and Scientists for Global Responsibility), and national media within member states lacking in the US. The GM issue reverses the transatlantic controversy flows of the 1970s when US expert and public concerns over nuclear reactor safety permeated the UK and other member states. The scientific controversy over GM food is far from over as demands for longitudinal epidemiological studies are unlikely to disappear. Should such studies fail to materialise then they will eventually be undertaken in some form given the increasing trend towards citizen initiatives and organisations such as the Soil Association.

In the US, examples of citizen science are calling into question the 'gold standard' cancer risk assessments which are cited as underpinning public confidence in US regulatory authorities handling GM (Tesh 2000; Vogel 2001). These developments coincide with increasing US public scepticism as awareness of the presence of GM in food products spreads, agricultural use of GM begins to be questioned by farmers and transgenic strains begin to be observed. In the GM case there is some time to go before the 50 years required for a reasonable scientific consensus to be negotiated elapses. US corporations and administrations have followed traditional US values and prioritised the apparent certainty of economic imperatives and market making in the GM sphere.

The planet is in effect the laboratory in which this experiment is undertaken on the basis of incremental extension of patenting principles developed from simple life forms to human biological materials. It is significant that ethical debate has primarily focused on issues relating to scientific and commercial access to human raw materials whilst issues associated with genetic enhancement remain relatively unexplored. Enhancement techniques are part of an assemblage of scientific agendas which intersect and interact. A US grant of $1m to UK scientists working on stem cell techniques with the potential to 'radiation harden' astronauts is one example of this unfolding nexus (NASA 2004).

Current EU regulatory stances merge with those of the US accepting both substantial equivalence and the right of member states to apply stringent risk assessments before granting new licences. Attention to the citizen within this regime is, however, limited to fulfilling the neo-liberal promise of 'perfect knowledge' through labelling. By adopting this position the EU remains locked in dispute with the US within the WTO and open to further internal charges of a technocratic top-down approach. The extension of the biotech enterprise into human genetics will increase these tendencies unless a significant shift in regulatory stances occurs.

One example illustrates this difficulty. The commitment to securing the interests of the individual irrespective of their stage of development takes on considerable significance in relation to the controversial process of harvesting embryonic stem cells. As Wertz (2002) points out different religions attribute 'life' to the developing foetus at different stages of development complicating the process of arriving at any global standard without transgressing the belief and value systems of both nations and members of multiethnic Europe. Europe-wide strategies continue to be pursued emphasising the need for common legal frameworks (Romeo-Casabona 2002), public trust in 'science-based regulatory oversight' and a 'rolling programme' of EU legislation (Commission 2002e).

Following the GM case, further divides between the EU and the US over stem cells are evident. The US ban on state-funded human stem cell work was immediately followed by the charge that certain EU member states, primarily the UK, were about to 'win a war' against the US. As the biotech age is slowly translated into material practices the external image of Europe as an economic threat in US eyes is likely to remain prominent. The incorporation of patent rights covering human genetic material within WTO patent regimes is an obvious forum within which these conflicts will become evident.

At the start of this chapter it was stated that the EU had the potential to develop a science-based trajectory consistent with the political ambitions articulated around the citizen and new forms of citizenship. A key challenge confronting scientific research and development, regulatory bodies and commercial interests, is the development of techniques resulting in flexible products adaptable to a diverse range of physical and cultural environments (Welsh 1994). Contemporary approaches, rooted in fordist mass production, are encountering the limits of acceptability associated with one-size fits all approaches.

Conclusions

This discussion of science and values in the EU has strayed far into political economy. Within the sociology of scientific knowledge literature economics is regarded as a science (Evans 1999) and there is increasing recognition that the boundary between politics and science is far less clearly defined than has been previously thought. The GM case suggests that the science/commerce boundary has wider implications for the biotechnology sector. The argument presented here suggests that the complexity of 'post-normal' regulatory science represents a major political and science policy challenge arising from the continued application to this process of an economic science based in centuries-old precepts where market dominance extended across the maximum spatial and temporal ranges possible. The relatively monolithic products resulting from this overreach transgress the values of so many social, cultural and ethnic locations that controversy and conflict are inescapable. The sanguine and detached lesson that must be learnt from this case study is evident in the assessment of the stakes associated with the GM debate by numerous US commentators, namely the risk that consumers will ultimately inflict significant commercial damage on the biotechnology sector (Pollack and Shaffer 2000).

The dominant external image of the EU in US eyes is likely to remain that of competitor intensifying internal concerns about the science base and economic competitiveness (Commission 2002e). These concerns have to be balanced with the internal images of the EU in the eyes of citizens upon which the legitimacy and viability of the Union ultimately depend. The Commission implicitly acknowledges this, noting problems of 'global governance' in the biotech domain (ibid.). Achieving this balance represents a major scientific and political challenge. The use of biotechnology in a diverse range of sites where genetically modified products interact with open biological systems makes the task of proper scientific risk assessment challenging, costly and time consuming given the potential for unforeseen synergistic consequences. In these circumstances the EU's commitment to the precautionary principle interfaces with other core elements of EU policy such as the primacy of the citizen and sustainability. The prominence given to ethical considerations relating to biotechnology is both welcome and a significant, principled, difference differentiating EU and US positions. However, the biotech revolution raises novel issues that challenge established ethical systems and principles.[9] Informed consent provides an example; here established uses protect the individual undergoing a medical procedure. These important considerations now have to be balanced against the potential collective risk to the wider human population arising from biotech procedures (Habermas 2003b).

Such ethical complexities extend far across space and through time when established systems of ethics, political philosophy and philosophy of science remain embedded in ways of thinking developed in the context of the nation state and national identities. Glasner and Rothman (2001) conclude that 'existing institutions of morality' are no longer sufficient to deal with the globalised nature of the biotechnology industry emphasising the inability of utilitarian approaches to 'deal with "multinational" issues such as the exploitation of the resources of the poorer countries of the South'.

Compared to US exceptionalism, EU thinking contains examples of principled stances that begin to address such concerns. Statements cited here about not simply transferring European ideas onto foreign soil are one example. Recognition of the indivisible relationship between human and environmental health represents another important dimension of such thinking with clear links to issues of inter-generational equity associated with sustainable development. Elsewhere EU documents discussing biotechnology have explicit recourse to 'deficit' models of the public understanding of science. Summarised crudely these assume that better-informed publics will increasingly accept complex technologies which re-order social norms, conventions and mores.

This is a profoundly problematic formulation. The UK's public consultation exercise on GM was based, in part, on this assumption. The outcome showed four in five people opposed to GM foods across the majority of response categories monitored, with public meetings and focus groups detecting no significant 'swing' constituencies (AEBC 2003). Other UK assessments suggest that there is little or no economic advantage to large-scale use of GM crops as there is no significant market.

The challenge confronting EU science policy in terms of both internal and external image involves translating the political ambitions revolving around the dignity and integrity of the citizen into practical policy measures with measurable outcomes. The sedimented traditions of 'old Europe', particularly those associated with action on behalf of collectives, are central here as is the importance attached to an informed and engaged public sphere. Whilst stakeholder dialogues have identified significant constituencies representing the biotech sector, the anatomy of the civil society actors to be included remains far less clearly defined (Commission 2003d). Effective inclusionary mechanisms and institutions with remits ensuring effective social inputs early within development cycles are in their infancy and require urgent proactive attention.[10] I have argued elsewhere that it is vital to broaden the social composition of the groups determining the scientific, technological and moral trajectories that colonise the future (Welsh 2000, chap. 8).

The scientific and technical trajectories, selected by national technocracies from within familiar economic, political, military and scientific elites, have been consistently presented as superior whilst simultaneously transforming war, wealth and welfare. In the post-11th September world the inviolable right to benefit from science and technology was invoked as a reason to wage pre-emptive war on the basis of the assumed intent to misuse some of the same techniques. The biotech age creates the potential for significant bio-weapon production using small, mobile and relatively inexpensive equipment. The problems associated with dual use in regulating nuclear technologies may well prove simple compared to the problems associated with the military potential of medical genetics.

The principle of pursuing progress and advancing civilisation through the use of military force against those suspected of possessing such technologies with malicious intent is one which 'old Europe' rejected. As the EU begins to formulate a collective foreign policy stance it is important to recognise the potential for the economic costs of pre-emption to undermine the civilisation in whose name such wars are conducted. In this regard the values, images and principles shaping science policy become supremely important as a means of articulating a future free from the values, images and principles derived from the long century of inter-state rivalry and war.

Discussions within Europe dating from the late 1970s recognised that certain science agendas would render the planet as laboratory; emphasised the importance of striking a balance between *local* and *world* technologies; recognised scientific and technological co-operation as an imperative not an option; and gave prominence to a range of ethical issues including inter-generational equity (Green and Griffith-Jones 1984). Elements of the associated values, images and principles continue to be nascent as political aspirations within the EU – the challenge is to translate aspiration into a material culture where science is more generous than either tradition or nature. This will require the skilful articulation of values revealing the importance of common interests over short-term political and market values driven by electoral and business cycles.

Notes

1 Nuclear power is one of the most prominent examples of this process in the post-war era being variously hailed as the triumph of Russian Communism, American entrepreneurialism and the start of a second age of Elizabethan splendour for the United Kingdom (Welsh 2000).

2 This has been prominent in physics projects particularly nuclear fusion research with considerable disagreement about the long term viability of the project and the physical configuration of a future fusion reactor (see EP-STOA-F1, EP-STOA-F2, 1998). European Ministers agreed a follow-on Fusion Project located in the South of France in 2003 though the final location remained subject to negotiation with international partners (*The Guardian*, 27th November, p. 17).

3 In the UK for example it was denied that nuclear waste would be a significant problem at the launch of the first nuclear power programme in the 1950s.

4 Whilst Hutton associates this process with Conservative American administrations others writing from both Conservative (Bacevich 2002) and radical stances (McMurty 2002) emphasise a continuity of purpose irrespective of the political composition of US administrations. For an initial discussion of the significance of different capitalisms within Eastern and Central Europe, including EU member states, see Baker and Welsh 2000.

5 The potential for retro-viral contagion arising from the use of genetically modified animal organs (xenotransplantion) in humans became a significant factor in the retrenchment of work in this area and the migration of commercial interests from the UK. This underlines the commercial risk associated with techniques based in recent scientific work (see Welsh and Evans 1999).

6 Rigorous scientific evaluation was one of the principal commitments of Michael Meacher whilst in post as Minister for the Environment, an appointment which was not extended in Tony Blair's 2003 Cabinet reshuffle and is a view present within the European Parliament. Recognising the importance of human epidemeologIical studies is one feature of EU stances.

7 This formulation was used in the UK government's public consultation questionnaire on GM crops reflecting the more pervasive presence of this tendency. Religious belief became an important issue in the drafting of the EU Constitution of 2004 given the prospect of incorporating Turkey as a member state.

8 See *Great Falls Tribune online*, www.greatfallstribune.com. Coverage (www.pcusa.org/pcusa/wmd/hunger/food/gmcrops.htm) reveals the prominent role of critical reports produced by the UK-based Soil Association in America – these now include studies of the transfer of GM plant material into the gut bacteria of humans (www.soilassociation/gm).

9 Bowring's (2003) argument for a 'deontological ethics' is one, controversial, attempt to reposition ethics to engage with such complexities.

10 Rothman's (2000) call for the inclusion of new social movement actors is important in this regard, implicitly recognising that such actors cannot be adequately regarded as simply 'antis' replete with the associated label of luddite or the contemporary 'terrorist'. At this early stage of an emergent risk controversy I would argue that such groups include the most informed sub-sections of the population which, like their anti-nuclear forebears, have the ability to come to sophisticated judgements on the complex issues raised (Welsh 2000).

5 Environmental values and climate change policy

Contrasting the European Union and the United States

Susan Baker

Introduction

This chapter examines the values and principles underlying European Union (EU) global environmental policy. This is contrasted with the United States (US), although the EU remains our primary focus. Global environmental policy refers to policy responses to environmental issues with global effects, which are managed through international regimes.

The chapter focuses on climate change policy, which is an excellent lens through which to explore the role of values and principles in international politics. Climate change is a critical global environmental problem, which exposes our limited knowledge about environmental systems, while simultaneously challenging the centrality of economic development relative to ecological and social well being. In this sense, climate change challenges the worldview of two global economic powers, the EU and the US.

In addition, climate change has resulted in international mitigation efforts by the United Nations (UN). While the establishment of a UN Framework Convention on Climate Change (UN FCCC) was relatively straightforward, its implementation has given rise to a bitter transatlantic dispute between the US and the EU. This makes the UN FCCC a rich source of empirical material for the investigation into the role values and principles play in shaping international environmental policy.

The investigation is motivated by a belief that the study of European integration has been too instrumental in nature. This has resulted in scholars defining European integration primarily in terms of its structural, procedural and material components (Weiler 1998: 60). To counter balance this, it is important to introduce a discourse on ideas into the study of European integration, not least because values and principles serve several important functions in the integration process.

First, they help the EU forge a sense of *group* identity. Identity formation is important for the EU, as it lacks roots in either state or nation, but is instead evolving as a unique combination of supranational and international forms of governance. As the European integration process gathers pace, values and principles act as a vehicle though which identity formation can take place.

Second, values and principles help in mobilising support for integration. In the early days of the European Community, this mobilisation was elite driven. However, in the post-Maastricht Europe, mobilisation of a wider support base is needed. Consequently, the EU is increasingly paying attention to the identification and articulation of shared values and legitimising principles. Here values and principles serve an additional, legitimising function (Weiler 1998; Manners 2000a).

Third, values and principles help to distinguish the EU on the international stage. The EU is increasingly making its external relations informed by, and conditional upon, a catalogue of norms. This marks the EU out as more akin to a normative power (Manners 2002: 241).

The focus of the chapter

This chapter has three distinctive focuses. First, it focuses upon the collective level: in the US, the study is of the US Administration at the federal level of government. Similarly, it explores the EU as a collective actor and sets aside a more differentiated investigation of the diversity of values and principles held by member states in relation to climate change (see Boehmer-Christiansen 1995; Manners 2000b). Thus, detailed discussion of the contributions of member states to EU climate change policy falls outside the scope of the chapter.

Second, attention is directed to the *declared* values and principles underlying EU climate change policy. Values are organising concepts that give meaning to our world. These values become principles once they become translated into general norms that govern behaviour. This study investigates two main sites where EU values and principles are located – declaratory political statements and the Treaty of Rome and its subsequent amendments. How these shape EU climate change policy is examined. This empirical investigation, however, comes with a methodological risk. A gap often exists, on the one hand, between declaratory intent and Treaty obligation and, on the other, actual practice. While the EU may declare itself to be guided by particular values and principles, these may be undermined by actions derived from a wider set of pragmatic considerations. Furthermore, the gap between intent and outcome may change across time, policy issues, within different institutional contexts, or within different negotiation settings.

The declaratory statements and Treaty obligations of the EU are taken as authentic, believing the EU to be honest in its statements of intent and aspiration. In other words, declaratory political statements or EU Treaty obligations are not taken as irrelevant or that, as the cynic may say, they aim to lead us into a state of false consciousness. On the contrary, such declaratory political statements and Treaty obligations oil the wheels of EU politics. They make the European integration process dynamic, articulating the base upon which Europe can build a shared future (S. Baker 2003).

However, concern about the gap between declaratory intent and treaty obligation and actual practice remains and helps shape the third focus of this chapter. While accepting that for too long the study of the EU has been one-sided and overly instrumental, we do not intend to contribute to this asymmetry by tipping the balance of research entirely in the opposite direction. Thus, in the exploration of the normative dimensions of EU climate change policy, we are careful not to entirely lose sight of the institutional perspectives needed to build a fuller picture of the role of values and principles in politics. This requires exploration of 'the fabric' of the political system, that is, the political and social context within which values are, or fail to be, realised. Thus, account has to be taken of how the 'constitutional' system, the distribution of authority, the institutional structures and the socio-economic system of both the EU and the US shape how values and principles are realised in political actions. Thus, the third focus is on the prospects for, and barriers to, the realisation of values and principles in political actions.

The chapter begins with a brief overview of international efforts to manage climate change under the UN FCCC, outlining the main areas of dispute between the EU and US. The values and principles that underlie EU environmental policy are considered, before turning to the example of climate change. Similarly, US environmental values are explored, before examining the values and principles that underlie their approach towards climate change.

International Climate Change Policy

The UN Framework Convention on Climate Change

The UN FCCC was one of only two Conventions to emerge from the 1992 Rio Earth Summit (the other being in relation to biodiversity management). It provides a convenient starting point for this study. Both the US and the European Community signed the UN FCCC. However, they did so for very different reasons. The US signed because, following lengthy negotiations, the UN FCCC did not contain any binding targets on reductions in greenhouse gas emissions. Indeed President Bush had threatened to boycott the entire Rio Summit until he had reassurance on this matter (Vig 2003: 110). In contrast, the EU had long sought binding timetables and quantified targets for reductions, particularly for carbon dioxide (CO_2) emissions (Commission 1997d: 3), including as far back as the 1990 Dublin European Council meeting (Bulletin of the EC 1990: 19). Other issues of dispute between the US and EU concern whether to include developing countries in reduction regimes and the use of carbon sinks as an implementation mechanism (Meadowcroft 2003). International efforts to deal with climate change have come to be dominated by the conflict between the US and the EU over the most acceptable approach towards the management of climate change. The conflict has structured the cleavage lines along which international bargaining, alliances and brokerage have been conducted between the contracting parties.

Working out the details: the CoPs meetings

Ten meetings of the parties to the UN FCCC, known as CoP meetings, have been held between 1992–2004, aimed at putting flesh on the general agreements outlined under the UN FCCC. The 1997 CoP-3 meeting in Kyoto was particularly divisive for transatlantic environmental relations. The EU arrived at Kyoto armed with a proposal for a binding 15 per cent reduction in emission levels. The US, in contrast, arrived armed with the belief that such targets were neither technically or economically feasible. Nevertheless, CoP-3 resulted in the Kyoto Protocol, which sets mandatory limits on emissions for the richer, including European countries, the US, Japan and the former Soviet Union. Because of the Kyoto Protocol, legally binding targets and timetables have now become an integral part of the implementation of the UN FCCC.

Despite this basic agreement, however, many issues were left unresolved by the Kyoto Protocol. The Kyoto targets were lower than the negotiating objectives of the European Commission (Commission 1996b: 110). The Commission feared that the US would meet its targets through emissions trading, especially with Russia, thus avoiding positive policy initiatives at home (Commission 1997d). The EU holds that emission trading should be 'supplemental to domestic action'. More fundamentally, the prospects of the US ratifying Kyoto were bleak because the Protocol lacked binding reduction targets for developing countries, which the US Senate believed gave these countries an unfair advantage in global markets (Bryner 2000: 293). Fears that the US would not ratify were confirmed in 1999, when the US Senate banned spending aimed at implementation of the Protocol.

Consequently, the agenda of the CoP-6 in The Hague in 2000 was heavily burdened and the talks broke up amid a much-publicised rift between the US and the EU. The US accused the Europeans of being inflexible, and the Europeans criticised the US for pursuing trading and sequestration schemes that would introduce numerous loopholes and measurement difficulties (Hempel 2003: 313).

The US withdrawal

A second blow was dealt in March 2001 when President George W. Bush announced that the US would not implement the Kyoto Protocol. While the EU believes that the Kyoto Protocol is an essential, albeit limited, step in putting the UN FCCC into practice, the Bush Administration saw the Protocol as having three fundamental flaws:

1   It does not oblige developing countries to cut their greenhouse gas emissions.
2   It does not allow developed countries to comply though investing in reductions in developing countries.
3   It is proposing action ahead of further research.

While the US position on developing countries was to change at the CoP-8 in Delhi in 2002, it has remained steadfast in relation to the third objection. This objection is particularly important for this analysis, as it goes directly to the disagreement between the US and the EU on the precautionary principle. This is discussed in some detail below.

Building upon these objections, the current Bush Administration has dis-associated itself from the Kyoto Protocol. The US has not disassociated itself from the UN FCCC, which it has ratified. Its alternative 'Blue Skies' policy, however, amounts to little more than 'business as usual' (Bodansky 2002). The EU, in contrast, holds that climate change policy should be technology forcing, believing that the problem of climate change can initiate a process of technolo-gical and behavioural change (Commission 1997e: 8; 2001a: 25). Consequently, the EU has gone on to develop a European Climate Change Programme (Commission 2000c; 2001i). This aims at the implementation of the Kyoto tar-gets through the integration of climate change considerations into Community sectoral policy, the adoption of energy efficiency measures and legislation (Commission 2000c) and, more recently, the introduction of an emissions trading regime. Emissions trading has become an essential mechanism through which the EU will meet its Kyoto targets (Commission Press Release, 'Climate change: projections show EU on track to meet Kyoto Protocol emis-sion targets', IP/04/1522, date: 21/12/2004). The EU has also played a key role in negotiations leading up to the 2004 ratification of the Kyoto Protocol by Russia.

A challenge to EU commitment

The US withdrawal from Kyoto has left the EU internationally vulnerable. Having ratified the Protocol in 2002, it remains challenged to continue its commitment despite the fact that the US is not introducing measured policies to address climate change. The Commission sees this asymmetry as potentially dangerous to European industrial competitiveness, arguing that:

> There can be no question of our European economy suffering the con-sequences of a unilateral global environmental protection policy while our trading partners could avoid measures influencing energy prices and hence the competitiveness of industry and employment.
>
> (Commission 1997f: 14)

The Commission also believes that unilateral action by the EU would dra-matically increase the costs needed to manage climate change and could result in the flight of energy-intensive industry to outside the EU. There is also con-cern that the US could act as a free rider, benefiting from costly efforts under-taken by others, without making any contribution (Commission 1997e).

The US withdrawal and its failure to develop an alternative, proactive climate change policy present not only economic challenges to the EU. It also calls into question the extent of the EU's commitment when this threatens other, eco-nomic goals. Here environmental values come directly in conflict with economic values.

The withdrawal also challenges the EU in a third way. The EU is determined to show itself as a global leader in the area of climate change (Haigh 1996), as it did in the early years of the IPCC (1988–91) (Bretherton and Vogler 1999). Its stance against the US has given the Community a heightened international role in climate change management. This was seen at the resumed CoP-6*bis* negotiations in Bonn in 2001 when, to the great surprise of the US, agreement was reached on implementation of the first commitment period of the Kyoto Protocol (Vrolojk 2002). The leadership role of the EU was also evident at the CoP-7 meeting in Marrakech, resulting in the Marrakech Accord (Meadowcroft 2003). Paradoxically, it would appear that the US disavowal of Kyoto helped galvanise the resolve of other states and the EU to reach agreement that would allow the Kyoto Protocol to come into force (Meadowcroft 2003: 13). Yet, global environmental leadership comes new to the EU, as was evident in its poor behaviour at the CoP-8 in Delhi, 2002. There is still much at stake as the EU struggles to ensure that its actions contribute to, rather than undermine, the desire to come of age on the international, political stage (see Grubb and Gupta 2000). The recent shift in the US from a rather benign to a more hostile approach towards Kyoto adds to this challenge (Ott 2003).

Such then, briefly, are the disputes between the US and the EU on how to implement the UN FCCC. Attention is now turned to an investigation of the underlying values and principles that drive their respective positions in the hope that this may cast light on how these disputes have arisen. This begins with an examination of the EU, exploring the general values and principles that shape EU environmental policy, and then turning our attention to the specific case of climate change management.

EU climate change policy

In this section, the declaratory statements of the two key EU institutions, the Commission and the Council, are explored for evidence of the values and principles that guide climate change policy. Such values and principles are typically found in Commission communications, Council declarations and in submissions made to the UN and the various CoP meetings. In addition, the values and principles enshrined in the Treaty of Rome are examined, particularly through its amendments following the Single European Act (SEA) 1986 and the Treaty on European Union (Maastricht Treaty) 1992, and the Amsterdam 1997 and Nice 2000 Treaties.

General values underlying EU environmental policy

Environmental Action Programmes (EAPs) are a key means for the Commission to develop and articulate environmental values and principles. The First EAP (1973–76) laid down the five main principles of EU environmental policy:

- the best environmental policy consists in prevention of pollution
- prevention is compatible with economic and social development

- environmental effects should be taken into account at the earliest possible stage in planning
- exploitation of natural resources must be avoided: natural resources are an asset that should be used and not abused
- the cost of pollution control must be borne by the polluter, that is 'the polluter pays principle'

(Commission 1973)

Later, the Fourth EAP (1987–92) adopted a distinctive set of values in relation to industrial policy, introducing the idea that 'ecological modernisation' could offer competitive advantage to European industry (Commission 1987). Ecologically modernised industry treats the environment not as a free resource, but as a factor of production that has to be priced. In the short term, this reduces natural resource inputs for a given level of economic outputs or valued added. In the long term, through promoting eco-efficiency, ecological modernisation can protect the resource base upon which further economic development depends. In addition, it links environmental protection with the stimulation of technological innovation, which can, in turn, open up or expand markets.

Amendments to the Treaty of Rome have also been important for the development and codification of EU environmental values and principles. The polluter pays principle, the precautionary and the preventative principles were all incorporated into the Treaty of Rome through the SEA. The SEA also enshrined the principle that environmental protection should be a component of other EU policies. This principle of environmental policy integration was subsequently strengthened under the Maastricht Treaty, which stated that 'that environmental protection requirements must be integrated into the definition and implementation of other Community policies'. The principle is very important for climate change policy, given that policies to address climate change need to be cross-sectoral in nature.

Of particular importance is the commitment to the promotion of sustainable development that was enshrined in the Maastricht Treaty. This was reinforced by the Amsterdam Treaty, which called for 'balanced and sustainable development of economic activities', and adopted environmental policy integration as a key means to achieving sustainable development. Treaty revisions have made the promotion of sustainable development the core principle that guides EU environmental policy, both at the domestic and the international levels. More importantly, the Treaty of Amsterdam made sustainable development one of the *objectives* of the Community, making it applicable to the general activities of the EU, not just its activities in the sphere of the environment. As a result, sustainable development is now a *norm* of EU politics, both domestically and externally (S. Baker 2000). This acceptance is reflected in the Fifth EAP *Towards Sustainability* (1992–2000) (Commission 1992b) and the present Sixth EAP, *Our Future, Our Choice* (Commission 2001a). Both programmes explicitly link economic development, environmental protection and climate change management with the promotion of sustainable development.

The Maastricht Treaty also strengthened the commitment to the precautionary principle, which, as discussed below, has become important in shaping transatlantic environmental relations, not just in relation to climate change.

Values underlying international engagement

The SEA also gave the EU a mandate to search for solutions to global environmental problems. This is not to deny the complexity of Community engagement in international (environmental) management regimes, where the boundary lines between Community competence and member state jurisdiction is often unclear (Bretherton and Vogler 1999; Jupille and Caporaso 1998), including within the UN FCCC (Macrory and Hession 1996). What the SEA made clear, however, is that the EU enters into international negotiations with an obligation to protect the environment and not merely to agree solutions that explicitly or implicitly are profitable to the European economy (see Krämer 2002). This is in marked contrast to the US position, discussed below. Furthermore, following the Maastricht Treaty, the EU can contribute to the pursuit of its environmental objectives by promoting measures at the international level to deal with regional or worldwide environmental problems. To this end, the Community is able to make binding international, environmental agreements, which, in turn, impose obligations on its member states.

The Community has identified climate change as a major, global environmental problem and is politically committed to stabilise greenhouse gas emissions. The Dublin Declaration (1990) encouraged this when it stated that 'the Community and its member states have a special responsibility to encourage and participate in international action to combat global environmental problems (Bulletin of the EC 1990: 19) and that:

> The Community must use more effectively its position of moral, economic and political authority to advance international efforts to solve global problems and to promote sustainable development and respect for the global commons.
>
> (Bulletin of the EC 1990: 19)

In part, this commitment is driven by a sense of moral obligation, with the Commission arguing that:

> As Europeans and as part of some of the wealthiest societies in the world, we are very conscious of our role and responsibilities. ... Along with other developed countries, we are major contributors to global environmental problems such as greenhouse gas emissions and we consume a major, and some would argue an unfair, share of the planet's renewable and non-renewable resources ....
>
> (Commission 2001a: 11)

To see how this moral imperative shapes practice, attention is focused on how one key EU environmental principle, the precautionary principle, is used to inform its policy preferences in relation to the international management of climate change within the UN FCCC.

EU climate change policy and the precautionary principle

As indicated above, the precautionary principle is particularly important for understanding the differences between the approach of the EU and US. The continued use of this principle by the EU has led to a series of disputes with the US, not just over climate change policy, but also in relation to trade, within the World Trade Organization. Indeed, disagreement over the precautionary principle has become one of the main arenas within which the value differences between the US and the EU are acted out, both in relation to environmental policy and, more specifically, climate change management.

The precautionary principle has been used in environmental policy for over two decades. It was first recognised in the 1982 UN World Charter for Nature and has subsequently been incorporated into several international environmental conventions. It is found in the 1992 Rio Declaration and the UN FCCC also refers to the precautionary approach, where Article 3 (Principles) states that:

> The Parties should take precautionary measures to anticipate, prevent or minimise the causes of climate change and mitigate its adverse effects. Where there are threats of serious or irreversible damage, lack of full scientific certainty should not be used as a reason for postponing such measures....

Since the 1980s, the precautionary principle has been progressively consolidated in international environmental management regimes, making it 'a full-fledged and general principle of international environmental law' (Commission 2000e: 10). This is despite growing US opposition to the use of the principle. The US feared that the EU could use the principle for (trade) protectionist purposes.

The explicit legal reference to the precautionary principle in the EU is in the environmental title of the Treaty of Rome (Article 174). However, one should not conclude from this that the principle applies only to the environment. Rather the Commission believes that the principle is 'a general one which should in particular be taken into consideration in the fields of environmental protection, human, animal and plant health' (Commission 2000e: 9). The EU regularly evokes this principle in matters relating to climate change (Commission 2000e: 8), dating as far back as the 1990 Dublin Declaration (Bulletin of the EC 1990: 18).

The EU has consistently refused to bow to US pressure over both its use and interpretation of the precautionary principle, with the Commission arguing that:

the Community ... has the right to establish the level of protection – particularly of the environment, human, animal and plant health, – that it deems appropriate. Applying the precautionary principle is a key tenet of its policy, and the choices it makes to this end will continue to affect the views it defends internationally on how this principle should be applied.

Commission 2000e: 2

In its simplest form the precautionary principle, as a tool of risk management, holds that in the face of scientific uncertainty, policy makers should err on the side of safety. The principle is related to the German '*Vorsorge Prinzip*' and has been used as a principle in shaping German environmental law since the 1980s. The German approach has since been adopted at the member state and the EU levels. In part, this policy transfer was due to its adoption by DG Environment bureaucrats who drafted the EU's Fourth EAP (Weale 1992). Its continued use by the Commission also owes much to the urging of the European Parliament and the Council 'to be in the future ever more determined to be guided by the precautionary principle' (Council Resolution, 13 April 1999).

This determination arises from growing social concerns about health and safety issues. Several food safety and public health scandals, especially the bovine spongiform encephalopathy (BSE) crisis ('mad cow' disease) in the UK, and growing public unease about biotechnological developments, strongly influenced the use of the precautionary principles by the EU. Member states have supported this development. The UK was not alone in experiencing public distrust in the state's ability to regulate for health and safety. The high profile case of contamination of blood supplies, especially in France, eroded public trust in the regulatory system governing public health in the country (Graham and Hsia 2002: 373). These incidences of regulatory failure have undermined the credibility of regulatory institutions at the EU level. The use of the precautionary principle in this context can be seen as an effort to rebuild public confidence. In addition, the EU's use of the precautionary principle can serve another important function. As a risk aversion strategy, it bypasses the need for regulatory management of risk through the establishment of EU-level institutions. Member states have been reluctant to allow the EU to develop such institutions. Thus, the use of the precautionary principle can also be attributed to the nature of the EU's governance structure, which frames a complex distribution of political authority and power between the EU, national, and sub-national levels.

Like many principles, the precautionary principle is deeply ambiguous, lacking a clear definition of such key terms as 'scientific uncertainty' and 'safety'. The Commission provided guidelines on the implementation of the principle by issuing a Communication in 2000 (Commission 2000e). The Communication offered official clarification of the principle, in part to enhance public confidence and in part to give the principle more legitimacy in international settings. The Communication was also produced amidst Commission concerns that, if not operationalised carefully, the principle could become a source of trade disputes among its own member states (Graham and Hsia 2002: 372).

The Communication argued that the principle should be adopted when there are '*reasonable* grounds for concern that the potentially *dangerous effects* on the environment, human, animal or plant health may be inconsistent with the chosen level of protection' (Commission 2000e: 10, emphasis added). This allows the EU to evoke the principle in a far wider range of circumstances than is indicated by the UN's interpretation, which holds that the principle should be used when there is a threat of 'serious and irreversible damage' (Majone 2001: 6). There is also an explicit expansion of the principle beyond environmental issues, to cover consumer and animal health and food safety.

The Communication places the precautionary principle within the EU's existing framework of risk analysis, linking it to a range of decision-making tools and processes already in use. These include the use of scientific evaluation, risk assessment and CBA. It lays down explicit criteria that must be met in order for the application of the precautionary principle to be justified. It also stipulated that, when applied, measures based on the precautionary principle should be:

- proportional to the chosen level of protection
- non-discriminatory in their application
- consistent with measures already taken
- examined in the light of benefits and costs
- subject to review in the light of new scientific data.

(Commission 2000e: 4)

The Commission also argues that the principle should be evoked to manage risk in the longer run and for the well being of future generations (Commission 2000e: 7). Consideration of the inter-generational dimensions of environmental management is one of the distinctive features of sustainable development. Here it can be seen that the commitment to the promotion of sustainable development influencing the Commission's interpretations of key, related policy principles.

The Commission's strong interpretation of the precautionary principle, found within the Communication, is in keeping with its views that policy making under conditions of uncertainty and risk is not a mere technical task. Rather 'judging what is an "acceptable" level of risk for society is an eminently *political* responsibility' (Commission 2000e: 3). This approach makes policy makers politically accountable for the way in which risks are managed. As will be seen later, this contrasts with the US position, where risk assessment and hence its management is seen as primarily a technical, *economic* task. This, in turn, makes it easier for policy makers to be disassociated from the consequences of their actions. Placing precaution in the hands of policy makers, it has been argued, lays the groundwork for democratic control of policy making in the face of risk, or rather, for accountability with respect to the degree of precaution exercised in risk management (Graham and Hsia 2002: 378).

The Commission is not the only EU institution committed to the use of the precaution principle. Justification of its use was also highlighted in a well-publicised report by the European Environmental Agency, *Late Lessons from Early*

Warnings (EEA 2001). This report revealed the costly and unforeseen consequences for the environment and human health of inaction by regulators across a wide range of issue areas. However, this is not to argue that the EU, having confirmed its commitment to the principle, has been entirely consistent in its applications. Indeed, there is strong evidence to suggest that there is much variation and even inconsistency in the relative precaution exhibited in US and European regulatory policy over time, especially in relation to consumer health issues (Wiener and Rogers 2002). We need also to be aware that the EU makes use of other risk management tools, such as impact analysis, and that it has been under some pressure to simplify its regulatory regime, particularly in the context of Eastern enlargement. The multiple Communications on Better Regulation in June 2002 (Commission 2002a–d) and the recent emphasis placed on impact assessment have been seen by some as a potential threat to the application of the precautionary principle within the EU (Löfstedt 2004). As is the case in the US, economic considerations also play a key role in guiding EU environmental policy. We can point in particular to the recent split within the Commission between DG Environment and DG Enterprise on the application of the precautionary principle, in particular with respect to the regulation of chemicals (Löfstedt 2004).

However, despite these problems, the precautionary principle is now written into Community law. In addition, the emphasis is different on the European side of the Atlantic. While both the US and the EU take economic considerations into account in risk regulation, for the Commission, taking account of economic factors entails:

> ... comparing the overall cost to the Community of action and lack of action, in both the short and long term. This is not simply and economic cost-benefit analysis: its scope is much broader, and includes non-economic considerations, such as the efficiency of possible options and their acceptability to the public. In the conduct of such an examination, account should be taken *of the general principle and the case law of the Court that the protection of health takes precedence over economic considerations.*
>
> (Commission 2000e: 4, emphasis added)

The US replied to the Commission's Communication on the precautionary principle with a long list of sceptical questions. To understand the rationale behind this questioning, attention is now turned to the exploration of the values that underlie environmental policy and, more specifically, climate change policy in the US.

US climate change policy

General values underlying US environmental policy

During the 1970s, the US was regarded as an environmental leader state. The Environmental Protection Agency (EPA) in particular pursued stringent environmental standards (Vogel 2003). Its tough enforcement policies made US environmental regulations the envy of environmental groups in other developed countries, especially in Europe. Much of this regulation was aimed at the protection of ambient quality and human health. However, the environmental leader status of the US was undermined during the Reagan Administration of the 1980s. Virtually all environmental protection and resource policies enacted during the 1970s were re-evaluated in the light of Reagan's desire to reduce the scope of government, shift responsibilities downwards to the states and rely more on the private sector (Kraft and Vig 2003: 14). Deregulation and decentralisation also undermined the power of environmental institutions, especially the EPA. This helped displace the lead role hitherto played by the US in setting global environmental standards and in the development of innovative solutions to environmental problems.

In addition, economic considerations have come to play a major role in shaping US environmental policy. Of particular importance has been the introduction of Order 12291, which requires the EPA and other federal regulatory agencies to conduct cost benefit analysis (CBA) of all regulatory proposals and adopt the most economically efficient or cost-effective alternative (Krämer 2002: 4). Despite the changes of administration since the Reagan era, environmental policy continues to be marked by the centrality given to economic considerations, especially under the current Bush presidency.

Environmental values

The assault of the Reagan Administration on environmental regulation has influenced the development of environmental values in the US in significant ways. The Reagan years have left a legacy of controversy about the regulatory role of the state in environmental policy. This controversy has crowded the environmental policy agenda with ongoing discussions about the acceptability of government regulation of behaviour that has environmental consequences. This debate is especially marked in relation to the role of government in the regulation of industry.

This crowding of the policy agenda has slowed down the development of 'second generation' environmental values. Ecological modernisation is a value typical of second generation environmental values. Here the perception that there is a trade-off between economic development and environmental protection is replaced by a new set of values that sees both as mutually reinforcing policy objectives. Such values help move policy beyond 'command and control' to stimulate the internalisation of environmental considerations at the level of government, the firm and the individual. As such, they exert a strong normative influence on environmental and related policy preferences.

The concept of ecological modernisation has failed to gain a foothold either among firms or policy makers within the US. In contrast, second generation environmental values, based on ecological modernisation, have taken hold in the EU. These values operate alongside the acceptance of the EU's regulatory role.

There is also some hint, albeit tentative, that in certain leader environmental states of the EU (Scandinavia and the Netherlands) environmental objectives are moving from 'de-coupling' of economic development from environmental harm (eco-efficiency), to considerations of 'de-materialisation' of society, thus paving the way for third generation environmental values to evolve (sustainable consumption).

Similarly, while the promotion of sustainable development has become a norm of EU policy, sustainable development is a term used only on the margins of debates in the US (Baker and McCormick 2004). Thus, although the Clinton Administration did establish the President's Council on Sustainable Development (PCSD) in 1993, it focused primarily upon the intersection of economic and environmental issues and failed to foster commitment to sustainable development, especially at the federal level. This is despite the growing interest at the local, state and regional levels in sustainable communities. The PCSD also failed to address broader social issues, or generate much discussion on moral issues (Bryner 2000: 297), such as the obligations of the US as a major contributor to climate change and to global resource depletion, to address the destruction of the global commons. Attempts to make sustainable development part of federal policy thinking were also undermined by the election of President George W. Bush, and his return to office for a second term.

Several deeply held values could explain, at least in part, the failure of the US to engage with the promotion of sustainable development. Regulation and 'big government' is anathema to US corporations. In a country that believes itself to be in possession of considerable space and untapped resources, the idea that limits should be placed on exploiting resources wins little corporate or public sympathy. Similarly, there has long been a belief that the exploitation of land and natural resources are central to the establishment of economic and personal freedom (Baker and McCormick 2004). The value of 'freedom' is central to US political culture. Freedom is realised by giving full expression to individual consumer taste, through the market and independently *from* the state. Consequently, environmental protection measures can be seen as restrictions on corporate and individual choices and freedom of behaviour. In contrast, in the European social democratic traditions, state (welfare) provision is understood to make freedom possible: in Europe, freedom is realised *through* the state. Environmental protection can thus be closely linked with the promotion of the collective common good.

Underlying US climate change policy

These value differences between the US and EU are reflected in their respective approaches towards climate change. The US sees itself as a resource-rich country and resource efficiency arguments have not received widespread acceptability, either among policy makers or among the public. At a minimum, they can be seen as leading to reduction in demands for energy and hence as harming US production interests. Thus, while increasing efficiency in resource use is a major part of the European Climate Change Programme, in the US there is suspicion that such policy could be used to enhance the opportunities for the state to interfere in citizen choices. In the US, climate change policy is marked by voluntary and market-led approaches. These approaches are to be found irrespective of whether or not the US Administration has a progressive or regressive environmental agenda. The voluntary approach dominated Clinton's Climate Change Action Plan ([US] Department of Energy 1994; Bryner 2000).

Principles guiding policy making under conditions of risk and uncertainty

As already indicated, the US rejects the precautionary principle as a guide to both domestic and international policy. It lobbied successfully against the use of the principle in the Rio Declaration, in favour of the less elevated words 'precautionary approach' (Krämer 2002: 10). In place of the precautionary principle, the US uses a science-based risk assessment strategy and strongly advocates its use within international regimes and as a principle of international, including environmental, law.

The science-based risk assessment strategy accepts that regulatory risk assessment takes place within the context of scientific uncertainty, particularly in relation to the protection of human health. The strategy aims at establishing 'safe' standards, for example, of levels of exposure to certain chemicals or products (Majone 2001: 5). Typically, risk assessment is followed by risk management strategies.

The use of risk-based decision-making is particularly important in the US EPA, where it has become 'the dominant language for discussing environmental policy' (Andrews 2003: 223). Like other forms of scientific knowledge, it has come to be used as both an ingredient in policy making and as a tool for policy legitimisation (Boehmer-Christiansen 1995: 7). For the EPA, risk assessment is used as a tool for evaluating the trade-off between environmental concerns and regulatory burdens and risk management has, in turn, come to mean choosing and justifying regulatory decisions.

Risk assessment can also tip policy in favour of business, because it implicitly accepts the view that proof rather than prudence is required to justify regulation. As Andrews has argued:

> The U.S. approach to risk-based decision making has been dominated by the use of detailed formal procedures ... to justify environmental regulatory proposals, and by a general principle of placing the burden of proof primarily on advocates of government action to prevent risk rather than on those who propose actions that might cause hazards.
>
> (Andrews 2003: 242)

From a comparative perspective, the EU's precautionary principle contrasts with the US approach because the former can more easily lead to the abandonment of use of a product and the decision not to regulate for 'safe standards' of use or exposure. In other words, faced with scientific uncertainty, the EU tends towards a more cautious, risk *aversion* strategy. In contrast, the US leans towards a *use-with-risk* strategy.

The centrality of economic values

In addition to differences in the US and EU approaches towards policy making under conditions of scientific uncertainty, different weight is given to economic over environmental values in climate change management. Order 12291 has led to several federal CBA studies of climate change impact. Overall, these have led to a view that costs, particularly of the Kyoto targets, would be prohibitive relative to the likely economic and local consequences of climate change to the US (Freeman 2003). Consequently, the introduction of federal-level policies is not seen as cost efficient and therefore not given priority.

In contrast, while cost-benefit considerations and considerations of proportionality require that the EU take account of the costs and benefits of environmental action or lack of action, they are not applied in the strict technical sense of a CBA. The Commission regards CBA as a rather inexact, somewhat blunt policy tool. More broadly, the idea that environmental policy should be narrowly based on economic theory has not gained much hold in the Commission and calls for the use of CBA as a tool for global environmental policy making are seen as somewhat misguided.

In addition, the strong Commission belief in the cost effectiveness of ecological modernisation pushes their time horizon well beyond the short-term view that is inherent in the time-discounted values given to costs and benefits within a CBA. Further, ecological modernisation, because it is seen as a powerful stimulus for innovation and modernisation, means that the narrow variables of CBA are supplemented by broader considerations.

Differences over the role and function of international regimes

The different weight given to economic over environmental values is reflected in the different understandings by the EU and US of the function of international environmental negotiations. The EU accepts environmental negotiations as being autonomous from commercial and foreign policy (Krämer 2002: 5). Since the early 1970s, environmental matters have been kept outside the direct influence of member states' foreign or trade policies. Thus, the environmental Directorate General and the environmental departments of member states mainly represent the Community in international environmental negotiations.

The US sees international environmental negotiations as primarily international trade negotiations (Krämer 2002: 13). As a result, the State Department and the Department of Commerce represent the US in international environmental negotiations, with a conspicuous absence of the EPA. Under the George W. Bush administration in particular, the US wants to see global institutions and instruments give greater importance to the economic aspects of free trade than to environmental protections. In addition, the US has consistently refused to accept negotiation outcomes that result in broad general texts on which it is hoped to base future, global environmental measures. These are perceived as the thin end of a wedge, inserting alien, value-driven environmental concerns into American political and economic priorities.

Value differences between the US and the EU guide their respective views on climate change policy. Nevertheless, implicit in this analysis has been an argument that factors other than values and principles direct climate change responses. It is to this wider context that focus is now turned, specifically to explore how such factors can act as barriers to, or help promote, the realisation of values through political action.

Barriers to and prospects for the realisation of values in political action

In this section, attention is paid to the wider political (institutional, constitutional and administrative) context within which policy is made, both in the US and the EU. Repeatedly in the discussion of the US case, consideration has to be given to the importance of administrative changes, the role of Congress and the division of authority at the federal level in shaping climate change responses. Similarly, the EU system of governance, and the sharing of competence between the EU and the member state levels, also act as important variables in analysis.

The US

The division of political authority in the US between the federal and the state levels can explain several features of the US approach towards climate change. Federal government has only limited competence over many policy areas and primarily only macroeconomic policy tools at its disposal. This makes the introduction of climate change policies very difficult, because they require both cross-sectoral as well as microeconomic policy changes. In addition, it has restricted the federal government's perception of the feasibility of climate change measures. For example, assessment of the cost of dealing with climate change has been restricted to options that are feasible given the limited range of policy tools available to federal government (Von Moltke and Rahman 1996: 331).

The distribution of power within Congress between the House and Senate and the granting of jurisdiction over environmental policy to dozens of committees and subcommittees also has major implications for climate management (Kraft and Vig 2003: 4). Curtailment of Clinton's more progressive environmental policy ambitions provides a noticeable example. Like Jimmy Carter, Clinton entered office with an ambitious environmental agenda and, like his predecessor, was forced by competing priorities and lack of congressional support to compromise his environmental plans (Vig 2003: 106), including his Climate Change Action Plan.

This is not to suggest that US administrations are incapable of progressive action. However, as Kraft and Vig have shown, certain conditions have to be met for the US political system to prove flexible enough to permit substantial policy innovation. These include that issues be highly visible, the public be supportive and political leaders act cohesively (Kraft and Vig 2003). These conditions have been lacking with respect to climate change. In addition, while institutional factors are important, the strength of the industrial, especially energy, lobby can also explain the failure of the US to adequately respond to climate change. The strong energy lobby, particularly within the oil-producing sector, plays a major role in shaping climate change policy under the current Bush Administration. This lobby continues to block both fiscal and efficiency measures aimed at reducing US oil consumption and greenhouse gas emissions, a third of which come from private modes of transport, including highly fashionable, high consumption, sports utility vehicles.

The US's own difficulties in implementing climate change policies are reflected in its scepticism about the capacity of other countries to effectively address the problem. Hence policy makers are deeply suspicious of EU promises to meet its Kyoto targets. However, the EU's competence over the use of a broader range of policy tools to address climate change means that it is not as hampered in its search for policy solutions as is the US federal government.

The EU

It should be noted, however, that Commission attempts to introduce an EU carbon tax were blocked by member states (Zito 2000). Thus, as is the case in the US, the ability of the EU to realise its values and principles in political action remains limited by its institutional shortcomings as well as the complex relationship that exists between the EU and its member states.

The values and principles laid down in the Treaty of Rome and its subsequent amendments and in the EAPs provide a basis for EU climate change policy. To be effective, however, EU policy must be embodied in legislation that places obligations on member states (Haigh 1996). While 'burden sharing' has become the acceptable approach to collective EU climate change policy, which recognises that the member states have to contribute to the preservation of the common or *climatic* good, there are nevertheless problems.

Effective implementation is weakened by two politically sensitive tasks. The first is the need to achieve horizontal coordination between the multiple sectors of EU activity, that is, to implement the principle of environmental policy integration. The second is to achieve vertical coordination between the levels of territorial competence that are to apply the principle of subsidiarity. In the first case, climate change policy is undermined by the difficulties of controlling emissions from sectors such as transport and agriculture and by the inconsistencies between member states' taxation and energy policies. In the second case, vertical integration is blocked by disputes over the respective competence of the Commission and the member states, particularly in the energy field. This means that the principle of subsidiarity has yet to be applied in a non-contentious manner. Because of these two factors, many member states still fail to meet the requirements of the burden sharing agreement, which sets out the contribution of member state to the achievement of the overall EU emission reduction target agreed at Kyoto (Meadowcroft 2003). Furthermore, many member states have used burden sharing as a means whereby they are able to increase their emission levels.

Thus, in contrast to its strong value-driven international stance, the link between values and principles and political action is weakest at the internal level within the EU. Horizontal policy coordination remains illusive, because environmental objectives frequently stand in conflict with the other, more traditional, aims of policy, particularly at the sectoral levels. As such, environmental values and principles often come in conflict with other values and principles. As a result, the Commission has admitted that reducing emissions of greenhouse gases remains one of the most intractable problems facing the Union today (Commission 2001a). While emission trading can help the EU to meet its Kyoto targets in the first commitment period (that is, up until 2012), this does little to force a direct reduction in emission levels in member states and can be criticised for breaking the principle of environmental integrity. Until these issues are resolved, the gap will remain between, on the one hand, the values embedded in the declaratory political intent and Treaty obligations of the EU, and, on the other, the ability of the EU to see its values and principles through policy implementation.

Conclusion

This chapter explored how differences in environmental values and principles underlie the dispute between the US and the EU over the implementation of the UN FCCC. While the election of President George W. Bush has done much to heighten transatlantic tensions, the highly publicised rift between the US and the EU over climate change management predate the decision of the Bush administration to withdraw from the Kyoto Protocol. Undoubtedly, there are specific differences over the UN FCCC implementation regime. However, these difficulties are also driven by marked differences in how the environmental *problematic* is understood and in the weight given to environmental and to economic values at either side of the Atlantic. Disputes over the role of international environmental regimes, including those operating through the UN, are a product of these value differences.

Despite differences within and between member states, there is a general consensus in Europe that environmental protection cannot be left to market forces and that environmental protection is a legitimate goal of government, or 'the foundation of any society' (Krämer 2002: 15). The European integration project has resulted in a gradual shift upwards of this task to the EU level. There is now consensus among member states that EU-level environmental policy should continue to develop and that this development forms part of the building blocks of the European integration project.

Since the 1970s, the EU has evolved a clearly defined and articulated set of environmental principles, primarily based around the commitment to the promotion of sustainable development. These now displace the centrality traditionally given to economic considerations by a set of wider social and ecological concerns. These principles guide both the domestic actions of the EU and its engagement in international environmental management regimes. Either the principles are enshrined in Treaty, and hence can be seen as Treaty obligations, or they are articulated through work programmes of the Commission, such as EAPs. EU environmental principles form part of a complex 'value set' that is held, either explicitly or implicitly, by the EU. Within this value set, the principle of sustainable development coincides with the principles of governance and of competitiveness to form the core values that currently drive the integration process. The components of this value do not always coexist in an easy relationship and thus the realisation of any one of these values through political action is not always ensured. Thus, a gap continues to exist between the declaratory intent and legal obligations of the EU and actual policy content. At one level, this gap exposes the value *differences* that lie at the heart of the European integration project. The gap also owes much to the complexity of the European integration project, with its requirements that, horizontally, sectoral policy integration be matched by the achievement of coordination and consistency along the vertical, territorial levels of governance. Despite this gap, values and principles remain important to the EU. They help consolidate the integration process. They provide a basis upon which Europe is articulating the values that will shape its shared, environmental future. More generally, they help legitimise the integration process, mobilising support for this unique and somewhat risky European political experiment.

Our study of the US has thrown up some rather different findings. While the EU needs legitimising values and principles but struggles to maintain consistency and coherence in their use, the US is shown to be far more consistent in its behaviour. It persistently attributes greater weight to economic over environmental values and to meeting individual needs over the maintenance of the collective good.

The US sees many so-called 'global' environmental problems as not global at all: they are problems for others. It sees the promotion of sustainable development as a task primarily for developing countries, not for itself. Domestically, environmental policy is still marked by controversy over the regulatory role of the state and, consequently, second generation environmental values have failed to develop. As such, environmental policy making is seen almost exclusively as a technical task, best seen as based on 'objective' processes, specifically CBA and science-based risk assessment techniques. The US's narrow perception of the nature of the environmental problematic, and the centrality given to economic values, stand in contrast to the EU's position. The EU sets climate change policy in broader social, economic, political and moral terms. As such, the EU has developed a highly principled approach, based upon a developed and articulated set of environmental values.

6 The European Union and the value of gender equality

Andrea Pető and Ian Manners

EU actorness is an interaction between presence, opportunity and capability (Bretherton 2002, 14) so this chapter analyses these three factors in a historical and comparative perspective as far as the value of gender equality is concerned, with special emphasis on enlargement and development, together with a reflection on the impact of EU gender equality mechanisms on the formation of European identity. Gender equality policy was born in Europe through the intellectual tradition of 'women's difference'. The EU is a young normative power, which is slowly transforming itself from an economic community into a post-national political actor (Manners 2000a; 2002). Its identity is based on universal human values such as equality in order to overcome the difficulties of diversity found in differing national traditions and lack of a common 'European' cultural tradition.

The value of gender equality may be the only value that was shared by political actors on both sides of the Iron Curtain during the Cold War. This value, that equal pay should be given to men and women for equal work, was one of the founding principles of the 'statist feminist' communist states in Eastern Europe guaranteed by the Stalinist constitutions. It was also a basic value of the European Community from 1957, located in article 119 of the Treaty of Rome guaranteeing 'equal pay for equal work' (Hoskyns 1994: 226). However, leftist intellectuals in Western Europe looked for inspiration on the other side of the Iron Curtain as far as implementing gender equality in the field of employment was concerned. Yet very few 'universal' European values are further from being institutionalised in reality than gender equality because of the paradoxical character of 'equality'. This chapter explores the value of gender equality in two areas of EU external relations: enlargement to include the accession countries of Central and Eastern Europe, and development policy with an emphasis on health, AIDS, and population policies. First, we will analyse the origins, history and institutionalisation of gender equality mechanisms in the European Union. Second, the impact of this value on the processes and consequences of enlargement will be considered. Third, we will look at the value of gender equality in development policy. Finally, in the conclusion we reflect on the values and principles of gender equality and feminisms in the EU.

Origins, development and institutions of gender equality in the EU

The history and transformation of European-level gender equality policy provides an explanation for the controversial character of present policy. The history of EU equality policy can be divided into three approaches (Rees 1998), perspectives (Booth and Bennett 2002), or historical periods (Bretherton 1999). The development of gender equality policy occurred in parallel with the slow, complicated processes of EU institutional negotiations, which initially resulted in adaptations to the principles of equal pay and equal treatment, including social security.

In the first phase of EU gender 'equality politics' the purpose was to achieve 'equality between sexes' in employment, thus acting as a starting point for policy spillover and further political action. In the European Community (EC) the principles of equality between sexes was institutionalised through flexible international arrangements, with the political support of the second wave of the women's movement during *détente*. Article 119 of the Treaty of Rome stipulated equal pay for equal work regardless of sex. This article was the focus of intense political action suggesting the likely interconnection between EU equality politics and social movements in the future (Hoskyns 1996). From this point onwards, equality in the workplace was a site where other gender equality demands were first formulated and later put into practice. Women's groups, using advocacy coalitions to lobby the EC and European Parliament, tried to expand equality policy into other fields such as childcare and violence against women, but the narrow focus of article 119 and resistance from member states prevented them (Mazey 1998). Empowerment of the EU as a supranational framework came from institutions such as the Commission and Parliament, which themselves needed public support from social movements for introducing and implementing new gender equality principles as the 'missionaries' of the new Europe. The shared vulnerability of both EU institutions and women's social movements created a powerful alliance for achieving equality between the sexes that was born in the 1960s movements and was institutionalised in the chain of World Conferences on Women (Pollack and Hafner-Burton 2000).

The frame in which gender equality policy was originally shaped in EC law poses a number of problems, not only within the EU itself, but also for its mainstreaming into external relations such as the enlargement process and development policy. Importantly, because equality of sexes was defined in an employment context, this pre-determined the site and the means through which gender equality might be achieved. Interestingly, this was the same frame, women's employment, in which 'statist feminism' in the eastern part of Europe was born. Historically, the demand for equal rights in work was part of the agenda of the liberal and social democratic women's movements from the end of the 19th century, which served as a common intellectual basis for European progress. After 1945, the Soviet type of women's emancipation in the form of the statist feminism dominated Eastern Europe through an equality policy based on *de jure* equality of sexes. In Eastern Europe, the most obvious indicators of the equality of women were achieved: equal opportunities in the labour market and in education; extensive and accessible family- and child-care institutions; encouragement and active participation in the political and public spheres. These achievements were presented as evidence of the 'state socialist' path to women's emancipation. Thus, equal social status of women and men was achieved, even if only through the actions of the centralised authoritarian power. This heritage of statist feminism eventually became a modifying factor in the adaptation to the value of EC gender equality for the accession countries. Because of this, the definition of gender equality in statist feminist terms rejected the concept of positive discrimination in a similar way to the first phase of EU gender equality policy. This rejection involved a serious challenge to the concept of gender equality by defining *women* as mothers through biological difference, which thus essentialised gender differences.

By the 1980s, it was becoming clear that the achievement of women's equality based on a policy of individual liberal rights for equal treatment was difficult to implement in reality. The concept of gender equality as equality of opportunity did not bring 'real equality' because of its utopian character. Because of this paradox the second phase of EU equality politics brought broad policy change – European-level NGO activists and EU 'femocrats' learned from both the successes and failures of implementing equality policies. A new policy frame was born with the collaboration with social movements in the shape of the protection of women's rights as a group. Learning from the failures of the struggle for equality based on individual rights, this new policy demanded positive action for women. These programmes were to use positive discrimination to implement change in systems of gender inequality and were based on the definition of women as equal, thus leading to the establishment of special programmes for women. In this context, the term 'equality' still really meant difference based on biological difference, similar to the first phase.

During the 1980s, it became apparent to the different groups active in gender equality politics that there was a serious difference between *de facto* and *de jure* equality of women. The use of the newly-coined term *'gender'* for describing socially constructed biological differences offered a good solution to break out from this fixed dichotomy. In the third phase of evolution of EU gender equality policy the experiences and critiques of women within equality programmes led to the formulation of 'gender mainstreaming' policy focused on transforming the systems and structures of discrimination instead of promoting individual or group rights. Gender mainstreaming aims to construct a routine procedure for promoting gender equality instead of on a case-by-case basis. This shift in focus should help to prevent setting up institutions for 'women' that appoint remote 'experts' for women's issues. Such political practices for the promotion of women's legal, economic and social rights are already familiar to women with a 'statist feminist' tradition and experience. It also became obvious that during the last decades it was difficult to differentiate between discrimination and personal lifestyle choices within the language of rights, and in particular the term 'equality' which could be interpreted differently, for example as justice, fairness, or autonomy. The previous definition and practice of equal opportunity as equal treatment handled public policy as gender neutral. The concept of gender mainstreaming challenges this 'gender neutrality' after the signing of the Amsterdam Treaty.

Before the unexpected fall of the Iron Curtain, the value of gender equality was based in legislation, and judicial institutional support in the EU. However, at the same time a network of experts and women's groups were acting to support and shape the EU's activities (Hoskyns 1996; Mazey 1998). No longer as a recommendation, but as a principle, mainstreaming was integrated in all EC policy developments following its introduction at Amsterdam, leading Susan Cox to argue that it entrenched 'equality policy as an integral part of the Community's economic and structural policies, and to promote women's full participation in economic and social life' (Cox 1993: 56).

Consequently, the EU's policies aimed at women now consist of two different aspects:

> a series of legislative measures which seek to promote equality of treatment in the context of paid work [and] a range of broadly based initiatives and programs which generally aim to enhance the social status and political influenced of women.
>
> (Bretherton 1999: 132)

However, the implementation of gender equality with gender mainstreaming policy and its impact inside EU countries (Hoskyns 1996), international organisations (Pollack and Hafner-Burton 2000), the EU institutions responsible for enlargement talks (Bretherton 2001), and development policies (Painter and Ulmer 2002) remains contested and has only recently become a focus of scholarly investigation. Critics emphasise that gender mainstreaming as a policy fails to acknowledge differences among women as far as race, ethnicity and class are concerned (Bretherton 2001; Hoskyns 2004). Gender policy advocates also point out the extent to which national policy makers remain unresponsive to the concept of gender mainstreaming. At the same time, critics underline the fragility of institutional enforcement mechanisms inside the EU. The criticism formulated against the EU can be generally divided into two schools: the first is the neo-liberal argument, which resists any type of outside regulatory intervention at the national level and the second one is the interventionist argument, which demands more fulfilment of the social mission (Bretherton 1999).

The EU's gender mainstreaming policy is a 'demanding strategy' (Bretherton 2002: 5) because it offers a chance to challenge deeply embedded cultural values and review the formation of policy issues. The EU also created a framework for reviewing national gender equality mechanisms, although in a humble way. This framework did go further than the Beijing obligations as far as the governmental level institutionalisation of women's politics is concerned. The institutional framework, legislation and the personal experience of political campaigns created powerful alliances, not only between different EU 'femocrats', but also helped to set up contacts between NGOs and international organisations. However, critics of 'agenda setting' underline the failures of the process, as gender mainstreaming failed to redefine the rules of the game and the terms of the gender contract (Beveridge, *et al.* 2000).

The EU was created with the original aim of ensuring peace between enemies (Manners 2005), as well as promoting economic integration and prosperity for all. For such a utopian project, the aim of achieving gender equality may not be so very far from the original aims of the European integration process. Both within and without Europe, the EU seeks to consolidate the rule of law and protection of fundamental human rights with a standardised and regulated market as part of enlargement, and the promotion of gender equality as part of its development policy. As the next two sections will illustrate, the implementation of gender equality proved to be an excellent policy instrument during the enlargement process, but is less successful in development policy. Both the enlargement process and development policy raise questions about the future of the EU as a post-national normative power, functioning at different levels of organisation, and the extent to which it is vulnerable to national political changes as well as competing political agendas.

Interpretation and value transfer during enlargement talks

Exporting EU gender equality policies eastwards means that EU policy makers assume that these policies are adequate and the only acceptable means to achieve gender equality in the East. However, one might argue that the controversial character of these EU values, as well as unclear EU institutional adaptation, undermine the assumption that the basic principles and causes of gender inequality are the same inside and outside the EU (Bretherton 2001). Also such half-hearted adaptation of the EU's gender equality policy strengthens a well-known phenomenon in the post-communist context: the difference between rhetoric and reality of policy implementation (Bretherton 1999). The possible failure of gender equality policy in the 'East' might have serious implications for gender equality in the enlarged Union. This failure might push the importance of the value of gender equality down to the level of lip service that endangers the controversial, but existing, institutions and achievements of gender equality policy in the EU.

Reviewing the literature on gender equality in Eastern Europe by Eastern European authors, the first impression is the striking absence of analysis of EU gender equality policy. Besides the government-sponsored translations of EU laws and descriptive, hence self-assuring, official governmental reports there are very few critical works that consider the implications of EU enlargement as far as the implementation of gender equality is concerned. These reports are uncritical of EU policies and urge their governments to comply with the technical conditions without any relevant suggestions as far as adaptation is concerned (Open Society Institute 2002). Following the 2004 enlargement, the external became internal, ensuring that the complex realities of post-socialist gender relations now contribute to the already pressing uncertainties and inconsistencies of EU gender equality principles and implementation policies that challenge the provisional facilitating instruments.

This intellectual silence about the value of gender equality during the enlargement talks was even more striking as we know that over the past fifteen years a very active discussion developed between women of the 'East' and 'West' regarding the direct application of Western gender equality mechanisms and Western gender theory to the post-communist reality. Some feminist intellectuals in the 'East' were opposing the style and means by which their Western sisters were considering the 'Eastern' social space empty. As Siklova commented: '[w]e object to some of the Western feminists' insensitive conduct towards us [...] this sometimes reminds us of the attitudes of apparatchiks or of those imparting political indoctrinations' (quoted in Watson 2000: 379). While activists and scholars were engaged in an emotionally charged exchange of ideas, their governments agreed to adapt the existing legal-technical mechanisms to promote gender equality through enlargement talks. During the enlargement talks between the Commission and the accession governments, formal technical criteria were created in order to measure and achieve gender equality within joining countries, without explicitly considering the political implications, consequences and costs of these attempts to alter historical patterns of discrimination. Equally, the enlargement talks defined neither a sanction system nor an institutional framework for implementation. This was despite the fact that the Amsterdam Treaty clearly defines two components of the *acquis* as anti-discrimination legislation and gender equality mechanisms. The governments of the accession countries interpreted gender equality within the framework of anti-discrimination legislation and the sole policy site of work and employment. Thus, the implementation of gender equality policy is problematic due to the interpretation and transfer of terms such as 'sexual discrimination' and 'indirect discrimination' not only linguistically but also institutionally.

The enlargement process highlighted the paradox of feminist advocates in the 'East' complaining about the gender-blind practices of their own governments, while the EU gender equality mechanisms in the framework of anti-discrimination legislation were accepted by the same national political elite. On reflection, this paradox is even more striking if we acknowledge that recent scholarship on Eastern Europe underlines the alarming worsening of women's position in these societies since the collapse of communism: their public, social and economic roles have diminished over the past 15 years. This social process is usually described as the 'masculinisation' of post-socialist Eastern Europe (Watson 1993). Over the past 15 years the position of women in the 'East' has converged towards the position of women in the 'West' as far as formal criteria of equality such as employment and participation in politics are concerned. For example, the number of women MPs in the first democratically elected Hungarian Parliament (7%) represented a dramatic decrease in comparison to the 'statist feminist' period (an average of 25%). Similar tendencies can be observed in the case of women's employment where the favourable economic position of women in Eastern Europe prior to 1989 worsened considerably after 1990 and converged towards the position in the West. These favourable conditions were due to greater gender equality in the employment sphere, as well as social security provisions such as free and accessible childcare that was available without restriction before 1989.

There are three levels of gender equality through enlargement that will be analysed here in order to make sense of the interactions between values, principles, policies and institutions. The first level of formulating gender equality as a policy is the general value of gender equality. On this level there is no serious debate. The rhetoric of acceptance in the governmental discourse is easy to identify. The political language went through a rapid transformation in the past decades in Western Europe partly because of pressure exercised by social movements and it has also been considerably changed in Eastern European accession countries through the processes of democratisation.

The diffusion of the value of gender equality primarily took place through accession negotiations as well as transnational dialogue involving national institutions. Such EU values were presented as fundamental and non-negotiable. There was never a question of whether the accession countries wanted to accept, but rather of how do they want to adopt such values. It was accepted that gender equality was one of the fundamental values of the EU especially since the EU was exercising normative pressure in this area. However, the mode of compliance was worth analysing because it raised criticism in both the West and in the East. EU enlargement experts and the accession government's representatives shared the consensus of adopting EU rhetoric as the negotiating minimum to the disappointment of the few women's representatives in the East. Thus, during negotiations the EU avoided exercising more pressure as long as East European elites unquestioningly accepted the necessary minimums. Gender equality, as an increasingly consensual public value, ensures that few European politicians now dare to say that it is not a universal value. But it is equally clear that setting up the legal framework of gender equality is only the first, but important step towards fostering change in the constructions of gender as ways of thinking. As Bretherton argued, during the accession talks governments followed a minimalist approach ensuring input from DG Employment and Social Affairs during screening and negotiations processes, in specific relation to the adoption of the formal equality within the *acquis*. Despite this, provisional closure of the relevant chapter was not impeded by failure to transpose this element of the *acquis* into domestic legislation. Thus, 'while even the minimalist position has not been assiduously pursued, the maximalist position was not attempted' (Bretherton 2002: 5).

The second level of gender equality policy implementation was the analysis of the current situation and existing governmental policies. The measuring process of gender equality is highly problematic because the comparison criterion is itself contested – how do we define gender? There appears to be an easy way to solve the philosophical problem of translation by interpreting *gender* as simply *women*. This is a simple, but problematic step as far as the concept of *gender* is concerned because it is a short sighted 'solution' that makes the term 'blind' to differences other than the biological. *Gender* is also a broader term because it shows how identity and subjectivity are constructed, it opens up ways of acknowledging other differences such as race, class, etc. Besides the simplistic translation of *gender* to *women*, which means its essentialist translation to *women* as biologically defined sex, it also hopes to avoid the complexities of meanings. It is too easy to collect gender segregated data with statistical methods if we mean under *gender* the biological division between men and women, and in that sense here *gender* means *sex*. Governmental officials and bureaucrats have clearly hoped to cut down the complexities of meanings of *gender* as much as they can, and have been sanctioned by the level of public discourse simply to make their life easier. Meanwhile scholars and academics (as advocates) are unhappy with the instrumentalised and/or simplistic use of *gender*. Even in a recent collection of articles on gender mainstreaming there are two different usages of gender: first in the introduction as 'differences between men and women' (Mazey 2000: 334) and later in one of the articles 'a principle which structures power relations between men and women under particular historical circumstances' (Watson 2000: 370).

In the case of legal guarantees the Constitution in the accession countries regulates the principle of equal treatment. However, the definition of meaning in gender discrimination is highly problematic. It should be noted that, despite the changing of compliance in labour codes, the notions of 'indirect discrimination' and the 'reversal of the burden of proof' are extremely complex and difficult ones to apply in every day legal practice. The definition of 'discrimination' should include the concept of 'indirect discrimination' not only in the labour codes but also in all the substantive laws relevant to the substantive scope of the directive. However, difficulties arise because disputes involving cases of discrimination under the substantive scope of the directive do not necessarily fall under the scope of the labour codes and the related procedural rules in civil proceedings according to existing laws. However, the EU pressure that forced Eastern European national elites to adopt gender equality policy and its facilitating institutions now offers a unique political opportunity frame.

The third level is the practical institutional implementation of gender equality: to force social, political and economic actors to implement the policy in practice through legislation and education. This programme involves the preliminary gender-proofing of different national legislation, using gender checklist manuals, as well as organising and requiring training for certain professions and positions. A quasi-independent national level institutional system should be set up for monitoring and evaluating this process.

To summarise: gender equality is a moving opportunity frame, which is dependent on national political developments and less on strength of pressure exercised by social movements. The *de jure* harmonisation of legal systems of the accession countries with the five Directives on securing gender equality is basically satisfactory but still the question remains open – what caused the unprecedented difference in women's opinion about enlargement in these countries?

During the accession talks it was agreed that the greatest shortcoming, and at the same time the greatest responsibility of the national legislation, is the enforcement of the principles enshrined in the legal regulations in daily practice. A future task is to achieve a breakthrough in the field of the practical implementation of equal treatment, based on the experiences of the member states. With regard to constitutional regulations, there were no serious differences between the accession countries and the regulations in the pre-2004 EU 15 member states. Unfortunately, this does not hold true in the enforcement of individual rights and positive action. Therefore, it can be concluded that the most serious problem was and is the lack of practical enforcement of basic constitutional principles in the 2004 accession countries.

One reason for the lack of enforcement mechanisms in the accession countries is the lack of an institution/organisation in charge of monitoring discrimination against women, the inspection of the enforcement of relevant legal provisions and the promotion of real equal opportunities through positive actions. East European feminist critics of EU enlargement talks often argued that there is an uncertainty regarding the concept of gender mainstreaming and it is half-heartedly institutionalised within the EU member states and the EU institutions themselves. This led to a 'double betrayal' – namely that both the EU officials and the national elites shared a common interest in not identifying the problems of implementation of gender equality in these countries when applying the principle of gender mainstreaming.

One possible approach is to strengthen the legal consciousness in the accession countries and to hope that EU membership will promote this process after the 2004 enlargement. The European Court of Justice (ECJ) is a key instrument with its binding decisions promoting the value of gender equality in guarding the implementation principles of equal pay in the labour market, equal treatment and equal opportunity. The ECJ, which became a powerful institution of implementation and an initiator of further progressive legislation, developed the legislative framework of 'equality politics', as well as reacting to changing social realities (Shaw 2000). The ECJ also has a political vision expressed in legal discourse as well, although certain criticisms have been raised against the ECJ's liberal feminist character and optimism that the Court is the primary instrument for constructing a fair society. This pragmatic liberalism is useful in understanding perspectives in which gender discrimination is best understood within the discourse of rights. However, it is difficult on a single case basis to construct a legal strategy, particularly in Eastern Europe with its scepticism towards the rule of law. The bitter and disillusioning experiences of enduring patterns of gender discrimination by Western feminists coincides with the similar feelings of easterners despite their experiences being born in a different social reality. East European women also experienced the gap between public discourse on women's equality and their lived experience of discrimination. Therefore, the first step should be to restore legal consciousness. In addition, most of the Court decisions are implemented within market-oriented national economies, which raises the question of intervention and enforcement from above. This interventionist heritage is a very sensitive topic in the newly built post-socialist market economies struggling to leave behind long decades of command economy.

In the case of Hungary, like most accession states, the national legislation relating to the principle of equal treatment was, *de jure*, found to be in conformity with the directives. Nevertheless, the implementation of these provisions was, *de facto*, far from favourable. While in other fields the EU intervention was considered to be undesirable by different domestic actors and interest groups, in the field of gender equality the EU was criticised for not exercising normative pressure in the interest of one 'imagined community', which is 'the women'. Similarly, the question of whether the EU Directives should have been understood simply as promoting *women's* equality, not *gender* equality, was unresolved. This mirrored the EU's equality policy itself as it consists of contradictory elements combining equal opportunities with positive discrimination, and mainstreaming (Bretherton 1999).

The last decade can be regarded as the decade of *formal adjustment* to the European Union, also in the area of equal opportunities. Similar to most accession states, the current system of Hungarian labour law provides the basic framework for legal guarantees of equal opportunities for women and men. Most of the relevant laws are concerned, however, with discrimination *in general* and formulated in such a way that sex is only one of several factors (other factors include, race, religion, etc.) that might be the basis of discrimination. Very few would disagree with the statement that the EU offered a favourable opportunity for feminist scholars and activists to increase their political influence in agenda setting, no matter how formalist compliance smuggled terms such as gender equality into the public discourse. With the open nature of EU decision making in the past decade there was a mode of direct communication between different actors in the field of gender equality: NGO activists, scholars, experts etc. All these generated the feeling amongst lobbying groups that the EU represents a socially progressive entity, thus expectations were raised by politicians and lobby groups that the EU would act as a modernising missionary. In practice the EU offered assistance in several forms to Eastern European countries to help compliance: Structural Funds (especially European Social Fund), various research and education funds (such as Socrates and Leonardo), and specific development policies, as well as the PHARE programme.

Empirical surveys suggest that the EU level of action on gender equality, although mediated by the domestic political context, is not currently successful at bringing 'Europe' closer to the people (Cram 2001: 597). Looking at a comparison of a experiences in a selection of EU states (see Table 6.1), it is suggested that that the non-confrontational character of women's groups on the one hand, and the institutionalisation of domestic gender equality mechanisms on the other hand, are promoting a relatively high level of pro-European opinion. If the institutionalisation of the gender equality mechanisms of the EU depends on dichotomies in party politics, then these mechanisms are not necessarily strengthening pro-EU opinion. Returning to the concepts of presence, opportunity

Table 6.1 Comparison of Greece, Ireland, UK, Hungary, and Poland on relationships between domestic political context, women's groups and pro-EU sentiments

	Greece	Ireland	UK	Hungary	Poland
Domestic political context	politicised party state	corporatist	competitive pluralism	politicised party state	politicised party state
Equal opportunity mechanisms	institutionalised	institutionalised	institutionalised	meta-institutionalised influenced by party dichotomy	non-institutionalised influenced by party dichotomy
Relationship between women's organisations and domestic politics	confrontational character	non-confrontational character	non-confrontational character	confrontational character	confrontational character
Pro-EU sentiments	Low	High	High	Low	Low

Sources: Bretherton 2002; Cram 2001

and capability from the introduction, it is clear that despite an opportunity for the EU in the promotion of gender equality, capability and presence were not exercised, because these factors were heavily dependent on domestic variables.

The analysis of these efforts to promote gender equality through accession suggests that the main obstacles to effective implementation are the controversial signalling and lack of a sanction system on the EU side of the relationships. During the enlargement talks, the EU failed to win the PR war in Eastern Europe in this context. It transmitted a general image of progress, equality and freedom, which combined with an unfavourable domestic political climate and structure as far as women's organisations are concerned (Bretherton 2001).

Gender equality and development policy

Attempts to introduce gender equality into EU development policy predate the eastward enlargement procedures of the 1990s. During the UN Decade for Women 1975–85, and following on from the Third World Conference on Women in Nairobi in 1985, the Commission established its 'women in development' (WID) approach, including WID desks, communiqués, and references in the Lomé Conventions (Pollack and Hafner-Burton 2000: 445; Booth and Bennett 2002: 438–440). These practices were accompanied by the inclusion of women through the Third and Fourth Lomé conventions (1984 and 1989) which first adopted welfare approaches, then moved to a more WID approach (Lister 2003: 97–98).

In the 1990s, the emphasis moved from women to gender equality in development policy, in particular through preparation and participation in the Fourth World Conference on Women in Beijing in 1995. This transformation away from WID and towards gender mainstreaming occurred in parallel with similar processes in the enlargement talks, thus immediately after Beijing, the EU began to gender mainstream its policies (Mazey 2002: 232). From 1993 to 1998, the EU worked on reaching agreement on a policy of integrating gender issues in development cooperation. This policy was finally realised in the Commission's 2001 'Programme of Action for the mainstreaming of gender equality in Community Development Co-operation' (Commission 2001j).

In parallel with these developments, issues of women's human rights and gender equality were also becoming established on the development agenda through the International Conference on Population and Development (ICPD) in Cairo in 1994 that led to the ICPD Programme of Action. The EC's Health, AIDS and Population (HAP) policy was initiated in 1987 and adapted in 1994 to take on board the ICPD agenda of gender equality. The ICPD programme and the HAP policy have increasingly led to gender equality issues being mainstreamed into development cooperation. Most important in this respect was the 1997 Council Regulation on Population (No. 1484/97 of 22 July 1997) which set out the basis of EU support for reproductive health and rights.

Despite these advances over the past two decades, there are still widespread criticisms of EU gender equality and development policy. Firstly there are concerns, expressed since the 1970s, that the solution to gender inequality was to be found solely through inclusion in the developmental processes (Hoogvelt 2001: 53–54). From this perspective, the idea that the inclusion of 'women in development' would lead to greater equality and lower birth rates is highly problematic because it overlooks structural inequality and the constructed nature of gender. Attempts to address this problem through the move from an emphasis on 'women' to the broader nature of 'gender' have been somewhat successful in that they have identified relations *between* gendered constructions of women and men as being important.

However, a second series of more specific criticisms have arisen over the way in which gender mainstreaming has been incorporated into EU policies through an 'integrationist approach' (Rees 1998) which has led to gender being 'everywhere and nowhere' (Painter and Ulmer 2002). The EU's integrationist approach has led to the existing institutional structures attempting to adapt to new practices without sufficient funding, staff or training in order to do so. Without these resources, it is clear that the structural and institutionalised character of gender inequalities and injustices will remain unrealised and unaddressed within the EU and its development policies (Pollack and Hafner-Burton 2000: 452; Booth and Bennett 2002: 443; Lister 2003: 99). As Painter and Ulmer argue regarding gender mainstreaming in EU development cooperation, the mainstreaming policy has sought to promote gender 'everywhere', but in practice the absence of resources, trained staff, legal provisions and the abandonment of positive discrimination has led to gender being 'nowhere'.

The EU policy on reproductive health and rights within HAP stands out as one of the few examples of the sustained promotion of gender equality in development policy under the most difficult conditions. With the clear international mandate of the 1994 ICPD, the EU has sought to promote its HAP policy in order to address the world's major causes of death in the developing world – HIV/AIDS, malaria, acute respiratory infections and diarrhoeal diseases, reproductive and sexual health and rights, and lifestyle-related causes of ill-health. Undoubtedly, these are the largest killers in the world and HAP is one of the EU's most important policy areas in addressing these endemic problems of poverty. Twelve years into the development of HAP policies the EU has encountered opposition from US religious groups keen to promote their ideology using the Bush Presidency and EU-based lobby groups. The relationship between these US religious groups and gender equality is clear as the groups seek to prevent EU support for women's reproductive health and oppose reproductive rights, as well as seeking to discredit contraceptive use, thus contributing to the spread of HIV/AIDS.

The first attack on women's rights came in January 2001 with the new administration removing US family planning funds from foreign NGOs conforming with the ICPD action programme in the provision of reproductive health services, and in July 2002 the US cut all funding to the UN Population Fund (UNPF). The Commission responded to this US undermining of the UN fight against disease and poverty by stepping in with €44 million to replace the lost support for the UNPF in Africa. From January 2001 until May 2003 the EU found its support for women's rights, children's rights and its development policies constantly under attack from US religious groups using US and EU front organisations, as well as the Bush Presidency, to promote their ideology. From May to October 2003 Commissioner Poul Nielson found himself under personal attack by EU front organisations for US groups who sought to discredit him and the EU in its support for HAP and women's rights. In May 2003 a campaign launched by 47 MEPs sought to oppose a fictional Commission 'unit' to monitor the activities of anti-reproductive health groups (Cahill 2003a; Nielson 2003). Then in October 2003 a campaign launched by the Vatican and the Bush Presidency sought to discourage the use of condoms in Africa (Cahill 2003b). Again, Nielson and the Commission found themselves forced to defend the promotion of contraceptive use in HAP, particularly in areas where the HIV/AIDS pandemic is widespread, by presenting research evidence on the effectiveness of condoms.

Despite such positive examples of EU promotion of gender equality in development policies, it is undoubtedly true that 'a declared commitment to gender mainstreaming tells us little of the political will or otherwise to include such a strategy in EU policies' (Young 2000: 91). Most critical voices suggest that gender mainstreaming in development policy has been more of a promise or idea than a reality (Young 2000: 91; Painter and Ulmer 2002: 6). However, in contrast Mazey identifies development polices as being one of the policy sectors in which gender mainstreaming has had the 'greatest impact' where 'the Commission's dedication to gender equality has been incorporated into policy guidelines and/or all calls for proposals and expressions of interest for programme funding' (Mazey 2002: 236–237). Mushaben identifies the HAP policy and the special budget line on 'Integration of Gender Issues into Development Cooperation' as being two of the 'best gender practices' in EU gender mainstreaming (Mushaben 2003: 9–11). Clearly, the EU's support for gender equality in development policies is mixed, but as the example of HAP policies illustrates, some aspects of gender equality are defended as a point of principle rather than an effect of gender mainstreaming.

The value of gender equality and feminisms

The value of gender equality cannot be separated from feminisms and feminists. The definition of feminism as a commitment to social change seems to be a consensual definition but it does not help us to understand the different traditions of Eastern European social movements, the relational feminism of the Mediterranean region, or the historical experiences within development policy groups (Offen 1992; 2000). In relational feminism, women are defining their social position through reproductive capacity, and other social institutions such as the family, while the individual feminists are using human rights arguments to fight for autonomy independently from biological determinations. These different feminisms are clashing in public discourse through 'double speak' – the language of equality vs the language of difference. This is the classic 'Woll-stonecraft Dilemma' in which we seek to find an answer to the question of whether gender equality should be achieved through the recognition of equality or difference (see Lombardo 2003). It would be a mistake to underestimate the historical roots and present attractiveness of the language of difference used by the different European conservative women's movements (Pető 2003). This discourse fits into government politics that defines equality through family by social policy. We would argue that redefining progressive citizenship rights in the new, enlarged Europe is one of the most urgent tasks. Because, as value surveys suggest, large numbers of women voters with 'conservative' values have joined the EU after the 2004 enlargement, this perspective requires the modernisation of the politics of difference. The sheer existence of the European Union with its supranational character, universal values and institutional system presents a serious challenge to feminist and other women's movements who consider themselves a progressive force of change. A new EU level of influence has been constructed in gender relations that raises challenges for both Western and Eastern member states coming to terms with membership and the obligations of EU relations with the rest of the world.

Our discussion of gender (in)equality also raises the question of whether it is appropriate to focus on just one, dominant social inequality such as gender in policy making when numerous other social differences are also constructed through race, ethnicity, or class, etc. The politics of recognition gives equal status of genders and cultures, all of which question the category 'women'. Due to the uncertainties of defining gender, the social and cultural costs of mainstreaming have never really been calculated. Similarly, the political costs and consequences of moving the focus from women's policy to gender policy has not been seriously considered in policy making communities. The fear of different women's groups losing financial and political support by the EU might paradoxically block the implementation of gender mainstreaming and strengthen conservative definitions of 'women' as biologically different, rooted in the first phase of EU gender equality policy. The politics of recognition is a crucial precondition for identity formation. In the case of women, self-confidence, self-esteem, and self-respect should be gained through identity formation and the recognition of difference. However, the conflict between the politics of equality and politics of difference has serious implications on current EU gender equality policy. In the case of European identity, questions should be raised regarding how to define the site of identity formation, where politics of recognition is happening, who is constructing these differences and who is defining the meaning of difference? In the case of the EU these questions are being shaped in the multilevelled EU institutions which foster European identity, together with rapidly developing EU law as a new scholarly field which is creating new 'rules of the game' (see Shaw 2000).

Gender equality policy is not necessarily a feminist enterprise. The problematic definition of equality politics is still based on a comparative dichotomy, which is relativising structural disadvantages. Institutionalised gender equality can be used against international feminist goals. Through accession negotiations, for example, to ensure full compliance with the spirit of the Directives, the introduction of provisions and positive programmes that facilitate the fair division of burdens between the two parents as regards taking care of and raising the child are advocated. By taking such measures, the state should actively support the stable labour market position of women who give birth to children. This policy might challenge women's exclusive role as caretakers, which is still a widely shared social norm and a practice in most of the countries. The support of introducing part-time work can influence women's lives in two radically different ways. If the concept of part-time work is interpreted in the difference frame, aimed at encouraging women to remain in their traditional gender roles, it does not strengthen, but rather weakens, gender equality. If, however, part-time work is an option for both men and women to harmonise their duties as parents and as workers, then it is certainly a progressive means towards achieving equality. It is recommended that part-time work be promoted by positive means not solely or primarily for women, but for both sexes. If the EU fails to acknowledge the conservative and relational traditions of equality politics, which are not necessarily dominant only in the recent accession countries, but also in earlier member states, then it threatens to lose the progressive social power behind it. Clearly, the rhetoric can be revolutionary in the short run, but very ineffective in the long run. In the 'state feminist' countries before 1989, measuring the equality by percentages (representation of women in different professions) might make social injustice visible but is not questioning of the system that constructed the inequality and leaves the correction mechanisms to the very same institutions. Thus, the common demand for the reformulation of policies 'recognising that what is taken as the norm is not necessarily gender-neutral' (Rees 1998: 189).

It should also be obvious by now that no other equalisation of social difference was as successfully institutionalised on the national and international levels in the EU as gender differences. The importance of this success story is that representatives of other social groups, constructed by other differences, have sought to replicate the gender mainstreaming strategies. However, there is the risk that their lobbying efforts at different political levels may become vulnerable to bargaining processes between different lobbying groups. For example, in Hungary the constitutional framework was used in 2001 to prevent any forms of discrimination and leave the technicalities to the sub/law codes, rather than introducing single-issue anti-discrimination laws such as the Law on the Disabled. Similarly, the conservative Polish government used one part of recent EU legislation to block another part, the equal opportunity legislation (Bretherton 2001). However, this type of behaviour is often governmental practice in both accession and existing member states – introducing anti-discrimination legislation without introducing gender equality policy. Similarly, in EU development policy, the introduction of conditionality clauses including human rights (and implicitly gender equality) without providing or assisting with the means to introduce such policies, often has a similar effect. Without a possible sanction system, it remains unsatisfactory that accession states or development assistance recipients are left to interpret and implement gender equality directives themselves. Despite the institutionalisation of gender equality practices through policies, conditionalities, and legal arrangements, in both the enlargement process and development policies, such aspirations remain largely unfulfilled. Within both accession and development partners, the values and principles of gender equality remain problematic without a welcoming epistemological space, and risk pushing domestic political actors into legitimation crises.

As we have seen in the case of the EU, the pressure exercised by the different levels of women's movements is crucial as far as the implementation of gender equality is concerned. The most decisive character of the women's movement of the East is the proactivity of local responses. The accession governments set the agenda, sometimes together with international women's organisations and networks, to which local women are reacting. Or perhaps Havelkova is right arguing that one of the reasons why there were no organised women's movements in Eastern Europe is because there were no 'women's issues' there – free abortion rights, high employment rate, high participation of women in higher education, etc., were all legacies of the 'statist feminist' period (Havelkova 2000). By now this legacy has gone and East meets West on the ground of declining women's employment rate and political participation rate. There are some who are still arguing the 'difference' between the East and West with the intention of protecting their feminist authenticity from the invading Western theory, but because of global social developments East and West are converging. Outside of the EU, gender equality policies, whether in development or health, are welcomed by local women, but opposed by those groups, both indigenous and Western, who feel threatened by women's liberation. However, it may be only a question of time before the scepticism of women based on their experiences of EU gender equality mechanisms will find a voice in the EU as a whole, despite potentially undermining the EU's 'best gender practices' outside of Europe. In this sense, the EU 2004 enlargement and 2005 reflections on relations between Europe and the world may come at the best possible time to force European actors to think about the value of gender equality in a more just world.

7 Principles of democracy and human rights

A review of the European Union's strategies towards its neighbours

Rosa Balfour

Introduction

> The European Union is well placed to promote democracy and human rights [...] *Uniquely* amongst international actors, all fifteen member states of the Union are democracies espousing the same Treaty-based principles in their internal and external policies. This gives the EU substantial *political and moral weight*. Furthermore, as an economic and political player with global diplomatic reach, and with a substantial budget for external assistance, the EU has both influence and leverage, which it can deploy on behalf of democratisation and human rights.
>
> (Commission 2001b, emphasis added)

The claim of the European Commission implies two issues: firstly that the EU, by virtue of *what it is*, can export its principles abroad; secondly that *what it can do* places it in a privileged position to pursue such objectives. Much institutional rhetoric has been spent on the EU's role in promoting principles of democracy and human rights, yet few analyses ascertain the extent to which the rhetoric is translated into political practice.

This chapter traces the development of the EU's civilian normative and instrumental apparatus – from aid to sanctions in the name human rights and democracy – in three of the EU's regional strategies: the enlargement process to the candidate countries of Central and Eastern Europe (CEECs), the stabilisation strategies towards South-Eastern Europe (SEE), and the Euro-Mediterranean Partnership (EMP). Sheer geographical proximity has demonstrated the importance of these regions to European stability: an examination of EU policies towards them will enable some understanding of the role human rights and democracy principles can play when elaborating policies which are also embedded in 'hard interests', from the prevention of conflict to the containment of population movements, risks that apply to all three cases. If the CEECs do not fall squarely in the category of EU foreign policy, the enlargement process does constitute a cross-cutting strategy between foreign and domestic policy, an important case of conflict prevention, and a laboratory of strategies developed towards third countries.

The literature on EU strategies for the promotion of human rights and democracy abroad points to the inconsistencies of the EU approach (K. Smith

1998 and 2001; Ward 1998) and how the principles are often trumped by other interests, such as security or economics (Olsen 2000; Youngs 2001b and 2002). Conversely, the EU has shown greater ease in resorting to negative measures for violations of human rights towards 'poor, marginal countries', such as sub-Saharan Africa (K. Smith 2001: 193). The tension between the treaty-based requirement for consistency and a more policy-based pragmatism runs through all EU external relations, and regards vertical consistency between the EC and its member states, horizontal consistency between policy fields (Missiroli 2001) as well as the gap between rhetoric and action and differential treatment of partners. It acquires particular salience in cross-pillar and cross-policy field activities such as the promotion of human rights and democracy. Here, these inconsistencies can serve to highlight the actual priorities of the Union when exercising political conditionality. They can also undermine the international profile that the EU is trying to build, the credibility of its commitments, and make it susceptible to accusations of 'double standards' or euro-centrism, despite the EU's appeal to the universalism of the principles it preaches.

Inconsistency remains one of the major setbacks in the EU's self-portrayal as a principled actor. The literature on the subject assumes a dichotomy between principles and interests in political terms, and between idealism and realism in analytical terms (Olsen 2000), an assumption that hides an implication that principles would reflect some 'genuineness' of the EU whereas interests would be inherently 'selfish'. From the case studies used here, this dichotomy appears tenuous, and the relationship between 'principles' and 'interests' should perhaps be challenged or seen on a continuum. The objective of this volume is not the search for the ethics of EU global action, and the extent to which the EU is 'genuine' about its principles, but for the values, images and principles (VIPs) that inform it: human rights and democracy should be understood as two of the principles and 'worldviews'[1] that play a role in EU external action, alongside and intertwined with specific conceptions of security and stability and of the ways to achieve them.

The relationship between the former and other principles and worldviews is no doubt dialectic, to say the least, and at times competing. As we shall see, while in the CEECs and the Balkans human rights and democracy were perceived as integral to a strategy aiming at stabilising the region from potential or latent conflict, in the Mediterranean the EU's security discourse left human rights and democracy relegated to the field of assistance and scarcely present in political and diplomatic relations. The apparent pay-off for not exercising conditionality towards the Southern Mediterranean states is to maintain a 'constructive dialogue' with countries with various degrees of authoritarian regimes, and to contain the risk of Islamic fundamentalist opposition gaining power.

The normative basis for human rights and democracy policies in EU external relations

In the 1990s human rights and democracy increasingly became a part of EC/EU relations with third countries (K. Smith 2001), and the process moved from the declarations of the 1980s to formalising treaty-based commitments and policies. 1991 marked an important turning point in this process. In June the Luxemburg Declaration of the European Council established that concern for human rights and fundamental freedoms 'cannot be considered as interference in the internal affairs of a state and constitute an important and legitimate part of their dialogue with third countries'. Some substantive elements of conceptions of human rights and democracy are made explicit: the 'indivisible character' of human rights, in their civil and political, economic and social dimensions, and respect for minorities, in line with United Nations conventions. In November 1991 the Council for Development and Human Rights issued a Resolution that outlined the positive and negative tools for the pursuit of human rights and principles abroad through political, diplomatic, economic, and aid means. The Resolution introduced for the first time the principle of conditionality, whereby the Community reserved the right to adopt negative measures 'in the event of grave and persistent human rights violations or the serious interruption of democratic processes'.

The Treaty on the European Union (TEU), which created the Common Foreign and Security Policy (CFSP), explicitly stated as one of the foreign policy objectives of the Union 'to develop and consolidate democracy and the rule of law, and respect for human rights and fundamental freedoms', (Title V, Art. J.1 TEU). In the field of development cooperation, the Maastricht Treaty also clarified that 'Community policy [...] shall contribute to the general objective of developing and consolidating democracy and the rule of law, and to that of respecting human rights and fundamental freedoms', (Art. 130u TEU). Finally, the Foreign Ministers agreed that the principles guiding claims for national independence should be firmly based upon the Helsinki Final Act, the Charter of Paris and the UN Charter, 'especially with regard to the rule of law, democracy and human rights', as well as the rights of minorities (EPC 1991).

The core principles and their legal basis were laid down in 1991. Over the next decade they were incorporated into the EU's most important regional strategies east and south of its borders, and some general policies and programmes were developed, such as the worldwide campaign against the death penalty (Manners 2002), sending electoral observation missions abroad, action against racism and assistance programmes. The overall and repeated objective of 'mainstreaming' human rights and democracy principles into external relations is still to be achieved, as Commission, Parliament and the Council all recognise.

Parallel internal EC/EU developments seem to have toed behind progress in including the principles in external policy. Article 6.2 TEC introduced by the TEU makes the European Convention for the Protection of Human Rights and Fundamental Freedoms (ECHR) part of the *acquis*. Article 7 TEC introduced by the Amsterdam Treaty contemplates a set of negative measures, up to the suspension of membership, in the case of violation of the principles outlined in Article 6. The political debate caused by the EU-14 sanctions against Austria did not deter the member states from modifying the article in the Nice Treaty from 'the existence of a serious and persistent breach to a *clear risk* of a serious breach' (emphasis added). Yet so long as the EU does not have a legal personality, it cannot accede to those international conventions whose principles it proposes to apply in external policy.

The source of legitimacy for its resort to principles in its global action thus lies outside its framework and can be found in international law and, where appropriate, regional agreements. The legal basis stems from the UN Charter (1948) and its International Covenants of 1966, the Charter of Paris for a New Europe approved in 1990 under the aegis of the Conference on Security and Cooperation in Europe (CSCE), and the Council of Europe's ECHR.

Together with this external legitimisation, the reasons moving the member states to include human rights and democracy stem from other considerations too. Within the broader European context, human rights became progressively part of political considerations towards the end of the 1980s and especially with the end of the Cold War. In 1990 the CSCE conceptualised the 'human dimension', whereby 'full respect for human rights and fundamental freedoms and the development of societies based on pluralistic democracy and the rule of law are prerequisites for progress in setting up the lasting order of peace, security, justice and cooperation' (CSCE 1990). An explicit link between democracy and human rights on the one hand and prevention of conflict and stability on the other was later made by the Commission in outlining its conflict prevention strategy: 'treating the root causes of conflict implies creating, restoring or consolidating structural stability in all its aspects'. And the definition of 'structural stability' includes 'democracy and respect for human rights, viable political structures [... and] the capacity to manage change without resort to conflict' (Commission 2001f).

In parallel, human rights and democracy principles were gaining ground at the multilateral level in the context of overseas development assistance. An influential 1989 World Bank report stated that donor programmes lost their validity in the absence of governance structures in the recipient countries capable of implementing reform: pluralism and good governance were seen as important factors in justifying aid (Crawford 1996). Both the Luxemburg Declaration and the November Resolution place democracy and human rights as a prerequisite for socio-economic development. The combination of these elements – the universal interpretation of human rights embedded in international law and reinforced by security and development concerns – provide the distinctive features of the EU's promotion of such principles abroad, together with the tools and means to do so.

Aid and diplomacy: the tools to promote human rights and democracy

The promotion of human rights and democracy can fall within the realm of diverse external activities of the EU, cutting across EC, member states and CFSP competences as well as the political, economic and aid dimensions. The main political and diplomatic tools and incentives to exercise pressure on the recipient governments range from the promise of accession or association, political dialogues at bilateral level or institutionalised through regional partnerships, support for the accession to international organisations, and economic and technical assistance through its regional and national programmes (Commission 1995b). The other side of the coin is the change, deferment or suspension of such incentives in cases of concern. The negative instruments at the EC's disposal too cut across first and second pillar tools and can include public or confidential démarches, changes in the content or channels of cooperation programmes, deferment of signatures or decisions, up to the suspension of cooperation agreements, trade embargoes and sanctions, as well as Common Positions and Joint Actions carried out under CFSP (K. Smith 1998).

Important steps occurred between 1992 and 1995, when the EU decided to include an 'essential element clause' in all cooperation agreements with third countries. By 2001 cooperation agreements concluded with 120 countries included the 'human rights clause', on the basis of which the EU can 'punish' the third country should those principles be breached (Commission 2001b). Sectoral agreements were excluded – and indeed important trading partners are exempt from such constraint (Ward 1998) – but the Nice Treaty established that the principles should be extended to economic, financial and technical cooperation measures with third countries (Title XXI, Art. 181a).

EU aid for democracy and human rights in third countries was first developed within the context of regional strategies, managed by different directorates of the Commission. In 1994, thanks to a European Parliament proposal, the European Initiative for Democracy and Human Rights (EIDHR) was created bringing together the separate human rights budget lines. With a budget of €100 million a year to complement regional programmes, EIDHR covers an expanding geographical area, with the countries of Central, Eastern and South-Eastern Europe and the Newly Independent States (NIS) receiving the lion's share.[2] As we shall see, priorities differ between countries and regions, but the regional distribution reflects the political importance attached to those areas.

Alongside projects aiming at strengthening the rule of law, pluralist civil society is perceived as a crucial pillar of democracy building and of raising human rights awareness, moving away from the more procedural approaches of the 1980s and early 1990s which focused largely on electoral assistance. But civil society is identified by and large with non-governmental organisations (NGOs) – the main channels for and recipients of EC aid – considered a bastion to check the processes of democratic transformation and a grassroots approach as a means to support local development and 'ownership'. This 'bottom-up' approach, however commendable, has its weaknesses: it narrowly identifies civil society with NGOs, especially of the Western advocacy-type (Youngs 2001b), while the role of institutions, especially the pro-reform elements of governments, watchdog and accountability functions, parliaments, trade unions and so on are far less supported (Crawford 2001). Secondly, the EU can use this method to avoid tackling controversial issues with partner governments, while maintaining a profile of an international actor keen on supporting human rights and democracy.

By the end of the 1990s a fairly broad range of tools had been put in place, though their use has been limited. The EU has proved reluctant to provide extra incentives to those countries demonstrating a good track record in implementing reform, in terms of positive conditionality, but also to use negative measures. Here lies one element of distinction in the EU 'style' (K. Smith 2003). In translating its principles into practice, a marked preference emerges for the use of persuasion[3] using dialogue with governments, and a reluctance to resort to negative or coercive instruments in the belief that engagement is more conducive towards stimulating democratisation than placing the country concerned into isolation. By contrast with the US, the use of 'socialisation' through political dialogue at a number of institutional levels and through the creation of a web of bilateral and regional relations even with countries with a lagging record on the principles is perceived in the EU as a valid route towards democratisation and the acceptance of human rights standards.

The blurred boundaries between the internal and external dimensions: the case of enlargement

Enlargement to the CEECs, inaugurated in June 1993 when the European Council made explicit what respect for democracy and human rights it was to expect from its future members,[4] represents an important case study for ascertaining the importance attached to promoting the principles of democracy and human rights abroad.

The tools through which the EU can press its conditions to the candidate countries have evolved over the years, from assistance through PHARE and pre-accession aid programmes to the Europe Agreements negotiated from 1994 onwards, and conditionality was gradually introduced. In view of the opening of negotiations, in 1997 the Commission started to publish its annual Regular Reports on progress made by the single countries in adopting the *acquis communautaire*. From December 1999 the Accession Partnerships indicated the short- and medium-term priorities for each country, and PHARE aid was increasingly geared towards tackling the weaknesses in the candidate countries. But it was only in March 1998 that the Commission was given the legal basis to suspend financial assistance if the country was not making sufficient progress, completing the range of tools through which conditionality could be exercised.

PHARE commitments between 1990 and 2000 were just under €12 billion, mostly directed to infrastructure and transport, private sector and economic restructuring, administration and public institutions, education and training (Commission 2000b). Conversely, allocations for human rights and democratisation occupied only 1 per cent of overall funding (ISA 1997). Between 1992 and 1996 priorities were the development of NGOs, awareness building, independent media, human rights (ISA 1997: 39–40). In the latter half of the 1990s the EU had been increasingly concerned with the functioning of the legal system and the challenges emerging in the whole of Eastern Europe regarding organised crime, illegal immigration, and the illicit trafficking of people and goods. Thus strengthening the legal system and its independence became one of the main priorities, absorbing over €6.5 million between 1996–99 (Commission 2000b).

Despite the gradual incorporation of ways of exercising conditionality in all the tools governing relations with the CEECs, the EC has avoided adopting the most vigorous methods. Since the signing of the Europe Agreements between 1994 and 1996, no punitive CFSP measure has been used against the candidate countries, nor has the EC suspended aid agreements or invoked the conditionality clause in the Accession Partnership for concerns over human rights or democracy in the candidate countries.

Slovakia was the only case in which negative measures were explicitly used: in 1998 it was considered not eligible to start negotiations solely on political grounds, though without suspending its Europe Agreement. The grounds to this decision had been prepared since the election of Vladimír Meciar to Prime Minister in 1994, who had been increasingly revealing authoritarian tendencies. In autumn 1995 the EU troika issued a démarche signalling its 'dissatisfaction', followed by a resolution of the European Parliament. EU concerns included the executive's campaign against the President, delays in the ratification of the Treaty between Hungary and Slovakia on accepting borders and standards on minority rights, the refusal to recognise a ruling of the constitutional court on the votes received by the new Democratic Union party, and hostility towards the Hungarian minority (Batt 1997; Henderson 1999). Importantly, the Commission's opinion distinguished formal and substantial democracy, underlining that while the skeleton of democratic institutions existed it was insufficiently applied in political life (Commission 1997c).

Romania too was subject to warnings over its treatment of the Hungarian minority, but treated differently. Due to the country's overall difficulties in reforming to meet the Copenhagen criteria, and fearing that too strong a condemnation of the government would negatively affect its difficult transition, the EU chose a smoother path of action by conveying its concern bilaterally and during Association Councils. It was nonetheless made clear that the deterioration of relations with the Slovak Hungarian minority and with Hungary, Romania risked its path towards membership. The signing of a bilateral treaty with Hungary in September 1996 and the change of government in November of the same year gave the green light to the Commission to conclude that Romania was on the way to meeting the political conditions (Commission 1997b). In March 1997 the European Investment Bank unblocked the freezing of a loan precisely because of changes in the provisions towards the Hungarian minority (K. Smith 1999).

One of the EU's political priorities that clearly emerged in the enlargement was respect for and the protection of minorities. While *per se* this has not warranted the application of explicit negative measures (in the case of Slovakia, the concern for the Hungarian minority was accompanied by preoccupations towards the functioning of democratic structures), minority protection does appear to be the sphere in which the EU exercised most pressure. This priority was reinforced in several ways. Firstly, the relationship between minorities and borders was also the subject of the Stability Pact for Europe launched in 1993–94 – the only CFSP initiative towards the CEECs. Focusing mainly on Hungarian minorities in Slovakia and Romania and on Russian minorities in the Baltic states, it played a significant role in the signing of over a hundred agreements, including those between Hungary and its neighbours (K. Smith 1999; Amato and Batt 1999). Secondly, the candidate countries are required in the Accession Partnerships to ratify the 1995 European Framework Convention for the Protection of National Minorities, despite the fact that not all the current member states have ratified it (Novak 1999).

What emerges is a conceptualisation of a strong link between minority protection and stability in Europe. As the Commission put it in *Agenda 2000*:

> minority problems, if unresolved, could affect democratic stability or lead to disputes with neighbouring countries. It is therefore in the interest of the Union and of the applicant countries that satisfactory progress in integrating minority populations be achieved before the accession process is completed.
>
> (Commission 1997a)

EU insistence on the consolidation of a system – democracy – guaranteeing those rights can be read as a long-term conflict prevention strategy (K. Smith 1999), a method similar to that embraced by the founding fathers of the EC, and strengthened by the fact that they were due to join in 2004.

From conflict to integration: strategies towards South-Eastern Europe

In the Balkans, the EC/EU has used virtually all the positive and negative tools at its disposal to try to stabilise the region, up to military intervention with humanitarian justifications. But its promotion of human rights and democratic principles in former Yugoslavia got off to a bad start. The first application of the principles it had subscribed to in the June 1991 Human Rights Declaration and in the guidelines for recognition of NIS was blatantly inconsistent: EC member states ended up ignoring their own guidelines and followed Germany's suit by recognising Slovenia (which, according to the committee satisfied the conditions) and Croatia (which did not), while they did not recognise Macedonia due to a Greek veto (though it did satisfy the criteria) (Zucconi 1996).

This chapter will focus on the post-Dayton Agreements period, when a more comprehensive strategy towards the region was gradually developed including human rights and democratic principles. The Copenhagen criteria formulated in the context of enlargement provided the blueprint for the Regional Approach, but the principles were further made explicit.[5] Prior to the 1999

North Atlantic Treaty Organization (NATO) intervention for Kosovo, the Regional Approach consisted of encouraging regional cooperation, renewing autonomous trade preferences (requiring compliance with the fundamental principles of democracy and human rights), various aid and assistance programmes (requiring compliance with the peace agreements obligations), and the establishment of contractual relations with the EU (subject to a number of general and specific conditions, such as the return of displaced persons).

After the NATO intervention, the Regional Approach was revamped, strengthened, and transformed into the Stabilisation and Association Process (SAP), which contains both regional and a bilateral dimension, the latter through the signing of Stabilisation and Association Agreements (SAAs) which could constitute a first step towards negotiating an Accession Agreement, as the EU member states at the Feira European Council eventually promised in June 2000. The prospect of accession – available to all countries of the region since the change of governments in Croatia (in January 2000) and in the Federal Republic of Yugoslavia (in October 2000) – provides the most important incentive for the governments to implement the reforms that the EU has spelt out.

EC assistance to the Western Balkans between 1991 and 2001 surpassed €6.8 billion of which about €63 million were destined to democratisation and human rights – the equivalent of 0.9 per cent of total assistance or 1.6 per cent if one excludes humanitarian aid and macroeconomic assistance from the total figure. EIDHR priorities in the whole of former communist Europe were discussed above in the section on enlargement, and unfortunately no evaluation of EC human rights and democratisation policies in the SEE region is yet available. Overall, in the SEE the EC's democratisation and human rights strategies followed the model adopted in the CEECs, with much support to local NGO projects, though the conflict prevention and confidence building dimension was much stronger, and the priorities for 2002 confirmed these objectives, tailored to match the perceived specific problems of the country. Thus, for instance, the Community Assistance for Reconstruction, Development and Stabilisation (CARDS) democratisation objectives in Croatia and Bosnia-Herzegovina were overwhelmingly geared towards the return of refugees and internally displaced persons, while in Macedonia towards inter-ethnic relations and civil society (Commission 2002f). In SEE too, attention was progressively paid to administrative structures and to issues relating to justice and home affairs, from the strengthening of the judiciary (with the fight against crime as a top priority) to border management.

The ways in which the EC/EU put pressure on the SEE countries is revealing both of the degree of inconsistency and of the ways in which the human rights and democracy discourse was woven into considerations of regional stability. With regard to Former Republic of Yugoslavia (FRY) and Croatia, after reaching the Dayton Agreements, only some economic and financial restrictions were lifted. A degree of 'discretion' became apparent in the treatment of the two countries between 1996 and 1998: while Croatian President Tudjman could hardly be considered a democrat, the country was penalised less than FRY for, among other things, its insufficient compliance in implementing the Peace Plan (Youngs 2001b), and for its continued support of the nationalist Croatian party in Bosnia. The country received small quantities of OBNOVA funds during this period though focused on reconstruction and on the return and integration of refugees and internally displaced persons. Yet extremely little or no progress was made in repopulating areas that had become ghost towns during the war. The three European Parliament Resolutions of 1996 and 1997 condemning, among other things, various kinds of violations of human rights in Croatia were not translated into the adoption of any further negative measures against the country.

Conversely, FRY was monitored more closely: throughout 1996 concern was repeatedly expressed through a number of declarations regarding compliance with the Peace Agreement, the independence of the media, and the legitimacy of the local elections of November 1996. EIDHR (and humanitarian aid) was the only programme that was kept running from 1994 onwards, while OBNOVA was either suspended or directed to support projects in Montenegro or Kosovo. From 1998, it suffered a UN arms embargo, a selective visa and travel ban on FRY officials, and a ban on EU investment. The reasons were the 'unacceptable violations of human rights [against the Kosovar Albanian community] [that] put the security of the region at risk' (CFSP 1998). These were maintained and reinforced until the change of government in October 2000. Thereafter, cooperation with the International Tribunal for Crimes in Yugoslavia (especially the extradition of Milosevic to The Hague) became a *sine qua non* condition for further aid to Serbia's new government.

In parallel to the negative tools, the EU offered incentives to the opposition that was gradually organising itself against the Milosevic regime, and some targeted programmes, such as 'Energy for Democracy' and 'Schools for a Democratic Serbia' to try to persuade the population that the sanctions were limited to the government only. The promise of integration into the Euro-Atlantic structures by becoming part of the SAP provided the opposition with an alternative to the isolation of previous decade.

Human rights and democracy priorities thus need to be understood in the context of the overall objective of stabilisation and containment of the region – still precarious, as the 2001 outbreak of conflict in Macedonia demonstrated. Security remains the paramount reason for EU involvement as well as for its development of human rights and democracy strategies. If regional stability was the core objective, the EU definition of stability requires further exploration. Tentatively, one can suggests two characteristics: FRY as central to regional stability, and the protection of national minorities. While Milosevic was in power, FRY was no doubt widely considered one of the major sources of regional instability (ICB 1996), justifying the negative action taken against the country. The case of Serbia from 1998 onwards 'served to highlight the EU's willingness to adopt coercive measures primarily where democratisation was pursued as part of a broad conflict resolution package' (Youngs 2001b: 24). National minorities also constitute a large part of the definitions of stability and instability and an important factor in shaping strategies towards the region. A very common perception of the wars in former Yugoslavia saw ethnic conflict as the cause and the solutions chosen reflect this belief: ultimately, the Dayton Agreements reflect an ethnically-based territorial division (ICB 1996). Protection of the rights of Kosovar Albanians was also the 'sound bite' over the 1999 NATO intervention, as well as in mediating the Macedonian 2001 conflict.

Turning a blind eye: the Euro-Mediterranean partnership

Launched at Barcelona in November 1995, the Euro-Mediterranean Partnership's stated objectives were to focus on three areas: a political and security partnership to create an area of peace and stability; an economic and financial partnership; and a social and cultural dialogue across the Mediterranean basin to encourage exchanges between civil society. The first basket of the partnership outlines the principles of political dialogue: human rights and basic freedoms, pluralism and tolerance, strengthening the rule of law and democracy. In contrast with CEE and SEE, where a universal approach to human rights was accompanied by special attention towards minorities, as well as with several EC/EU declarations, the list of principles introduces some elements of cultural relativism, such as 'due regard for the characteristics, values and distinguishing features peculiar to each of the participants' and proposes to 'refrain, in accordance with the rules of international law, from any direct or indirect intervention in the internal affairs of another partner' (Euro-Mediterranean Conference 1995).

One of the main aspects of the partnership is the bilateral Association Agreements signed with the individual countries of the region, all of which include the 'human rights clause'. Relations with the Mediterranean are also governed by a CFSP Common Strategy of June 2000, which reiterates the principles and objectives of the EMP. The tools in place for the EU to pursue objectives relating to human rights and democracy thus range from economics (through the Association Agreements), economic and financial support through the MEDA programme, EIDHR aid, political dialogue through the meetings at various levels to discuss the three baskets of the Partnership, as well as CFSP tools.

Yet EU commitment has been lagging on most aspects, including in the most advanced economic basket. Regional security and cooperation have been held hostage by the long-standing conflicts over Palestine–Israel and the Western Sahara. The European Parliament has declared that the Barcelona Process has seen 'no significant progress in the past years' (European Parliament 2001). The Commission itself has admitted that the dialogues on human rights, the prevention of terrorism and migration have not been 'sufficiently frank and serious' (Commission 2000b). Thus, the EC/EU performance on promoting human rights and democracy in the Mediterranean should bear in mind the overall problems of the process.

Prior to the 2000–01 reform of the Commission, even aid provisions have been disappointing: only 26 per cent of the €4 million committed between 1995 and 2000 under the MEDA programme (more or less tripling previous commitments) was paid (Commission 2001e), half of which was earmarked for structural adjustment, economic transition and private sector development, while 41 per cent was directed to development projects. Similarly to CEE and SEE, the Commission privileges almost entirely the use of civil society organisations, with 96 per cent of projects implemented by NGOs, while only 4 per cent is contracted to public bodies such as government ministries or international organisations (Karkutli and Bützler 1999). Thus it avoids tackling controversial issues, with the recipient governments often extremely hostile to substantial assistance aiming at political institutions (Youngs 2001b). Many of the objectives in the Mediterranean are also similar: between 1996 and 1999 the headings that received most funding were: education and awareness in human rights issues, the strengthening of NGOs, the legal system and its independence, legal assistance aimed at protecting civil and political freedoms, the empowerment of women, conflict prevention (Commission 2000f; Karkutli and Bützler 1999). In 2000, direct support to NGOs and human rights education continued to take the bulk of funding, and the empowerment of women remained a top priority. Assistance to strengthening the legal system, instead, was cut and focused on the abolition of the death penalty, while greater assistance was used for other target groups, such as support to the victims of torture, the military, police and security forces, and children (Commission 2001h). Compared to the other geographical areas, specific themes that emerge in the Mediterranean are a greater emphasis on gender equality.

Yet such priorities cannot be evinced from political and diplomatic relations, revealing a gap between bottom-up approaches based on assistance and a political and diplomatic exercise of conditionality, undermining the value of the 'human rights clauses' as well as the commitments the EC and its member states undertook during the 1990s. Where the EC has shown some muscle has been largely in condemning individual cases of human rights abuse. With the exception of the European Parliament, officially documented episodes of expression of concern are few and far between. In addition, many of those few cases were not forcefully put. Apart from Libya, isolated from the international community up to the very end of the 1990s, no negative CFSP provisions have been adopted, economic and technical assistance has not been suspended or officially threatened to be made conditional, and the 'human rights clause' of the association agreements has never been invoked.

Tunisia was the first country with which the Agreement entered into force in 1998, yet, in the name of the fight against fundamentalism, the human rights situation seems to have deteriorated. There has been increasing evidence of restrictions on civil and political rights during 2000, such as the targeting of human rights activists, restrictions on the media, repression of dissent and unfair trials (Amnesty International 2001), to which the European Parliament responded with two resolutions, one adopted in 2000 and a further one in 2002. Yet no negative measures have been taken to try coercing the government into respecting the international standards of the treaties and covenants to which the country is party, though the EU does address the topic of cooperation with international institutions and NGOs on human rights issues at the level of the Heads of Mission in Tunis.[6] This said, at the start of 2003, some signs of change became apparent in the Commission's strategy towards some countries. During the visit of its President to Algiers and Tunis in March, in the midst of war against Iraq, Romano Prodi underlined unequivocally that the fight against terrorism should not be used as a 'pretext to reduce public liberties, nor to renounce improving human rights in Tunisia' (Prodi 2003).

Algeria is one of the most problematic countries in the region. The military coup of January 1992, soon after the EC had made its landmark decisions with regard to promoting human rights and democracy abroad, was not followed up by any punitive action (Olsen 2000). International human rights organisations and the UN Human Rights Committee have repeatedly signalled their preoccupation over massacres of civilians, allegations of torture, disappearances, and the European Parliament has issued numerous resolutions throughout the 1990s. The EU member states also intervened with a number of declarations condemning terrorism.[7] Eventually, in 1997 negotiations for the Association Agreement were suspended, but then resumed in 1999 under the new President Abdelaziz Bouteflika, when the country seemed to have achieved a degree of stability, though progress in political pluralism was still absent (Youngs 2002). In the name of the fight against terrorism, Algeria has violated basic human rights for over a decade (Amnesty International 2002), and although the EU heads of mission have raised the issue of the 4,000 'disappeared' (Commission 2001e), there is no evidence that human rights and democracy considerations played much of a role in signing the Association Agreement in 2002.

It has been argued that security (Olsen 2000) and stability (Youngs 2002) are the central priorities of the EU member states in the region: political change towards democratisation was perceived as potentially destabilising and would thus be subordinated to the maintenance of regional stability. There is no doubt that the EU has not lived up to its rhetoric and principled commitment in its relations with the Southern Mediterranean states. The fear that political liberalisation could lead to Islamic fundamentalist organisations winning power through open electoral competition, given that they constitute the bulk of opposition across North African Arab states, is shared by Arab and European governments alike. But this has meant that the EU has frequently turned a blind eye to violations of fundamental freedoms: 'by focusing on the "terrorist threats", southern regimes have been very successful in branding all manifestations of opposition – violent and non-violent – as a threat to the stability of the region' (Lia 1999: 49–50). This ensures limited EU meddling with the internal affairs of the Mediterranean partners bilaterally – a trend reinforced since September 11 in the context of the fight against terrorism. The issue of the Occupied Territories and the plight of the Palestinians also contribute to making any discussion over human rights at the multilateral level a source of increased tension between Israel and its Arab neighbours.

The trade-off for this view of 'stability' – or maintenance of the *status quo* – is that democratic opposition and dissident groups receive little international support, undermining the very foundations of the democratisation efforts that the EU pursues in other parts of the world. In the southern Mediterranean, the political and ethical problems surrounding the promotion of human rights and democracy abroad are caught in the dilemma between maintaining some kind of regional stability and the perceived destabilising consequences of encouraging pluralism.

Conclusions

The Commission's claim quoted at the start of this chapter implies that the nature of the EU as well as its capabilities put it in a privileged position to pursue human rights and democracy abroad. This claim needs to be further explored.

A 'comprehensive human rights policy' has been defined as one containing two distinct elements. The first regards the ratification of international human rights treaties and the submission of internal human rights practices to international review. The EU member states have accepted the jurisdiction of the European Court of Human Rights, although, as we have seen, the EU as such cannot (yet). The second dimension involves:

> the projection of human rights values internationally through an external human rights policy. An external policy exists when explicit human rights legislation or executive policy regulates aspects of foreign policy making so that human rights are incorporated in the foreign policy calculus.
>
> (Sikkink 1993: 143)

On the one hand, the EU has developed a legal basis for promoting human rights and democracy abroad, has formalised its commitments in its treaties and foreign policy objectives, and has equipped itself with sets of tools for this purpose. From this point of view, the commitments do stand out – in words and moneys, but also in terms of making these principles a part of relations with all third countries. No other large state has put on paper that its foreign policy objectives include international action in support of human rights and democratic principles and has created a legal basis to do so; no other state has tied its relations with third countries to 'human rights clauses', no other regional or international organisation can wield the same power or influence to do so. The process of formalising such principles in the structures and policies of EU foreign relations makes them more resistant to political change and less vulnerable to manipulation. The degree to which it has incorporated principles of human rights and democracy are part of the model that the EU presents to the world, even though they are not always or necessarily resorted to in the actual politics of its external relations.

This shift partly reflects the experience of the Member States in creating a 'democratic community' model of integration and conflict prevention based on sets of liberal institutional principles (K. Smith 2001; Lucarelli 2002a). This logic is reinforced in the case of enlargement to the CEECs and eventually to SEE. Additionally, it reflects the ways in which the EU engages with the international environment. Objectives of promoting human rights and democracy can perhaps be best understood through the lens of 'structural foreign policy' (Keukeleire 2002), whereby the EU pursues amongst its many foreign policy goals, milieu and long term objectives aiming at influencing, through a range of pacific and civilian means, structural and long term changes (Keukeleire 2002; Telò 2001; Lucarelli's introduction). In other words, if not by choice, the EU has developed, by default or by necessity, extensive sets of civilian tools and a normative strength that allow human rights and democracy to be included in its external objectives. In 2001, human rights and democratisation objectives were firmly included in the EU's conflict prevention strategy as a crucial building block of sustainable stability.

In terms of means, the EU has shown a clear preference towards supporting the growth of NGOs to foster civil society development from below, accompanied by the development of institutionalised relations which can include 'constructive' or 'critical' political dialogues, even with governments whose human rights record ranges from the debatable to the abysmal. Even if the bottom-up approach through democracy assistance and the top-down approach based on the concept of partnership do not always proceed symbiotically and in a mutually reinforcing fashion, they do constitute two characteristics of the EU's promotion of human rights and democracy abroad.

On the other hand, the drawback of maintaining relations with countries with chequered democratic records does represent a breach of the principles, highlighting the political need for flexibility in the EU's external relations. One should therefore not assume that the EU's commitment towards including such principles stems simply from the nature of the EU, with an idealist turn (Sikkink 1993) as its main source of change. If this were the case, human rights and democracy would figure far more prominently in the Barcelona Process, notwithstanding the challenges of finding a balance between maintaining consistency of principles and engagement with non-democratic states.

The cases of Central, Eastern and South-Eastern Europe also illustrated some limitations to the notion that the EU is simply idealistically projecting its norms abroad. Here, security concerns ensured an important role to human rights and democracy principles, but the standards advocated were higher than those applied within the EU, reflecting an unresolved tension between the member states on the relationship between conceptions of human rights (individual versus collective) and the democratic structures to guarantee those rights (for example, counter-majoritarian rules or positive discrimination). The empirical results from the case studies reviewed here also challenge the dichotomy between idealism and pragmatism. In other words, despite the Treaty-based requirement for consistency, the actual politics of the EU's external relations show a stronger tendency towards a 'flexible adherence to principles'[8] exercised by the EU when it comes to deciding where, when, how, and why to press for the principles it proposes to stand by. In Chris Brown's words, however, 'because the goals are multidimensional, governments are never able to judge relations solely on the basis of human rights, and it would be wrong to expect them to do so' (Brown 2001: 29).

Notes

1 According to Goldstein and Keohane (1993: 8), worldviews 'are embedded in the symbolism of a culture and deeply affect modes of thought and discourse'.

2 35 per cent between 1996–99 and 24 per cent in 2000 (Commission 2000g); the Mediterranean region received during the same periods 24 and 11 per cent (Commission 2001b).

3 Persuasion too can be a double-edged sword: from the point of view of the third country, EU persuasion can be perceived as imposition of its norms with little space for bargaining or finding alternatives (Lucarelli 2002a; Elgström 2000).

4 The political criteria include: 'stability of institutions guaranteeing democracy, the rule of law, human rights and respect for and protection of minorities' (European Council 1993).

5 They include 'representative government, accountable executive; government and public authorities to act in a manner consistent with the constitution and the law; separation of power (government, administration and law); free and fair elections at reasonable intervals by secret ballot'. Under the subject heading 'Human rights, rule of law' are: 'freedom of expression, including independent media; right of assembly and demonstration; right of association; right to privacy, family, home and correspondence; right to property; effective means of redress against administrative decisions; access to courts and right to fair trial; equality before the law and equal protection by the law; freedom from inhuman or degrading treatment and arbitrary arrest'. 'Respect for and protection of minorities' are also included in the political criteria: 'right to establish and maintain their own educational, cultural and religious institutions, organisations or associations; adequate opportunities for these minorities to use their own language before courts and public authorities; adequate protection of refugees and displaced persons returning to areas where they represent an ethnic minority' (Council of the EU 1997).

6 See 'Fiches pays tiers: Tunisie'. Available online: http://www.consilium.eu.int/pesc (accessed 01 January 06).

7 See the 'Fiche pays tiers: Algerie'. Available online: http://www.consilium.eu.int/pesc (accessed 01 January 06).

8 I owe the phrase to Knud Erik Jørgensen.

8 Promoting human rights and democracy in European Union relations with Russia and China

Stefania Panebianco

Introduction

In the last decade, the debate on the responsibilities that the European Union (EU) has in world governance and the roles it has to play to face the challenges of the global system has become intense both in political and academic circles. Several EU documents illustrate the paths for new EU roles in world politics and some of them are worth recalling. The European Commission's White Paper on the European Governance of July 2001 raised the need for the Union to 'seek to apply the principles of good governance to its global responsibilities'. The Laeken Declaration on the Future of the EU adopted in December 2001 urged the EU to play 'a stabilising role worldwide', exporting the EU 'humane values' which include – *inter alia* – human rights, fundamental freedoms, democracy, respect of diversity, etc. More recently, the Title V on the Union's external action contained in the Constitutional Treaty offered a general framework for the EU to act as a multilateral actor, human rights and democracy promoter, security-provider, and stabiliser of the EU neighbourhood. These EU normative documents reflect the process the EU is experiencing of progressively strengthening its foreign policy by developing a wide range of political, economic, trade, humanitarian and diplomatic actions.[1] The literature on EU foreign policy – reflecting this 'widening process' – is focusing more and more upon the projection and roles of the EU in the international scene. Thus, the nature of EU participation in international politics has been variously regarded as 'actorness' (Sjöstedt 1976), 'presence' (Allen and Smith 1990; 1998), 'role' (Hill 1993; 1998), 'impact' (Ginsberg 2001), and 'normative power' (Manners 2000a; 2002). The EU's role as human rights and democracy (HRD) promoter will be the main focus of this chapter.[2]

The European Commission depicts the EU as an international actor with 'political and moral weight' (Commission 2001b: 3) with EU values and principles to be supported and diffused by means of EU foreign policy. Among the values and principles upon which the EU foreign policy is based, HRD have emerged as distinctive features of EU *principled* foreign policy, and the promotion of HRD is depicted as an EU foreign policy objective *per se* (see Article III-193(2) of the Constitutional Treaty). With the inclusion of the human dimension in EU foreign policy, the EU tends to export to the international system the EU domestic political and socio-economic development model which is based – *inter alia* – upon democratic principles, minority rights, equal opportunities and solidarity. The EU assumes that the EU model will also prove successful in third countries, as it did first in Western Europe and more recently in Eastern Europe. This is even truer in the post-Cold War era which has experienced the failure of the political and economic communist model of development. For this reason, principles and values such as liberty, fundamental freedoms, democracy, human rights, the rule of law and good governance are included in EU official documents and international agreements as a key dimension of EU foreign policy. There is an assumption that poverty reduction can only be achieved with functioning democratic institutions and accountable governments, and that democratic, pluralist governments respecting minority rights lead to domestic stability (Commission 2001b: 4).

But it is not necessarily the case that EU values and principles can be easily exported to third countries. Notwithstanding its originality, the principled approach to EU foreign policy can be successfully applied provided that the partners are willing to accept EU norms with unilateral adaptation instead of negotiation (Cremona 1998: 86). In this respect, the incentives to comply with EU norms and standards which are offered to EU partners play an essential role. By implementing the *acquis communautaire* and the *acquis politique*, the Central and Eastern European countries (excepting Romania and Bulgaria until 2007) have obtained full accession to the EU; Turkey has become a candidate EU member; the Mediterranean countries can create a free trade area with the EU by 2010. As far as Russia and China are concerned, since the incentive for the approximation of legislation can only be market access, adherence to HRD seems instrumental to obtain economic benefits, trading advantages and stability conditions.

In order to contribute to the conceptualisation of the EU as an 'international actor with a principled behaviour in foreign policy' (see the Introduction to this volume), this research aims to verify to what extent values and principles such as HRD can be regarded as a motivating factor in EU foreign policy. This chapter provides some empirical evidence which questions the coherence of the EU as an international actor with a distinctive principled 'international identity' (Manners and Whitman 1998; 2003). In particular, attention is focused here upon EU relations with Russia and China, two increasingly powerful actors in world affairs which in the last decade have become EU strategic partners. The main argument is that, beyond the discursive dimension of EU foreign policy, the EU is not always able (or willing) to exert its capability to 'extend its norms into the international system' (Manners 2002: 252), and concrete action in defence of HRD lags behind overriding security and economic interests in the cases of Russia and China.

What the analysis of the promotion of HRD in EU relations with Russia and China shows is the limits of the 'exportability' of the EU model. Not all EU partners are necessarily ready to change their traditions and specificities to adopt EU values and principles, as a result of an external interference. For Russia and China, it is not a question of contesting *tout court* the universal definition of human rights or opposing the democratisation process. The dilemma between universal ethics and cultural relativism emerges when, for instance, the EU insists upon the universality and the indivisibility of civil, political, economic, social and cultural rights, as reaffirmed by the 1993 World Conference on Human Rights in Vienna (Commission 2001b: 3), while China tends to prioritise human rights by affirming the supremacy of economic and collective rights over individual rights. Moreover, the EU promotes pluralistic democracy, but the implementation of democratic processes in Russia are accompanied with autocratic tendencies leading to the weakening of opposition and limits to freedoms of the media.

Values, principles and images of the world are usually reiterated and defended through political discourses (this is true both on the EU and its partners' sides). Analysis shows that when dealing with HRD, EU normative power is challenged by third countries' views, beliefs and different priorities. In most cases, the EU makes extensive use of 'declaratory measures' (Manners 2002: 248) to sanction human rights violations in Russia and China, where ethnic minority rights are not guaranteed (respectively in Chechnya and Tibet). The discourse of Russian and Chinese political élites express the political will of two emerging global powers who state their diversity in order to affirm their influential role in the international system. Our primary hypothesis is that strategic and/or economic considerations often prevail over HRD promotion, thus proving the existence of boundary problems (White 1999: 50) among political and HRD issues. Defence of human rights and democratic principles is an important component of EU foreign policy, but when setting priorities in relations with third countries such as Russia and China, strategic and economic objectives stand higher on the agenda.

A wide definition of EU foreign policy

The EU is acting in the international scene as an emerging global power (Piening 1997: 1) whose major interests are not only international trade and economic cooperation, but political, security and human affairs as well. The Union's power now resides upon a variety of tools that constitute EU foreign policy, such as economics, trade and aid, although not exclusively. Before focusing upon the transposition of HRD into EU relations with Russia and China, a preliminary analysis of the comprehensive approach the EU has elaborated for its relations with third countries is provided to illustrate how the promotion of HRD has become an issue of EU foreign policy.

The change of nature of EU foreign policy reflects a concept of security which since the end of the Cold War has 'broadened' to become comprehensive and multidimensional.[3] Since threats to security often have a transnational origin and go beyond a purely military dimension, EU foreign policy has expanded to include cooperation in the political, economic, social and environmental fields.

The EU has adopted strategy documents that include – alongside cooperation on trade and commerce, a wide range of 'new' political security issues, with international terrorism as one of the most recent issues in the agenda of political cooperation. EU foreign policy has therefore acquired a horizontal dimension which includes political and diplomatic initiatives, development and humanitarian aid, trade and HRD promotion. The basic assumption of the comprehensive approach to EU relations with third countries is that economic development in EU partner countries cannot take place without taking into due account political instability and socio-economic disparities, deterioration of the environment, threats to security deriving from illegal migration, terrorism, organised crime, etc. Along with international security, third countries' domestic security and stability is now being regarded by the EU as a crucial field of bilateral cooperation.

Since the 1990s EU relations with third countries have adopted a 'comprehensive approach' which assumes as distinct but interrelated fundamental components: (a) political and security cooperation, (b) economic and financial cooperation, (c) cooperation in social and human affairs. The innovative aspect of this approach consists in the coexistence of political and economic cooperation with the human dimension. The European Commission (Commission 2001b) in particular has stressed the linkage between traditional trade relations and human rights standards, support for democracy and fundamental rights, all issues addressed by EU foreign policy.

The EU Strategic Partnership with Russia reflects this three-fold approach. By relying on a comprehensive concept of security, it addresses common security threats such as terrorism, transnational organised crime, customs, taxation fraud, communicable diseases, etc. (Commission 2004). It is also to favour domestic security and stability that EU cooperation with Russia aims at developing democratic processes and institutions, the rule of law, protection of minorities, the rights of children and women, etc. For this reason, in the EU Strategic Partnership Agreement with Russia, economic instruments to develop a free trade market economy to replace the state-planned economic system are accompanied by political cooperation to manage domestic political crises and support to democratic reforms. EU–China relations are also based upon a three-fold approach: the political and human rights dialogue, technical assistance and cooperation, and trade and economic development (Commission 2003a). However, although the human dimension has been added to trade and economic development, the latter still prevails.

Promoting human rights and democracy in EU–Russia relations

Since 1991, when Russia gained sovereignty, EU–Russia relations have seen enhanced political and economic cooperation on the basis of a mutual interest: the EU is Russia's most important trading partner and the most important partner for providing foreign direct investment; Russia represents a strategic EU partner in many areas of cooperation and, in particular, supplies the EU with energy (Hubel 2004: 351). EU–Russia interdependence in trade, energy and finances significantly affects their definition of interests and behaviours (Hubel 2004: 352). There is also a mutual interest in strengthening EU–Russia security cooperation, since the EU's long-term objective is to integrate Russia in the European security system, and Russia favours a pan-European collective security system in which it claims an active role to play, reflecting the prevalent Russian idea of a multipolar world (Forsberg 2004: 254).

The key EU–Russia agreements have to be briefly recalled to illustrate the normative cooperation framework and the principal cooperation areas. In 1994 the EU and Russia signed a Partnership and Cooperation Agreement which offered the general framework for EU–Russia relations; but the ratification of the agreement was delayed by EU countries as a protest against the war in Chechnya and it entered into force only in 1997. At the Cologne European Council in June 1999 the EU adopted a Common Strategy to organically structure the EU–Russia relations by initiating a Strategic Partnership. The Common Strategy considers consolidation of democracy, the rule of law and public institutions in Russia as key EU objectives and seeks a further reinforcement of political dialogue at all levels in which questions of common interest are tackled, including Chechnya (Council of the European Union 2003).

Russia was originally part of the European Neighbourhood Policy (ENP) launched by the Commission in March 2003 and later endorsed by the EU Council to promote cooperation with Europe's Eastern and Southern neighbours (Commission 2003b). Through the ENP, the EU seeks to provide its neighbours with a new framework of cooperation, to extend the EU's internal market and to promote free movement of persons, goods, services and capital; moreover, the ENP seeks to enhance EU relations with the neighbouring countries on the basis of shared values, notably democracy, human rights respect and the rule of law. However, Russia has expressed its lack of interest in this cooperation framework, preferring instead to foster bilateral relations with the EU via the Strategic Partnership.

At the St Petersburg Summit in May 2003 the 'four common spaces' (a Common Economic Space; a Common Space of Freedom, Security and Justice; a Common Space of Cooperation in the Field of External Security, and a Common Space on Research, Education and Culture) have been identified as the main goal of EU–Russia relations. The EU seeks to reduce Russian political and economic instability and anchor Russia to the European political and economic system without full accession. The EU is interested in Russia's internal stability because it is aware that, due to the increasing political and economic interdependence of the global system, threats to EU security can easily derive from political instability or financial crises in neighbouring countries. Thus, EU–Russia cooperation includes political and economic development, know-how transfer, humanitarian aid, support for democratisation, transnational organised crime (including people, arms and drug trafficking), nuclear insecurity and deterioration of the environment.

As far as HRD are concerned, direct reference is made in all documents regulating EU–Russia relations. The 1994 Partnership and Cooperation Agreement added for the first time the political dialogue to the economic dimension. Moving beyond economic cooperation, the political dialogue was intended to help cooperation on matters pertaining to the observance of the principles of democracy and human rights, particularly the rights of minorities. The agreement considered democratic reforms granting pluralism and the establishment of a multiparty system with free and fair elections as the necessary basis for the economic liberalisation aimed at setting up a market economy.

Also the TACIS (Technical Assistance to the Commonwealth of Independent States) programme, which was initially conceived to provide Russia with technical and financial assistance to favour the passing from a state-led economy to economic liberalism, has expanded its objectives to develop a pluralistic political system. Now TACIS largely relies upon the consolidation of democracy by strengthening the role of civil society and non-governmental bodies. Support for institutional, legal, administrative and judicial reforms, support to the private sector and assistance for economic development, and support in addressing the social consequences of transition are currently regarded as priority areas of EU assistance to the Russian transition process (Commission 2003c).

Going beyond the economic dimension, the 1999 Common Strategy was conceived to embrace cooperation in justice and home affairs, visas, internal security (i.e. institutional development, democratic processes and rule of law) and international security (i.e. fight organised crime, including people, arms and drug trafficking, illegal migration, money laundering, etc.). The Common Strategy proved too wide in scope and too detailed on methods to act as an effective tool. Despite this the EU declared political commitment to anchor Russia to the European political and socio-economic system through the creation of a strategic partnership. So far the instruments adopted by the EU within the framework of the common strategy have not proved successful.

Unfortunately, despite this panoply of initiatives and the generosity of Western countries, due to the lack of 'skills, legal traditions, commercial contract experience, and investment banking infrastructure that could benefit from a Marshall Plan' for Russia, so far Western funds proved unable to help the transition to a modern free market economy (M. Walker 2001: 121), democratic reforms provided no guarantee of good governance and the situation concerning human rights still remains critical.

The difficulties the EU encounters in the promotion of human rights and democracy in Russia

The official documents that shape EU–Russia relations refer to a strategic partnership based upon 'a series of shared values among which paramount importance is given to the respect for the rule of law and the defense of democracy and human rights' (Council of the European Union 2003). The Joint Declarations regularly adopted at the EU–Russia biannual Summits stress the importance of

freedom of speech, independence and pluralism in the media as essential democratic conditions for the EU–Russia partnership; the situation in Chechnya is also discussed during the EU–Russia Summits. But human rights support and democratic principles defence are just some among several areas of cooperation, with security, political and economic issues being the priority areas. Security concerns, the fight against international terrorism or economic self-interests seem to take precedence over fostering HRD. To some extent, Russia's adherence to the supremacy of human rights seems to be more the result of external pressure than a genuine domestic strategy of political development. Since the EU strongly emphasises human rights defence and democracy support, it is as if the rhetoric adherence to HRD provided Russia with higher credentials as an EU partner.

The promotion of HRD in EU–Russia relations is affected by several difficulties. For many years EU–Russia relations have been marked by a stop-and-go progress, slowed down by the Chechnya crisis, or by Russian political and financial instability. Despite Western political and economic support, the development of a viable democracy in Russia is far from accomplished and minority rights are still not fully guaranteed. Russia has started its transition towards democracy, but the road to a pluralistic democratic political system seems long. The European Commission is aware that democracy and civic institutions as well as media pluralism still need to be consolidated (Commission 2004), but the EU 'gentle pressure' towards democratisation (Mahncke 2001: 435) appears deficient when faced with strategic interests and political priorities. Russia is dealing with the first stage of the democratic institution-building process and its political system still combines democratic institutions with authoritarian practices of the state administration. Yet, the Russian political regime can be regarded as 'authoritarian-presidentialist, further aggravated by a widespread disregard for legal norms, constitutional rules, institutional power sharing, and accountability of decision-makers' (Mangott 2001: 380). In 2003 its records of respect of political rights and civil liberties were both ranked by Freedom House as 5 on a 1–7 scale (where 1 represents the most-free and 7 the least-free rating), thus considering Russia just as a 'partly free' country (Karatnycky 2004: 91).

On the socio-economic development side, there are some deficiencies as well. At the end of the Cold War Russia had turned towards Western countries to 'import' a successful system of political, economic and social development. Yet the implementation of the EU model has not been easy. The reforms carried on during the last decade produced mass impoverishment of the population, a big gap between the few rich and the majority of the population, widespread corruption, violence and criminality (Yurlov 2000: 56). The European Commission acknowledges that Russia has experienced a difficult transitional period, since 1990 poverty rates have increased considerably and inequalities between groups of population and regions have been growing.[4] Moreover, the Russian economic system has developed some peculiar traits: it is not based upon an emerging market economy which is 'liberal' in the Western sense, it is based instead on a mixed economy strongly influenced by the state, with direct bureaucratic influence in economic processes. The giant state enterprises have simply become nominally privatised monopoly firms, and the soviet *nomenklatura* have retained political and economic power (M. Walker 2001: 117).

Despite this tortuous path towards an open Russian political and economic system, Russia remains an increasingly important economic partner and a crucial partner in the area of security and defence. The EU has significant strategic and economic interests in Russia's economic development, mainly due to its dependence on energy supplies from Russia (Commission 2004: 1). Moreover, EU relations with Russia are strongly influenced by security concerns, being the EU's largest neighbour since the 2004 enlargement, and the EU is interested in finding common positions on security and stability in Europe. The most recent EU documents on the European Security and Defence Policy (ESDP) foresee association procedures for countries such as Russia with which the Union maintains a political dialogue. On the other hand, Russia attaches great importance to cooperation with the EU in the security and defence field to counterbalance a hegemonic global system run by the United States (Webber 2001: 415).[5] This mutual interest prevents the EU from adopting a confrontational strategy on violations of human rights (minority rights in particular) and the lack of transparency and democratic practices.

In particular, security considerations have strongly affected the EU position vis-à-vis the excessive use of military force against the Chechen minority. Since 11 September the war against international terrorism has also become a crucial field of cooperation in EU–Russia relations. But due to the war against terrorism, or more exactly because of it (Allen and Smith 2002: 105), Russia has a red light on the question of Chechnya, where it claims to be fighting terrorism. With the war in Chechnya, Russia moved back from the declared adherence to the European countries' approach and definition of human rights; it proved instead that, in practice, it considers human rights issues to be the exclusive internal affairs of Russia. Russians regard the Chechnya question as part of cross-border terrorism (Yurlov 2000: 47), and the EU accepts that Russia deals with this crisis as an 'internal' crisis rather than an 'international' one, acknowledging that it has direct implications for territorial integrity and national sovereignty of the Russian Federation. On several occasions the EU has reiterated its blame for the military intervention in Chechnya on Russia and expressed its concern over the need for an urgent political solution to the conflict, but it has never questioned the territorial integrity of Russia, nor considered cutting off its financial assistance to Russia as an effective lever in order to put pressure on the Russian authorities. Instead of a firm political reaction, the EU only adopts symbolic measures (e.g. by reallocating TACIS means to other areas such as the advancement of democracy and humanitarian assistance). The former EU Commissioner for external relations, Chris Patten, in his 'Declaration on Chechnya' (Patten 1999) illustrated the dilemma in EU–Russia relations as 'retaliation *vs* strategic friendship', with the latter still prevailing.

NGOs (such as Amnesty International or Human Rights Watch) and even the European Parliament repeatedly denounced that the EU is turning a 'blind eye'

in the name of the fight against transnational terrorism. This attitude clashes
with the EU's claim of respect of minority rights as one of the main basis of EU
foreign policy. The Parliament has recalled that '[p]rominent politicians [...]
have warned of a repetition of the mistakes of the Cold War era, when dicta-
torships were supported in the name of the fight against communism' (European
Parliament 2002a: 22).

Despite the declaratory emphasis upon EU values and principles contained in
EU foreign policy documents, in EU–Russia relations the EU model of political
development which includes consideration of HRD has been adjusted according
to the prevalent security needs. With great pragmatism, in the EU the issue of
Russian respect of (or lack of) HRD standards is prominent among political
discourse, but hardly dominant (Neumann 1997: 122). Even the European
Commission questions 'Russia's commitment and ability to uphold core universal and European values and pursue democratic reforms' (Commission 2004:
1). Analyses of the EU–Russia Strategic Partnership tend to converge on the
same evaluation: the EU and Russia do not share the same strategic culture and
values. Some analysts explain the low performance – compared to the high
expectations of the 1990s – of the EU–Russia Strategic Partnership by pointing
out the 'structural incompatibilities between these two unequal partners' (Hubel
2004: 354). Due to the different standards of HRD, Hubel argues that there are
'fundamental differences in political culture' (Hubel 2004: 354). In the same
line, Forsberg's critical view of the EU–Russia Security Partnership relies upon
the different perspective of the two partners: for the EU the Strategic Partnership
should rely upon common *values*, while for Russia it should rely upon common
interests (Forsberg 2004: 261) (emphasis added). The different values and strategies is inevitably part of the 'lack of substance' of the EU–Russia Security Partnership: 'values, particularly regarding human rights, are perceived as being
much more central for the EU than for Russia, and strategic culture and practices related to the use of military force different' (Forsberg, 2004: 262). Thus, in
EU–Russia relations political discourse seems to prevail over concrete political
measures:

> the relationship between the EU and Russia has fallen short of expecta-
> tions because it has been guided more by visions than concrete measures.
> Both the EU and Russia have a culture of building partnerships that
> revolve around speeches and documents. The finest of the ideas are how-
> ever poorly implemented.
>
> (Forsberg 2004: 265)

The EU 'constructive engagement' with China

EU–China relations are marked by a commonality and a difference between the
two partners: both the EU and China are reshaping their role in the international environment in order to affirm themselves as key players in the global
system (Moeller 2002: 10); however, the EU – in order to avoid being only an

economic power – is seeking to increase its global political weight, while China is focusing primarily upon its global economic weight. At a time of economic crisis and slow global economic growth, the fast Chinese economic growth is helping China to become a key actor of the international system. As far as bilateral relations are concerned, China is an EU strategic partner and vice-versa: China is the EU's second largest export market, and the EU is China's third largest trading partner and the major supplier of advanced technology and foreign direct investment (Lan 2004: 115). Trade has been a fundamental aspect of EU–China relations since the mid-1990s, when the rapid growth of the Chinese economy attracted European investors keen to profit from a huge market with prospects for development.

For many years EC–China relations had been influenced and limited by the East–West competition, but unlike the Soviet Union, China was never totally closed to Europe (Piening 1997: 155). China was already recognised in the generalised system of preferences in 1980; in 1985 a trade and economic cooperation agreement was reached granting China a broader framework for cooperation and trade, but it included no provisions about democracy and human rights. In the 1990s EU–China relations developed towards a comprehensive partnership defined by a series of Strategic Papers adopted by the European Commission.[6] The 1998 policy paper adopted by the Commission to establish a 'Comprehensive Partnership with China' (Commission 1998) and the policy paper adopted in 2003 to create a 'Maturing Partnership' (Commission 2003a) list a wide spectrum of cooperation areas. The EU supports the Chinese political and economic reform process mainly through technical assistance, legal and judicial cooperation, and a special dialogue on human rights. In fact, the EU Strategy for China relies upon a comprehensive approach based upon three main headings: (a) political dialogue, including a specific dialogue on human rights; (b) economic and trade relations; (c) technical assistance (Patten 2002).

Despite this three-fold approach, in EU–China relations there is an imbalance between political and economic cooperation, with the latter neatly prevailing (Xiang 2001: 94). The EU-China policy of 'constructive engagement' is based upon the neo-functionalist assumption that increased contacts with European partners should almost automatically bring more liberalisation in the Chinese economy and eventually in the Chinese political system. The neo-functionalist approach that assumes political changes as a result of economic reforms has been clearly expressed by the former EU Commissioner Chris Patten, who recalled that interdependence and economic growth would transform into political stability via a spill-over effect (Patten 2002).

The EU prefers the 'engagement' approach based upon persuasion to the containment relying upon the imposition (or threat) of sanctions. The EU constructive engagement strategy does not imply continuous pressure upon HRD issues; it is limited instead to strengthening cooperation in all existing sectors. For this reason the EU approach to China has been more tolerant than the US one, the former insisting more upon economic reforms than upon human rights standards. A different approach between the US and EU has emerged also concerning China's entry into the World Trade Organization (WTO). For many years the USA applied the conditionality principle to the Chinese application, while the Europeans favoured the entry of China into the WTO in order to have China in the multilateral institutions and to 'control' it from inside.

The EU promotion of HRD in China mainly relies on an approach based on dialogue. The EU political dialogue with China was formally established in 1994 and a specific human rights dialogue was initiated two years later. As a reaction to the EU's denial to drop a China resolution at the UN Commission on Human Rights, the human rights dialogue was suspended by China in 1997 and resumed later that year. The human rights dialogue allows for a candid exchange of views on a broad range of issues of EU concern, such as China's cooperation with UN mechanisms, freedom of association, freedom of expression and belief, torture prevention, the death penalty, administrative detention, the treatment of refugees, ethnic minorities' rights (especially in Tibet and Xinjiang) and individual cases. Upon request, the Chinese authorities have to provide written information on individual cases raised by the EU. This dialogue is held twice a year and is complemented by human rights seminars which bring together academic experts, NGOs' representatives and other participants from the EU and China. The EU–China Human Rights Seminars provide an opportunity for exchange of views on specific violations and on the role of national human rights institutions. The EU regularly evaluates the results of the dialogue to determine to what extent its expectations have been met. In addition to dialogue sessions, the EU raises human rights concerns in bilateral summits, ministerial and experts' meetings with China. Public statements of concern, including at regular sessions of the UN Commission on Human Rights, as well as démarches made on specific issues of concern, are other means of expressing EU views.

The EU–China human rights dialogue, together with pressure from other international partners, has produced minor concrete results such as visits to China by the UN Commissioner for Human Rights; the signing (but not yet the ratification) of the UN Covenant on Civil and Political Rights; the signing and ratification of the UN Covenant on Social, Economic and Cultural Rights; the release of prisoners and setting up of Commission cooperation projects. While recognising some changes in the Chinese political and economic system due to the opening of the economy and the ongoing reform of the judicial and legal system, the EU remains concerned about continuing violations of human rights. The widespread use of the death penalty and torture as well as the continued system of administrative detention, significant shortcomings as concerns freedom of expression, assembly, association and religion, freedom of speech and press, ongoing violations of the human rights of pro-democracy activists, proponents of free trade unions and followers of Falun Gong, and the repression of persons belonging to ethnic minorities in Tibet and Xingjiang continue to figure high on the EU agenda vis-à-vis the Chinese government. China still has to achieve more substantial improvements on the ground.

There is no sight yet of a considerable improvement of HRD standards. Political reforms to introduce greater grassroots democracy and improve human rights' records are slowly implemented and still far from meeting internationally recognised standards in the area of civil and political rights. Moreover, similar to the Russian conduct in Chechnya, China justifies the denial of basic freedoms in Xinjiang on counterterrorism grounds. China's modernisation is characterised by a very slow process of democratisation in favour of economic liberalisation. China's record of respect of political rights and civil liberties remains very low and in 2003 Freedom House ranked the level of political rights and civil liberties, respectively, 7 and 6 out of a 1–7 scale (Karatnycky 2004: 91).

Nevertheless, the EU has not modified its strategy of constructive engagement with China and still opts for a pragmatic reaction to human rights violations. Instead of a confrontational strategy to react to this picture, the Council regards the EU–China human rights dialogue as the best instrument to promote improvements in the human rights situation in China (Council of the European Union 2003). The dialogue is a channel of communication which allows the EU to express concern about human rights abuses and seek information about human rights developments in China. It is also a way to expose the highest level of Chinese government to international human rights standards and EU best practice and a vehicle to identify concrete cooperation projects under the EIDHR and other instruments. The Council appreciates the cooperation of China within the EU–China human rights dialogue process, but expects the dialogue to produce measurable results and progress on the ground – not least with regard to individual cases and China's stance towards UN special procedures (Council of the European Union 2003).

On the one hand, the European Commission welcomes the positive developments of the EU–China human rights dialogue which arise from 'detailed and frank exchanges of views' on individual cases of human rights violations (Commission 2003a: 12). On the other, it acknowledged that the human rights dialogue has produced poor results. The former Commissioner Chris Patten pointed out the difficulties of implementing effectively the EU HRD policy in relations with China and expressed the need to make the human rights dialogue more results oriented by focusing upon specific projects, such as cooperation projects on village governance, the provision of technical assistance for the ratification and implementation of the UN Human Rights Covenants, enhancing the Chinese legal system concerning detention and rights of the defence, small projects facility to support emerging Chinese civil society, the EU–China academic network, etc. (Patten 2002).

Among the EU institutions, the European Parliament stands out for being the most critical towards the lack of respect of human rights in China. In the aftermath of Tiananmen, the Parliament had contributed to slowing down the normalisation of EU–China relations. Yet, the Parliament keeps a watchful eye on the slow progress made by Chinese democratic reforms and human rights respect; it regularly expresses concern on human rights violations and restrictions to fundamental freedoms (European Parliament 2002c).

The weaknesses of EU promotion of human rights and democracy in China

The overall picture of HRD standards in China remains unclear and there is evidently a difference between the rhetoric of EU support for a stable, prosperous and open China that fully embraces democracy, free market principles and the rule of law, and the concrete use of political tools to raise human rights standards and implement democratic processes. The effectiveness of the EU grassroots-level strategy to build mutual trust and confidence and foster HRD in China, which is very much praised by constructivist analysis, seems to be challenged by facts. Several other elements need to be recalled as well.

Firstly, the EU and China clearly do not share the same view of foreign policy and international cooperation on security issues because they have different security cultures. EU security culture relies upon the concept of comprehensive and cooperative security, while China's strategic culture has historically exhibited a relatively consistent hard realpolitik which translates into a preference for offensive uses of force (Johnston 1996: 217). Significantly enough, the human dimension of security, which is one of the components of the European security culture based upon the concept of comprehensive and cooperative security, is not part of the Chinese security culture, which is instead primarily focused upon economic growth and traditional security (Attinà and Guichang 2001: 92).

Secondly, there is a double standard in Chinese international and domestic policy. China wants to appear receptive to foreign ideas, values and principles in order to gain easier access to the international community, but the slight Chinese opening to the international scene has not granted more freedoms at the domestic level; in fact, despite China's involvement in the human rights dialogue with the EU, a deterioration in China's human rights practice has been registered (Baker 2002: 62). The EU promotion of HRD as a way to achieve political stability clashes with the *rationality* of the Chinese policy of economic development without political reforms and pluralism. According to some analysts, much of the governance contradictions that China is facing in its transformation from a centrally planned economy to a market-driven economy are embedded in the nature of the Chinese regime. The one-party system cannot open to pro-democracy movements or organised interests. The Chinese Communist Party is probably not prepared for the emergence of autonomous social forces such as organised interest groups, which are inevitable actors of industrialised economies (Pei 2002: 98). On the contrary, the EU is committed to establish in its partner countries a pluralistic democratic system and allow for the dispersion of political power among political parties, NGOs, interest groups and associations, along with governmental institutions; the EU attaches high importance to pluralism and considers civil society as an important actor of reform. But China remains a one-party state with the Communist Party of China retaining its monopoly on political power and not tolerating direct challenges to its authority.

Thirdly, Chinese civilisation is coming to terms with globalisation, not only in the economic field but also at the cultural level. The Chinese establishment has adopted a 'selective adaptation' strategy, trying to 'import Western techniques and equipment while keeping out new cultural and political values' (Saich 2001: 273). In their official discourse Chinese leaders often claim the necessity of preserving essential Chinese values from foreign influence and stress Chinese distinctiveness from other cultures. It is true that the Western and Chinese society are different due to the important role given, respectively, to the individual or to the community. Western liberalism, which is based upon individualism, differs sharply from the Chinese collectivism which relies upon centralised nationalism and tradition (with the important role played by the 'clan society'). The difference between the Western individualistic society and the Chinese community-oriented society sheds light on a different conception of human rights.

The EU insistence upon 'persuasive' measures is also destined to have poor results because the two partners have a different approach to HRD. The EU and China differ sharply on their approach to human rights protection. The EU adopts a comprehensive approach to human rights, which includes political, economic and social issues. In the Chinese human rights' conception, rights related to the economic growth (relying upon domestic political stability) are the key object of concern. In the Chinese vision of human rights, economic collective rights are more important than individual political and civil rights, with the right to development and subsistence as state priorities to be granted to the citizens. The Chinese interest of engaging in the international system and 'paying the costs' of interdependence derives from the gains of entering into the world economic institutions, but this is not to be done at all costs, particularly not if this translates into domestic interference in sensitive areas such as extending political and economic rights. Economic development remains a top priority of Chinese domestic and foreign policy, and political external influences on domestic policies can be regarded as an interference and a limitation to sovereignty (Miaofa 2001: 48).

Questioning the universality of human rights is not a new phenomenon. Historically, the development of human rights international law after World War II was characterised by a clear-cut human rights ideological divergent interpretation. During the Cold War the UN human rights regime creation had to cope with two approaches: the communist economic rights *vs* liberal capitalism and individual freedoms. Now that capitalism has emerged from the end of the Cold War as 'the' economic development model and also China, with entry into the WTO, is opening to market economy, closure towards fundamental freedoms and civic political rights has remained the distinctive feature of the 'Chinese' way to development, a difference which reflects 'contrasting perceptions of the individual and of society-state relationships' (Bretherton 1996: 251). This attitude clearly emerges when Chinese delegations attempt to reject universal human rights in international fora (as happened for instance at the World Conference in 1993).

Moreover, the exportability of a EU polity model based upon HRD has to come to terms, for instance, with values such as national dignity, state sovereignty and territorial integrity, which are strongly felt in China (Jiaxuan 2000:

20). In contrast, once EU states have adapted to the post-national nature of the EU, they have lost their link to the sovereignty of the nation-state. The political discourse of Chinese leaders instils nationalism as a legitimising core value; they regularly recall the importance of mutual respect and equality as founding principles of EU–China relations, and human rights are regarded as a purely domestic issue.

Finally, it is not our intention to adopt cultural relativism as a conceptual tool for the analysis of human rights' low respect in China (and Russia), since in its extreme this might lead to denying the existence of universal human rights, but undeniably moral values that lie behind human rights are socially constructed and politically reinforced. Unfortunately, in some cases they are constructed more for the establishment's sake than for the citizens' interest. When the Chinese leaders refer to the 'Asian Way' to human rights, EU attempts at modernisation and imposing globally human rights tend to be depicted as the result of a contested Western hegemony. For this reason, resolutions adopted by the European Parliament denouncing the low respect of human rights and democratic principles in China always annoy the Chinese establishment. We are not interested in the moral implication or philosophy behind this approach, rather we seek to illustrate why it is so difficult to export the EU HRD standards to third countries. In the Chinese case, prioritisation of economic and social rights at the expense of civil and political rights is the justification for political repression. The political reforms China has adopted to launch the democratisation process which has been strongly encouraged by the international community seem too often a lip service to counteract international pressure. And the EU does not react to effectively defend human rights and democratic principles to profit from economic and trade benefits. If we compare funds allocated to financial and economic cooperation with funds destined to HRD, we come to the conclusion that economic and trade cooperation remains the driving factor of EU–China relations.

Conclusions

Russia and China are becoming powerful actors in the global system and two crucial partners of the EU. Although the EU had never completely neglected these two countries, since the 1990s there has been a fervent cooperative relationship as a result of the mutual interest of the parties. These concluding remarks will briefly recall the reasons that inspired this comparative analysis on the EU promotion of HRD in its relations with Russia and China and will explain the argument on the EU's weak role as an HRD promoter.

Russia and China have many elements in common. First of all, they share the same vision of the international system after the Cold War: a multipolar world in which they can act as a 'pole', thus they welcome the EU as a global power contrasting the current hegemonic structure of the international system. Moreover, they prefer an enlarged EU to an enlarged NATO, and the EU to the US as a security provider in Europe (Moeller 2002: 20). In the evaluation of the norms regulating the international system, Russia and China attach great importance to the respect of sovereignty and territorial integrity arguing that there should be no interference by other countries – EU included – in their domestic affairs. As far as the visions and practices of HRD are strictly concerned, Russia and China often adopt the 'cultural filter' (Manners 2002: 245) and share some views and behaviours. In both countries there is a reluctance to adopt outside practices, because they tend instead to see the EU promotion of HRD as an undue interference in their domestic affairs. In addition to that, Russia and China support each other respectively on the Chechen, Taiwanese, and Tibetan questions. Both Russia and China attach much importance to the economic areas of cooperation, which override the human dimension. All these factors explain the half-hearted commitment of these EU partners to implement EU values and principles.

For the EU countries it is difficult to elaborate a common position to go beyond the rhetoric of being in favour of human rights and consistently reacting against human rights violations. The EU does not react with a coherent defence of HRD because, when dealing with crucial political or economic partners, pragmatism prevails over the defence of values and principles. Although the EU conceived the 'human rights clause' as an instrument to spread EU common values to third countries, it has been seldom applied. Analysis of the cases of aid suspension for violation of human rights and democratic principles shows that the EU is often inconsistent and treats third countries differently, i.e. poor, marginal African states tend to be subjected to negative conditionality more easily than strategic countries, even if they have similar human rights records (K. Smith 2003: 205). The European Parliament shares this critical view and raises concerns for the EU double standard adopted in the promotion of HRD. In particular, the Parliament has repeatedly criticised the European leaders' 'soft' position on Russia's conduct in Chechnya and human rights violation in China.

As this analysis of relations with Russia and China has illustrated, the EU *principled* foreign policy has been clearly conceptualised and overtly asserted. The EU regards HRD as important, inspiring principles of EU foreign policy and in all documents regulating EU relations with Russia and China, human rights protection and democratic rules and principles are mentioned as EU concerns. In acting as an HRD promoter, the EU clearly prefers the engagement strategy to the containment one. This translates into an EU approach that insists more on persuasion through political discourse than imposition through the threat of sanctions. To promote HRD the EU relies on the involvement of practitioners and civil society representatives in cooperation programmes conceived as an instrument for a 'socialisation process' at the grassroots level. In practice, the EU is exerting 'gentle pressure' to act as a HRD promoter. But, the literature on democratisation (see, among others, Schmitter 1996) has clearly pointed out the key role of the local political leadership for political change to take place, since a synergy of politicians, administration and civil society is required to change the political system via 'velvet' revolutions.

There is a gap between political discourse and political change in the EU HRD external policy. Although the EU is supporting cooperation at the grassroots level as an engine for further political cooperation regarding HRD, favourable political conditions are required to develop higher standards in the HRD field. Moreover, the EU and its partners do not share the same definition of HRD; the question of the universality of human rights remains a crucial aspect of the spreading of EU values and principles via EU HRD policy, but in practice EU partners are more prone to instrumentally defend cultural relativism and strategic domestic interests. When EU partners express different interests and/or definition of values and principles, only the agreement on, and the implementation of, 'minor' specific projects is possible, such as the creation of human rights academic networks and NGOs cooperation, instead of directly addressing thorny issues such as political pluralism, fundamental freedoms and minority rights. In such a suspicious context the EU strategy of persuasion will have a hard time to be successful.

Notes

1 See K. Smith (2003: 2) for a wide definition of EU Foreign Policy.
2 In this chapter the two aspects of human rights protection and democracy promotion are taken together. First of all, because in the EU vocabulary they are assumed as part of one single policy. Secondly, and more importantly, because human rights and democracy are strictly related and feed each other. Notwithstanding, the operative tools to foster democracy are distinctive from the human rights agenda.
3 The Copenhagen School first elaborated on the broadened concept of security (Buzan 1991; Buzan and Waever 2003 and Buzan, *et al.* 1998). This study will make just an operational use of 'comprehensive security'.
4 In 2001, about 50 million Russians were still below the subsistence level.
5 China shares the same vision of a more balanced multipolar international system (see note 6).
6 In 1995 the Commission adopted the Communication 'A long-term policy for China–Europe relations'; in 1998 the Communication 'Building a Comprehensive Partnership with China'; in May 2001 the Communication 'EU Strategy towards China: Implementation of the 1998 Communication and Future Steps for a More Effective EU Policy'. Finally, in 2003 the Commission adopted the Policy Paper 'A maturing partnership. Shared interests and challenges in EU–China relations'.

9 The use of force as coercive intervention
The conflicting values of the European Union's external action

Sonia Lucarelli and Roberto Menotti

Introduction

The use of force can be seen as the ultimate expression of willpower: it reflects the determination by an individual or a group to impose someone's will on someone else, or at least to resist such imposition from the other side. Viewed in this light, the connection between values and coercion is all too evident. Despite this, values and identity are rarely analysed with respect to an actor's pattern to recur to force, particularly when the actor is the EU.[1] This is a significant gap since political values are invariably incorporated in the justification and rationale for resorting to force. George W. Bush launched the US campaign against Iraq first claiming a violation by Iraq of international rules regarding weapons of mass destruction (WMD), then emphasising the different rationale of toppling a bloodthirsty tyrant. In early 2005, he inaugurated his second term calling for a US role in the world aimed at exporting freedom.[2] International rules, democracy and liberty are the values Bush has most often referred to.

Such values are also European values, but the option of resorting to the use of force in furthering them is severely constrained in the EU case. The prevailing security discourse in the EU context tends to relegate the problem of coercion and forceful means in the area of extreme measures that only very few circumstances could conceivably justify. Part of the origin of this stance is to be found in the EU's initial *telos:* the construction of an area of peace and prosperity among its members. Indeed, having realised this founding aspiration is rightly seen as the EU's greatest achievement to date. Given such *telos* and the peculiar understanding of the EU's international role as that of a 'civilian power' (Duchêne 1972, 1973) or a 'normative power' (Manners 2000a, 2002), with the aim to shape the external environment helping to erase the deep causes of conflict (Keukeleire 2000, 2002; Telò 2001a; also Lucarelli in chapter 1), the dilemma of coercion is uniquely challenging for the EU. As a matter of fact, if on the one hand the use of force seems to openly contradict the goal of a structurally peaceful and regulated international system, on the other hand intervention in support of shared norms and values could be regarded as a necessary requirement for the EU's credibility. Thereby consolidating its internal political identity (which, as we have seen in the introduction to this volume is constantly affected by the EU's actual policies) as well as its international role.

The point is recognised also in the EU Treaties. Without marking any major break with existing Treaty provisions, the text of the Constitution for Europe stated:

> The Union's action on the international scene shall be guided by the principles which have inspired its own creation, development and enlargement, and which it seeks to advance in the wider world: democracy, the rule of law, the universality and indivisibility of human rights and fundamental freedoms, respect for human dignity, the principles of equality and solidarity, and respect for the principles of the United Nations Charter and international law.
>
> (Constitution for Europe, Article III-292, Part III, Chapter I)

As can be seen, the EU is guided by a markedly liberal approach to international affairs, reflecting the Union's own experience and historical background. And yet, even the cautious wording of the Constitution has been adapted to include tasks (beyond the original 'Petersberg Tasks') that broaden the possible range of military commitments:

> The tasks ... in the course of which the Union may use civilian and military means, shall include joint disarmament operations, humanitarian and rescue tasks, military advice and assistance tasks, conflict prevention and peace-keeping tasks, tasks of combat forces in crisis management, including peace-making and post-conflict stabilisation. All these tasks may contribute to the fight against terrorism, including by supporting third countries in combating terrorism in their territories.
>
> (Constitution for Europe, Article III-309; Part III, Charter II)

This chapter focuses on those situations where 'from time to time hard cases arise' (Frost 2001: 38). The hardest cases for the EU are instances in which its core values and principles recalled above (democracy, the rule of law, human rights, equality and solidarity, and international law) are at risk. More specifically, the type of intervention that has been central to the EU's identity formation and evolving conception of security over the past decade is the use of force to prevent or stop severe violations of human rights. We argue that this is the underlying concept behind the more neutral and technical notion of *crisis management* – the one most often adopted in EU policy statements. Indeed, the kind of crises around which the EU has designed its Common Foreign and Security Policy (CFSP) and more recently its European Security and Defence Policy (ESDP) are precisely those with a predominant humanitarian dimension. In addition, the way in which actual involvements in crisis situations have been officially explained is by referring specifically to humanitarian concerns. This type of intervention, contrary to the use of force for territorial defence (which is not contested[3]), requires the enforcement of specific values on the basis of an optional and highly discretionary determination, as in the small and brief 'wars of choice' that the international community has experienced in the 1990s.

The rest of the chapter will first retrace the evolution of the EU approach to the use of force as a result of external critical junctures that pushed the EU to begin to develop a practice of intervention and its first security strategy. It will then go on to show how this *securitisation* of human rights and other core values and principles has been only partial, based more on discourse than practice, and applied with double standards in the EU area and outside it. Finally, the chapter will point to the political and identity problems of such a halfway securitisation.

A steep learning curve: from former Yugoslavia through 11 September to Iraq

It would be simply impossible to make sense of the evolution in the EU's concept of security without tracing the practical learning process of the Europeans which has started in the Western Balkans a little more than a decade ago. The wars in the Balkans (Bosnia, Kosovo) and the American invasion of Iraq in 2003 represented critical junctures, that is situations which challenged the ideational structure of the EU and that forced both policy and institutional adaptations.

When confronted with the violent collapse of former Yugoslavia, the Union had at its disposal only embryonic instruments, since its CFSP was still a fledgling institution under construction. Some useful learning did occur on the ground, in a rush and through improvisation, but the tools at hand did not allow a prominent role: failing the early attempts at mediation, the EU thus retreated into a low profile supporting role.[4] After some hasty conflict management through diplomatic/declaratory policy in 1991, what followed was a sort of burden-sharing arrangement with the UN and the OSCE until Spring 1994, when NATO made a formal commitment. Then there was the post-conflict peacemaking/peacekeeping of the post-Dayton phase – essentially under US leadership, with the EU focusing on humanitarian aid and reconstruction assistance (Garde 1996; Lukic and Lynch 1996). The unique case of the EU Administration of Mostar (Monar 1997) was a great leap forward and a precious experience for the Union's maturity as an international stabiliser and security provider. But the mission ought to be put in perspective, given that the US and NATO presence in the region was very significant at the time.

The brief military action in Bosnia of 1995 (conducted by NATO under a UN umbrella) did not pose fundamental questions for the EU with regard to military coercion, given the institutional arrangements that solved both the practical problem of capabilities and decision-making, and the political-legal problem of international legitimacy. However, it is undeniable that the Bosnian experience was broadly perceived as a European failure: the European performance was far below initial expectations captured in Jacques Poos's famous expression 'this is the hour of Europe' (S. Anderson 1995: 340). Furthermore, Bosnia demonstrated to the Europeans that the US was no longer available 'on request' to manage European security crises and that France and Britain had to improve their cooperation on the ground. This lesson had important consequences for shorter- and longer-term institutional developments in EU security and defence policy. First, the Bosnian experience pushed the EU member states to improve on the deficiencies of the CFSP as defined in the Maastricht Treaty and create the High Representative and a Planning Cell (Amsterdam Treaty). Second, it slowly convinced French and British political elites that the Western European Union (WEU) was neither sufficient nor adequate for the changing needs of European defence, but also that a strong direct link between the EU and NATO was necessary. As Howorth observes (2004: 218–219), France and Britain had different goals (to strategically aim at an EU military capacity in the case of France; to tactically find a middle ground between the two sides of the Atlantic, in the case of Britain), but the result was a fundamental step forward. For a qualitative leap to take place, the combination of three elements proved essential: the election of Tony Blair in May 1997, a new call from Washington for the strengthening of a European pillar in NATO, and the risk of being caught once again unprepared in the Balkans, where a serious crisis in Kosovo was materialising (Howorth 2004: 221). France and Britain at their bilateral Summit in St Malo (December 1998) issued a declaration calling for the definition of a security and defence component within the CFSP pillar (ESDP) and the end of the historical function of the WEU. The declaration was 'a paradigm shift in European Security thinking' (Howorth 2004: 222) in that it attributed to the EU 'the capacity for autonomous action', but it was still destined to suffer from the 'constructive ambiguity' on which it rested: Britain's and France's different understandings of the document and its implications.

Only a few weeks after St Malo, the Kosovo crisis reached its culmination. Without getting into a detailed story of the EU's involvement, suffice to recall that the Union had to take hard decisions. In the first place, the decision to get politically involved on the basis of a relatively solid consensus which envisaged forceful action at a much earlier stage than in Bosnia. The EU never took on a primary direct role in 'diplomacy backed by force' – leaving that to NATO and the Contact Group. In the second place, it agreed to assume most of the burden of reconstruction and stabilisation, in the framework of the 'Stability Pact for South-East Europe', i.e. a comprehensive and 'holistic' approach to the region, to be progressively linked to the enlargement process. The most acute military phase of the crisis, consisting of NATO air operation Allied Force, was – from the EU's viewpoint – a sort of pact with the devil: NATO was put in charge of a bombing operation lacking a specific mandate of the UN Security Council, despite significant and sometimes public reservations among at least some European allies about the specific military course chosen by the Alliance as a whole, and primarily set by the United States.[5] What resulted was, to many Europeans, the right war fought in the wrong way. 'Humanitarian bombing' stretched the concept of humanitarian support to its outer limits. Yet, a majority of EU members did agree with, and actively contribute to, NATO's limited use of force, for lack of better alternatives and in order to keep the US engaged.

The Kosovo experience, however, functioned as a legitimisation of St Malo/ ESDP in that it dramatically showed the need for a European capacity to handle crises in its neighbourhood. It also encouraged further the definition of actual capacities beyond the agreed institutional engineering (Howorth 2004: 225). The Helsinki Council meeting of December 1999 established 'Headline Goals' and the creation of a European Rapid Reaction Force (60,000 personnel deployable within 60 days for Petersberg-like tasks), then added the Political Committee and a Military Committee to the CFSP decision-making when dealing with ESDP issues. All these institutional changes were eventually incorporated in the Nice Treaty.

At the same time, the Kosovo experience convinced even the most reluctant protagonists of the need to finalise the negotiations for the possible use of NATO's military assets in operations which would not involve the American ally (the so-called Combined Joint Task Forces, or *Berlin Plus*). The Presidency Conclusions of the Cologne European Council of 3–4 June 1999 stated that ' ... the Union must have the capacity for autonomous action, backed up by credible military forces, the means to decide to use them, and a readiness to do so, in order to respond to international crises without prejudice to actions by NATO' (European Council 1999; see also Missiroli 2000, 2003a; Howorth 2001). Approximately between late 1998 (St Malo) and September 2001, the peculiar relationship between the two organisations appeared at least to encourage gradual adaptation: NATO would be in charge of 'collective defence' and the EU could (on a case-by-case basis) tackle 'crisis management' when the Alliance as such was not involved, by relying on some US assets. The EU and NATO's involvement in early crisis management in Macedonia in 2001 represented a case of close coordination between the EU and NATO – particularly between Javier Solana as High Representative for CFSP and George Robertson as NATO Secretary General – on the basis of the understanding that NATO was needed as an irreplaceable political-military backup to the EU. In turn, NATO (and the US) recognised that the EU could play a unique role in offering all Macedonians a credible prospect of 'Europeanness'. In other words, a degree of self-restraint and division of labour prevailed in both organisations.

A formal agreement between the two organisations, however, required lengthy negotiations and was reached only in December 2002. On the basis of the agreement, the EU is now assured to have access to NATO's planning and other capabilities if necessary. A form of constructive ambiguity was adopted on the procedures to grant the EU access to NATO assets, as the US preferred a case-by-case decision, while the EU preferred an automatic access. The agreement was initially conceived as a sort of stepping-stone to more ambitious achievements. However, the agreement has undeniable shortcomings. In the first place, the arrangement has essentially spared the EU the task of developing its own distinctive discourse and doctrine on the use of military force across the entire spectrum, from 'low end' to 'high end'. This could not continue indefinitely, however, since the institutional arrangement (particularly the controversial issue of EU 'autonomy' from NATO in a possible military operation), and operational features (command responsibilities and the inadequate European capabilities) have a direct bearing on the question of the Union's 'international identity' (Manners and Whitman 1998, 2003). Indeed, key questions remain: on whose behalf is the EU going to act in the field of military intervention, given the *de facto* veto power held by the US on indispensable assets? On the basis of what criteria, given the lack of a full-fledged debate on a European security and defence policy complete with a threat assessment, scenarios of operations and operational doctrine? These issues were deliberately left unresolved both by the St Malo agreement and the EU–NATO agreement, but an attempt to provide a threat assessment and an EU security doctrine was soon to be made, as we will see below.

Despite its ambiguities, the EU–NATO agreement permitted the deployment of the first EU military operations, mostly in the Balkans. In March 2003, the EU launched operation *Concordia* (later *Proxima*) – in Macedonia, the first EU *Berlin Plus* operation. The operation, requested by Macedonia and endorsed by UNSC Res. 1371, took over NATO's operation Allied Harmony with the aim of contributing to a stable environment and ensuring the implementation of the 2001 Ohrid Framework Agreement between Macedonians, Slavs and Albanians. In December 2004, a second EU operation with NATO assets, operation *Althea,* was launched in Bosnia-Herzegovina, substituting NATO's *Stabilisation Force,* on the field since the 1996 Dayton Peace Agreement. Meanwhile, the EU launched several other operations with exclusively European forces: the EU Police Mission in Bosnia-Herzegovina (launched on 1 January 2003 for three years), the first CFSP Civilian crisis management operation, substituting the UN *International Police Task Force* in place since 1995. In July 2003, the EU launched Operation *Artemis* in the Democratic Republic of Congo (DRC) (July–September 2003), a peacekeeping operation in support of an ongoing UN effort, with France acting as 'framework nation'. The aim of the operation was to prevent a large-scale humanitarian and civil crisis in Ituri (a region north-east of the DRC), under UN Resolution 1484. Finally, in July 2004, the Union launched its first EU 'rule of law mission' (EUJUST): Operation *Themis* in Georgia – again, on a very limited scale. These operations, although rather diverse, have some common characteristics: they are all low intensity (i.e. the use of force is foreseen – when it is – only for self-defence, protection of local civilians and international operators), take place in the context of a peace-building or a conflict prevention effort, frequently involve non-EU states, and are embedded in the legal framework of a UN authorisation. They also suffer from a series of constraints: they are limited in scope, they depend on the leadership and commitment of major EU member states (when they prefer to use their assets outside the EU, there is no EU operation, such as in the Ivory Coast or in Sierra Leone); they are financed on an *ad hoc* basis. However limited, they represent a major breakthrough for ESDP. As Missiroli notes (2003b), these operations show an EU 'proactively engaging in security affairs, covering a variety of tasks that stretch from policing to military intervention [...], capable of reacting to ongoing or emerging humanitarian/security crises and to contribute to peace enforcement, reconstruction and stabilization'. Furthermore, *Artemis* and *Althea*, contrary to the other operations, are operationally complex and seriously test the EU's military capabilities and political will. However, the jury is still out on the final result of this evolution. The assumption of global responsibilities has so far remained limited to Congo and East Timor, which might indicate that the geographical and strategic scope of future EU operations will encompass the immediate proximity of the EU or post-colonial areas, the same areas that are currently the main recipients of EU aid and preferential trade arrangements (Missiroli 2003b). Furthermore, an absence of intervention in Sudan or the Great Lakes is also politically relevant and puts the EU credibility at risk.

While the first EU operations were unfolding on the operational level, in the political field a severe crisis affected intra-European relations in 2002–03. The Europeans had demonstrated cohesion in their solidarity to the US after 11 September, and offered to use NATO following the activation of article V; but President Bush decided to rely on a coalition of the willing for Afghanistan (US-led), then proclaimed the existence of an 'Axis of Evil' in his 2002 State of the Union address (Bush 2002) and declared a right to pre-emptive war in the United States' 2002 National Security Strategy (NSS). Understandably, as the issue of the use of military force came to the fore with such intensity, many Europeans began to feel uneasy. Even before the transatlantic crisis over Iraq, the debate across Europe on how to react to 11 September became inextricably linked to a rising concern with US unilateralism and excessive reliance on military tools.

These concerns were prominent all over Europe during the debate on a possible US attack on Iraq, in the course of 2002. However, when the US eventually decided to invade Iraq without a UN resolution, the European governments divided sharply, despite the fact that, in principle, they all supported the idea of a UN resolution as by far the best option. Various political actors tried to show that a difference existed between the use of force in Kosovo and Iraq, although both occurred without an explicit UN resolution (Prodi 2004).

Furthermore, the internal fragmentation of the EU and Europe on Iraq provoked a further push ahead in the security and defence sector (Menon 2004) – albeit in ways that did not necessarily prove fruitful. In April 2003, France, Germany, Belgium and Luxembourg agreed in principle to launch a close cooperation on defence issues, with plans to set up a headquarters near Brussels, which was clearly perceived (and presented) as an alternative to NATO and lacked British support. The result was that all the underlying tensions (including the inherent ambiguity of the original St Malo arrangement) were brought to light; in effect, the core countries – Britain, France and Germany – were forced to find a compromise on crucial areas of disagreement to avoid permanent damage. This effort led to the decision to create a planning cell within NATO's main headquarters (SHAPE); limit the 'enhanced cooperation' foreseen in the draft EU Constitution for Europe essentially to the development of new military capabilities; and adopt a mutual assistance clause among the EU member states while still leaving, at least on paper, a core defence role to NATO. At the same time, CFSP High Representative Javier Solana was given a mandate to write the first ever European Security Strategy (ESS) (European Council 2003), which he presented to the member states in June 2003, just as negotiation of the new Constitution entered its final stage. Solana's Strategy, though with minor changes, was adopted in December 2003: it is the most specific official EU document to date attempting to explain how a civilian power can play an active role in the construction and maintenance of world security.

What does the ESS say? To what extent does it provide a strategic concept for the EU? The document is the first of this type for the EU and in this respect it should be regarded as an unprecedented achievement, but it is also a 'light' document in that its effectiveness suffers from three structural EU weaknesses: (a) limited capabilities, (b) internal conceptual and political difficulties in combining the traditional EU role as a civilian power with new international challenges and responsibilities, and (c) the different interpretation that EU countries, particularly France and Britain, attach to the ESDP and NATO's role therein.

The document recognises that 'the EU is inevitably a global player [. . . that] should be ready to share the responsibility for global security and building a better world'. Globalisation, poverty, aids, security as a condition for development, competition for natural resources and energy dependence are the challenges the EU is facing. Key threats include terrorism (regarded as a phenomenon with deep and complex causes), the proliferation of weapons of mass destruction, regional conflicts, state failure and organised crime. In order to face such challenges and threats, the document states, the EU strategic objectives should be threefold: assessing threats, building a secure neighbourhood and developing an international order based on effective multilateralism. At a first glance, the document does not seem to differ dramatically from the US 2002 NSS, on the contrary a closer look reveals two quite different security concepts. Despite the fact that the two documents differ in length, language and depth, a comparison is possible, as emerges, for instance, from the analysis of Felix Berenskoetter (2004). In the first place, the world depicted in the ESS, despite being recognised as being complex and replete with security challenges, is not depicted as one of a 'new kind of war' as in the NSS. To the contrary, the ESS affirms that Europe has never been so secure. In the second place, although both documents refer to universal values and principles such as liberty and justice, the crusader's tones and universalistic attitude that we find in the NSS are absent in the ESS. In terms of geographical scope, contrary to the global reach of the NSS, the ESS defines a precise EU responsibility only as far as Europe (and the Middle East) is concerned: here the Union has a duty to promote liberal values and well-governed societies (beyond it there is a generic call for global responsibilities). In terms of threats, despite similarities, some relevant differences are telling. In the first place, terrorism is treated as a 'strategic threat' rather than the new global 'enem[y] of civilisation' (US Presidency 2002: 11). It follows that the division of the world into liberty-loving countries and rogue states supporting terrorism finds no equivalent in the ESS. In the second place, the ESS dedicates much more attention to the deep 'complex causes' of terrorism which are identified as 'the pressures of modernization, cultural, social and political crises, and the alienation of young people living in foreign societies', further recognising that 'this phenomenon is also part of our own society' (European Council 2003: 3). The implications are huge: if the enemies are primarily poverty, the collapse of the rule of law, social and political crises, the tools to be employed should be economic, social, diplomatic, more than military. Furthermore, even in cases when force is necessary, the ESS indicates that a UN authorisation must be obtained, while the NSS underlines the US right and duty to resort to pre-emptive action (US Presidency 2002: 6, 15) – a type of action with a significant military component which would be incompatible with the EU's preventive strategy of primarily constructive engagement. Indeed, the only time that the use of military force is envisaged is in connection to failed states to restore order after a conflict has occurred (European Council 2003: 6–7). The 'biggest departure' from the NSS (Berenskoetter 2004: 14), however, is the ESS's stress on multilateralism and the rule of law: 'our security and prosperity depend on an effective multilateral system. The development of a stronger international society, well-functioning international institutions and a rule-based international order should be our objective' (European Council 2003: 9–10). Multilateralism takes on various forms in the text: support for the UN system, adherence to multilateral treaty regimes, widening membership in international organisations, efforts to approach countries that have abandoned international law with incentives to rejoin the international community (constructive engagement first). On the contrary, the NSS does not contain reference to multilateralism or to the specific international role of the UN (beyond considering it an arena),[6] is rather critical of the International Criminal Court (US Presidency 2002: 31) and affirms a US right to unilateral and pre-emptive action (US Presidency 2002: 6). From a prescriptive point of view, the EU document recognises that Europe needs to be more active, more capable (in terms of resources and common threat assessment), more coherent (across EU instruments, EU pillars, member states, regional policies) and work with partners (not only the US, but also Russia, neighbours and others).

On one level, the document can thus be seen as a natural development for an international actor – the EU – which is increasingly aware of its responsibilities, has a holistic view of threats and their causes, has a preference for longer-term instruments in meeting such threats, and strongly favours partnerships and multilateralism. On a more specific level, the ESS has a dynamic dimension: it is the first attempt at threat assessment, specifying that multilateralism also requires effectiveness (as coordination *per se* is not sufficient), and indicating a readiness to use all possible options at the Union's disposal. Such reasoning produces an openly proactive approach but differs from the US approach due to a much-reduced emphasis on military tools. The scenario of forceful action is not absent, but strictly constrained:

[We need to be] More active in pursuing our strategic objectives. This applies to the full spectrum of instruments for crisis management and conflict prevention at our disposal, including political, diplomatic, *military* and civilian, trade and development activities. Active policies are needed to counter the new dynamic threats. We need to develop a strategic culture that fosters early, rapid, and when necessary, *robust intervention.*

(European Council 2003: 11)

But again, the precondition for the use of force is recognised to be a UN authorisation, something which is not stated in the NSS.

The document, though an important first step toward developing an EU security concept, has not solved once and for all the problem of the EU's approach to the use of force, which is recognised to be one of the tools of foreign policy. In the past (Kosovo) a humanitarian focus had allowed a degree of cohesion, despite the lack of legal legitimacy. In 2003, the doubtful humanitarian character of the Iraqi war and the breach of multilateralism by the US Administration, provoked strong opposition by the EU institutions and several EU member states, but also saw other members side with Washington, thereby creating an internal crisis nearly as serious as the transatlantic one. It is now legitimate to ask: where is this experience leading the EU? Where do we go from here?

The EU's *securitisation* dynamic and recurring dilemmas

It seems that certain key features must be present for the Union to consider the option of threatening or actually using military force. The dynamical nature of values turning into forceful action can be understood as a process of *securitisation*, as laid out by Buzan, Waever and de Wilde (1998) and defined as 'the move that takes politics beyond the established rules of the game and frames the issue as a special kind of politics or as above politics' (Buzan *et al.* 1998: 23). In this understanding, security is 'a particular type of intersubjective politics' (Buzan *et al.* 1998: 19).

The securitisation mechanism is particularly useful to interpret the EU's policy making process because the Union lacks a shared and historically grounded tradition as a 'hard security' actor: therefore, we need an interpretive tool which allows for a complex communicative and negotiating dynamic to produce a working (if temporary) definition. In the securitisation process, different situations create unique dynamics, in terms of short-term domestic politics, geographical setting and political stakes, economic interests, cultural conditions, etc. As will be seen in the last section, the (evolving) notion of a 'European space' is a central determinant of European behaviour in how values are applied and how they inform policies. The EU as such has so far contemplated direct intervention only in areas that present a spin-off potential affecting its own borders or where a compelling case for humanitarian rescue can be applied – hence the recurring references to sub-Saharan Africa in speeches by Javier Solana, for instance.

Protecting – i.e. *securitising* – the 'European space' and enforcing – i.e. *securitising* – human rights and the rule of law are thus emerging as the two pillars of the EU's external action beyond the economic field. Both, however, are problematic: the former requires a shared threat assessment regarding the likely spillover from sources of local instability; the latter can turn into practice only if the Europeans embrace costly global responsibilities, which may overload the fragile CFSP/ESDP. For instance, even the deployment of a limited number of military forces in a non-combat mode, as in Macedonia, requires an escalation capability. Furthermore, even the very specific task of protecting civilian populations can rarely be accomplished without defeating (or at least deterring) an enemy on the ground (whoever opposes or hinders these goals), i.e. staging a classical military operation, however limited in scope. This, in turn, tends to produce a need for external control of a geographical area and key local authorities also for some time *after* a successful military engagement.

In some – probably rare – cases (witness Bosnia and Kosovo), 'normative power Europe' may actually get a chance to largely dictate and enforce its own norms (albeit in cooperation with other local and international actors), i.e. to rule and administer a given entity. Here, the stakes are at the highest level, putting to the test the seriousness and effectiveness of the EU, as well as its moral coherence. Thus, political and moral responsibility entails the need for coercion (enforcement), while coercion often entails the assumption of new responsibilities. Additional tasks will require additional capabilities, in an upward dynamic of international activism.

When the protection of the European space and the enforcement of fundamental human rights have converged, as in the Balkans, the case for some form of intervention has become overwhelming. But when the two pillars remain separated the whole construct tends to become paralysed. Jolyon Howorth has rightly suggested that ESDP represents the construction of 'a radically new discourse on European security', and notes that key EU countries have eventually shifted 'towards a common acceptance of *integrated European interventionism*, based not solely on the classical stakes of national interest, but also on far more idealistic motivations such as humanitarianism and ethics, thereby introducing a new normative paradigm into international relations' (Howorth 2004: 213). Howorth's argument is persuasive as far as it goes – in terms of the prevailing narrative. But in terms of behaviour, the EU's interventionist impulse should be better specified to understand where differences with the US lie. First, force is regarded as a 'last resort' tool and intervention has more frequently taken the form of economic and political reconstruction, peacekeeping through presence on the ground, as well as the enlargement process itself. Second, the area of intervention is limited to the Union's neighbourhood (as evidenced by both actual performance and the ESS) – though with the significant exception of former European colonies. Third, intervention should (most likely) take place in a legal framework. These elements taken together convey the image of an international actor unwilling or unable to enforce its values efficiently and worldwide. The EU's inability to intervene in Darfur to stop what certainly amounted to deliberate mass killings (despite the UN's nuanced official position on the 'genocide' issue), reduces the EU's credibility, as is true of its intention to lift its arms embargo against China (initially adopted to condemn human rights violations linked to the Tiananmen repression).

Clearly, the EU's limited interventionism is not just due to its interpretation of its values and worldviews, but also depends on the peculiar institutional structure of the Union, where foreign policy decisions always require tough intra-EU bargaining, testing the level of solidarity in case of a deterioration or escalation of the conflict, and mutual trust to enable one or more individual countries to lead at the operational level (as in the case of France in the EU operation *Artemis* in the Congo). It also implies internal agreement on the acceptance of imperfect compromises regarding the crisis at hand, such as the *de facto* partition of Bosnia or the postponement of the settling of the status of Kosovo. Compromises also take the form of political-military choices on which side in a conflict should receive more support in order to facilitate a resolution of the crisis or at least an interruption of violence: it goes without saying that in these circumstances, minorities can hopefully be protected but never entirely satisfied in their aspirations.

These difficulties illustrate one of the unresolved problems of international liberalism as a political theory (Hoffmann 1998: 77–80), which the EU has fully incorporated. As Stanley Hoffmann argues in general terms, the debate among liberals on outside intervention is more open than ever, with a specific dilemma over the use of force:

> Traditionally, liberalism has tried to limit legitimate force to self-defense and collective defense against aggression. But the scope of state chaos, as well as the murderousness of some contemporary tyrannies, has led many liberals to endorse in principle the idea to an outside resort to force whenever domestic chaos threatens the peace and security of other states (for instance through the mass flight of refugees) or whenever domestic chaos or tyrannical government results in massive violations of human rights, such as ethnic cleansing and genocide.
>
> (Hoffmann 1998: 80)

There are, therefore, questions of consistency and double standards, proportionality in the use of coercive means, and overall correspondence between means and ends, which cannot be ignored or easily circumvented. The rejection of military force (as a violation of a constitutive value of the EU – peace) on one hand, and the use of limited military force (as a means to secure other constitutive values) are the Scylla and Charybdis of Europe's debate on intervention. The weaknesses of the EU's capabilities and the intergovernmental decision-making are the troubled waters that make the trip to this particular Ithaca all the more complicated.

The securitisation process as formulated by Buzan and colleagues captures the incremental adoption of these conflicting principles as guidelines for action by the EU. The mechanism casts in sharp relief the communicative (discourse) basis of security policy, focusing on the level of priority attributed to a certain chain of events. Clearly, there must be a crucial turning point so that coercion is taken into consideration; some important threshold must be crossed for this to occur, particularly since the EU is certainly no 'trigger-happy' international actor, and in fact has no tradition as a military player (thus very limited credibility vis-à-vis outside actors, as well).

The EU had identified no such 'threshold' until the early 1990s. It did so, mostly by default rather than by design, under the pressure of events in former Yugoslavia. The end result was quite apparent well before it became enshrined in the ESS: a democratic and prosperous EU resting on its founding values cannot exist in a larger regional context in which democratic politics is absent and human rights are systematically violated. One could argue that the absence of democracy, *per se*, poses a risk, while a steep escalation in the extent of human rights violations (certainly of the kind and scale observed in former Yugoslavia after 1991) constitutes a threat (on the contrary the US NSS treats both as threats).

This transition from generic risk to actual threat is where the securitisation process comes in, and the protection of basic human rights can become the object of security policies. In other words, an issue that may require the threat or actual use of coercion, including military means. A liberal political philosopher, Michael Walzer, has presented this dilemma in the most precise form:

> Grossly uncivilized behaviour ... unchallenged, tends to spread, to be imitated or reiterated. Pay the moral price for silence and callousness, and you will soon have to pay the political price of turmoil and lawlessness nearer home ... Now obligation is seconded by interest.
>
> (Walzer 1995: 60)

In the case of the EU, we ought to further specify this general observation: obligation is always seconded by interest in the 'European space', and possibly in areas adjacent to it – which adds a complex dynamism to the concept of 'Europe'. Identity is being shaped by stating what we do not tolerate, thus setting boundaries to acceptable behaviour – not just to physical territory. Put in a different perspective, the Union's boundaries may become wider than the sum total of the member states' national boundaries as regards the application of the EU's core norms. In this perspective, 'Europe' is an inherently outward-bound project.

As Gwin Prins has forcefully argued (2002: 60), it is primarily through the experience of former Yugoslavia that we have moved from the notion of a symbolic and consensual use of limited force (mostly under the moral authority of the UN), called peacekeeping, to a 'sharper reorientation toward enforceable human rights'. Clearly, the actual use of military force puts significant pressure on the basic norm of peaceful resolution of international disputes that lies at the heart of the EU's collective identity. Beside the conceptual and ethical difficulties of reconciling protection of rights and coercion (i.e. violation of those rights, if only temporary or by *collateral damage*), there is also a technical problem: the requirements of military success (however limited) tend to clash with the requirements of a highly 'surgical' and restrained form of engagement.

The central point here is that accepting the logic of a constrained use of coercion in support of values and political objectives presupposes a continuum of political instruments that are both civilian and military, both cooperative and coercive. Most specialised observers agree that the Union currently possesses inadequate military capabilities when compared with its stated international ambitions. The objective limitations can be viewed either as a coherent civilian power choice, or – rather – as the resource-wise constraints imposed by the Cold War legacy of dependence upon the US and the focus on domestic expenditures. In any case, the conclusion we can draw from this observation must be cautious: the lack of public support for higher defence spending in most EU countries may well be a sign that there simply is no appetite for a higher profile security role when this clashes with other priorities. This open question of priorities brings to the fore, once again, the issue of the 'European space'.

European space and beyond

The EU is struggling to reconcile its 'civilian power' roots with the recognition that force has a role to play in the creation and maintenance of peace (defined as peaceful order based on human rights). A distinction – somewhat arbitrary, yet useful – can be drawn to describe where we stand today: respectively inside and outside the expanding 'European space'. Inside, a sort of zero tolerance policy has been asserted – though only by trial and error – and values are systematically enforced by all available means. Outside, compromises are the rule and values are subordinated to the art of the possible – politics as the pragmatic matching of means and ends depending on circumstances.

The paradox has been partly captured by the famous article by Robert Kagan 'Power and Weakness' (Kagan 2003), which argues that the US acts according to the maxims of a Hobbesian world, while the EU acts on the (mistaken) assumptions of a Kantian world. Kagan gets half the picture, because the EU is also committed to transforming the European space (which today clearly includes the whole of South Eastern Europe) into a Kantian province, even by force. There is certainly no enthusiasm for a prominent role of military power, but 'crisis management' is all about stabilising Europe's immediate periphery and the Europeans have become pretty serious about this business. Where Kagan may be right is in characterising the EU's relations with the 'outside' world: there, the EU is inclined to stick to its civilian power (Kantian) approach. More precisely, it is not (yet) willing to take the lead in forms of coercive intervention beyond extremely limited engagements and preferably in areas of historical interest for some European states (e.g. Congo).

The question of different – and increasingly diverging – attitudes toward the use of force in Europe and the US is largely treated in the literature. For a taste of the US approach under President Bush, a passage from the 2003 State of the Union address is telling:

America is a strong nation and honorable in the use of our strength. We exercise power without conquest, and we sacrifice for the liberty of strangers. Americans are a free people, who know that freedom is the right of every person and the future of every nation. The liberty we prize is not America's gift to the world; it is God's gift to humanity.

If we were to focus on the key issues bearing on the possible use of force, we can pinpoint a few which the EU probably does not feel comfortable with: the emphasis on strength (even if guided by honour), on power *per se* (even if not used for conquest), and the focus on freedom and liberty detached from any reference to justice. In addition, instead of religious faith we would usually find a reference to 'European values' in the EU context.

We found another interesting hint in the comparison between the NSS and the ESS, where to the lack of reference to multilateralism in the former, we juxtaposed a reiterated reference to this concept in the latter. In the ESS and in many other EU documents, multilateralism is not only meant as the existence of international institutions – such as the Bretton Woods institutions, the United Nations, or NATO – but also meant as a *practice*, a way of managing international order. In a seminal study on this issue, John Ruggie defines multilateralism as 'an institutional form that coordinates relations among three or more states on the basis of generalized principles of conduct' (Ruggie 1993: 11). Multilateralism thus defined has become a constitutive feature of the EU: through the integration process political identity, interests and institutional mechanisms have been reshaped giving origin to an unprecedented process of polity-building. Such a process regards not only institution-building, but also significant elements of cross-influence between EU/EC level and the member states as well as among the latter. Furthermore, current research on EU foreign policy shows that even in this area, usually the realm of state sovereignty, processes of Europeanisation are underway (M. Smith 2004: 99–100). Multilateralism has become a praxis of behaviour which represents normality; defections from normality occur, but are denounced as infringements of acceptable behaviour. This also explains the depth of the current uncertain status of transatlantic relations and its intra-European repercussions.

Here the challenge before the EU is huge: how to combine multilateralism (a constitutive value for the EU) with a will to adopt a value-led foreign policy even when it is not acceptable to other international actors who might block the EU's decision exerting their veto power in multilateral fora? To what extent is the EU willing to accept major constraints to its foreign policy action due to an external veto, particularly cast by the US (whose veto would also preclude access to NATO assets)? If the EU were to take the lead in calling for a coercive intervention somewhere, it would have to deal with the US. This problem has never materialised in the face of large-scale conflicts, so it is difficult to discuss it on the basis of practice. What can be said, however, is that so far the EU faces a dilemma between two core values that at times might conflict: multilateralism and the active protection of human rights. A second dilemma is the type of 'humanitarian intervention' the EU is ready (if not to perform on its own initiative) to at least consider acceptable.

The 2002–03 Iraqi crisis has exposed the strong European reluctance to follow the US along the road of 'democracy by force', 'regime change' or the kind of coercive Wilsonianism that the Bush administration seems to pursue. The EU appears to have major reservations on the specifically American brand of 'neo-imperialism', to borrow Robert Cooper's provocative term; but it has yet to reach agreement on what other form of external projection it wants and can afford. Explaining to a wider public how similar values can be safeguarded through different foreign policies is a task the EU has just begun to face, but not yet accomplished. A key question is: how to produce order out of disorder on the basis of the EU's 'postmodern' conception of international politics? And what role can be played by coercion and military force in this framework?

Some answers can be provided by a reference to standing international law and the multilateral imperative, but these will only be partial answers: as Solana has argued, 'law and power are two sides of the same coin. Power is needed to establish law and law is the legitimate face of power' (Solana 2003). In this framework, it is obvious that the ultimate decision to resort to force (coercive power) to 'establish law' is an eminently political choice, in which legal considerations provide only limited guidance.

If the EU's willingness to transform international politics is taken rigorously as a guide to action, the EU's Kantian ambition is going to produce growing entanglements and commitments. Once the EU gets in contact with destabilising areas which might require the application of forms of hard power, it is precisely the structural – i.e. transformational – nature of the EU's external projection that may encourage the Union to engage directly in conflict-prone situations. However, the EU has not made a definitive choice on whether it will skirt international responsibilities that might require the exercise of military coercion.

In the meantime, the Union is already caught between the global horizon of its values and the mostly regional focus of its well-tested structural policies. In this connection, the notion of a 'European space' (i.e. the EU proper and its immediate neighbourhood) seems an attractive solution to formulate a realistic framework for external action, with a more selective role in global security affairs mostly to be mediated by larger international institutions. However, we should not take it for granted that an expanding Europe will enjoy the luxury of picking and choosing where and when to get involved in a steady and orderly progression. Especially after 11 September 2001, it is worth recalling Leon Trotsky's ominous warning that 'you may not be interested in war, but war is interested in you'.

Conclusion

This chapter made three main arguments with respect to the VIPs affecting the EU's external action. First, that the EU's concept of security excludes, for the time being, certain forms of coercive actions: punishment, as well as 'pre-emptive' actions designed to signal resolve in a preventive mode, are currently outside the scope of EU security policy. This fundamental choice is decisively affecting the whole approach to security and the use of force, but it is accompanied and indirectly reinforced by the lack of sufficient capabilities to engage in large-scale war fighting without US support. As we have seen, this circumstance greatly complicates the interpretation of European values with respect to security policy.

The second argument is that a distinctive political dynamic – not a static set of criteria – explains how values are turned into a specific approach to the use of force. This dynamic has manifested itself for the first time in the course of the 1990s and early 2000s and thus is a recent development, not fully crystallised into an established practice. However, because there is a degree of path-dependency in security practices, the formative years have left their mark.

The third argument is that this very political dynamic is now pushing the EU toward gradually accepting a wider notion of intervention, designed to provide order and stability in still vaguely demarcated regional, macroregional and global contexts. A whole new phase in the evolution of the EU as international actor is opening up, because the type of security role that the Union may want (or have) to play is rather open-ended. In the fluid global environment of the early 21st century, the pressure for major change in the security field is growing, and the intra-European debate is already venturing into uncharted waters. The current transatlantic crisis and the EU military deficiencies are complicating factors. Furthermore, grave dilemmas are unresolved regarding the relationship between EU values which at points might conflict with each other (e.g. multi-lateralism and forceful protection of human rights). Finally, the EU needs to clarify how its peculiar transformative understanding of foreign policy can deal with severe violations of its core values. Humanitarian imperialism might be as dangerous as other types of imperialism. The EU now needs to clarify how it can be a different type of actor, even when 'hard cases arise'.

Notes

1 The literature on EU identity rarely refers to the use of force. Two excellent collections on EU identity (Cederman 2001) and ethics in EU foreign policy (McSweeney 1998) do not touch on the issue of the use of force.

2 The word 'freedom' was repeated 26 times, while 'liberty' 15, in his inaugural speech (Bush 2005).

3 What is contested, of course, is 'pre-emptive' action in view of a possible, but not immediate or ongoing, attack.

4 For the following reconstruction of events, see Lucarelli 2000; Menotti and Balfour 2001; Owen 1995; Zucconi 1996; Woodward 1995. For some of the lessons learned by the EU, also see Gnesotto 1994; Tindemans, *et al* 1996.

5 The largest part of the literature on the management of the Kosovo crisis focuses on the impact that such management had on NATO (Caplan 1998; Carpenter 2000; Daalder and O'Hanlon 2000). More broadly on NATO's development since the end of the Cold War: Yost 1998.

6 The word 'multilateralism' is never used, and all references to multilateral cooperation are qualified or put in a strongly functional context – i.e. multilateral efforts are evaluated on the basis of results.

10 Values in European Union development cooperation policy

Federico Bonaglia, Andrea Goldstein and Fabio Petito

Introduction

[W]hy does Europe do this [development co-operation] at Community level? The individual 15 member states do their part in development co-operation, so why do we also do it together? The answer to this is that it is simply a projection of the values on which European co-operation has been founded. These are the same values we want to project into the world, and also our own self-perception makes it natural for us to do these things. There is a strong moral aspect in this, but there is also ideology and some enlightened self-interest; promoting stability, co-operation and prosperity in the world is definitely also part of making it a better world for us to live and work in.

(Nielson, former EC Commissioner for Development and Humanitarian Aid, 2001)

This paper aims at identifying values, images of the world and principles (VIPs) which influence (or at least emerge from) the Development Cooperation Policy (DCP) of the European Union (EU).[1] In investigating the role of VIPs in EU international action, DCP is a key case study for two main reasons. First, the aims of DCP, namely fighting underdevelopment, improving international distribution of wealth and enhancing global distributive justice, have become core issues in the debate on how to build a more principled world order (Rawls 1999; Beitz 1999; Falk 1995). Second, DCP is a policy axis in which the importance of Europe cannot be understated. At US$ 22,497m, the 2000 combined development aid budget of the 15 member states and the European Community (EC) is twice larger than Japan's and 2.7 times the United States' and accounts for well over half of world aid. In particular, the contribution of the EC as such has grown in real terms from US$ 1,761 million (10.8 per cent of total) in 1980 to US$ 4,763 million (21.2 per cent of total) in 2000, making it the largest multilateral donor. The EU is also the largest provider of international humanitarian aid. But is the EU successful in conveying a certain image of Europe in the world through its DCP? And, even more critically, if the EU aspires to become a global 'civilian power' (Duchêne 1972, Whitman 1998) should not this be first of all visible in its DCP?

The chapter is organised as follows. The first section briefly traces the historical evolution of the EU's DCP from the 1957 Treaty of Rome until the 1993 Maastricht Treaty that officially included DCP among the main functions of the EU. In the second section we identify the VIPs informing the EU's DCP by analysing the official goals and the institutions of EU aid policy and then looking at how money is allocated functionally and geographically. In the third section we test empirically if deeds meet words by estimating the determinants of EU aid policy in the case of sub-Saharan Africa, so as to gauge the relative importance of the VIPs identified previously. Finally, we conclude with some general comments and briefly explore the implications of our findings for the EU identity building process.

Europe's development cooperation policy before and after Maastricht

From association to partnership

In 1957, at the creation of the European Economic Community (EEC), the legal bases of aid policy were enshrined in the so-called 'association system' established under part IV (Art. 131–136) of the Treaty of Rome. Together with the Food Aid Convention (1967), these articles (and the following Conventions) constituted the only legal basis for EC aid until the Maastricht Treaty. The Treaty *unilaterally* established a *reciprocal* free trade agreement between the EC and the associated countries and ensured the right of establishment for citizens and enterprises from both sides (Grilli 1993). The aim was to use aid to ensure the six EC members – four of which (France, Belgium, Italy, and the Netherlands) still had responsibilities for colonies or UN mandates – a continuation of their privileged trade relations.

The EC associationism suited well the ideologies of the political forces that dominated Europe at the time. Depending on the emphasis, the system could be seen as incorporating elements of humanism, solidarity and moral responsibility (socialist and social Christian traditions), as well security, economic interest and cultural nationalism (conservative tradition). Besides the 'trade pillar', the system established the collective responsibility of the EC to provide financial assistance to the colonial dependencies of its member states through the European Development Fund (EDF). Funding of the EDF was granted by specific contributions of the member states and not from the Community's budget but the Community did administer it. However, the *Europeanisation* of EC aid was only *partial*, as the EDF was to coexist with the aid bilaterally distributed by the member countries, and be additional and complementary to it. This *additionality* of EC direct aid was an aspect that the Commission never ceased to emphasise.

In 1963, 18 newly independent Francophone countries that were no longer bound by the association system, but wished to keep preferential access to the EC market and receive economic aid, concluded the Yaoundé Convention. With this the association system went from being *involuntary* and *unilaterally granted*, to being *voluntary* and *negotiated* (Grilli 1993). Given the new nature of the association – a freely negotiated agreement among independent states – its administration could no longer be left to Community institutions alone and had to be *multilateralised* throughout a formal institutional structure. In 1967 Food Aid was established within the EC as the first development cooperation instrument outside the framework of existing cooperation agreements and directly financed from the EC budget.

Following the entry of the United Kingdom into the EC, the 1974 Lomé Convention extended Yaoundé to 46 developing countries from Africa, the Caribbean, and the Pacific (ACP).[2] Although trade cooperation and financial assistance remained the most important pillars of EC external cooperation, Lomé also contained some new features: *stability, contractuality,* and *non-reciprocity.* Stability meant that preferences are granted for long periods, while contractuality guaranteed that preferences were jointly agreed and could not be modified unilaterally by the EC. Finally, non-reciprocity meant the ACP countries were not obliged to extend reciprocal preferences to EC exports, thus the Convention ensured free access to the EC market for all products originating from ACP countries with the exception of agricultural products covered by the Common Agricultural Policy, which were nonetheless granted preferential treatment.

Lomé, by recognising some of the goals of the New International Economic Order – namely stabilisation of receipts from commodity exports and non-reciprocal trade concessions – and basing cooperation on equality between two sets of countries at a very different stage of development, has been considered the most advanced system of North–South cooperation and a sincere European response to the core demands of developing countries (Grilli 1993: 27).

Privileged cooperation agreements were signed with non-ACP countries in the following years, starting with the neighbouring countries of the southern Mediterranean. Bilateral arrangements were made with countries in Asia and Latin America. Recently the countries of Eastern Europe gained their own regional programmes. The historical legacy of this evolutionary process of incorporation of development objectives into the EC/EU organisational system has been *regional differentiation* of policies, budgets, administrative procedures and aid instruments (OECD 2002a).

The EU's DCP since Maastricht

Four elements are important for understanding the evolution of the EU's DCP in the 1990s. First, the fall of the Berlin Wall and the perspectives of enlargement have blurred the boundaries between DCP and foreign policy and raised EU ambitions to become a more influential global player. Second, globalisation has increased the strategic stakes of the insertion of developing countries in the geography of capital, production and trade flows. Third, a series of UN conferences have identified poverty reduction as the overarching objective of development cooperation and shaped a new consensus on development thinking.[3] And fourth, criticism has mounted over the inefficiency, lack of vision and clear priorities, complexity and fragmented structure of EU aid – as highlighted most notably in 1999 when the Santer Commission resigned *en masse* following allegations of incompetence and corruption relating to the EU's development and humanitarian aid programs.[4]

In fairness, aid has come under considerable criticism from various and different sources: the World Bank (1999) in particular argues that aid can only be effective in raising *growth* and *reducing poverty* in a good policy environment and that aid cannot buy such an environment. In the EU case, there is a perception that its stance vis-à-vis aid recipients is ineffective because the EU has proved unable to clarify its policy vision, set clear priorities, and build a development cooperation identifiable as its own (e.g., OECD 1998 and Santiso 2002). According to aid practitioners, policies are guided by legal and financial instruments instead of clearly defined objectives, cooperation priorities and adapted country-level, regional or sectoral strategies (Lehtinen 2001). Also, many political priority areas (e.g. the fight against poverty, support for civil society, cooperation with conflict-affected countries, and support for decentralisation) lack coherent strategies. Most of these criticisms have been identified by the Commission itself in its *Green Paper* (Commission 1996a), which formed the basis for the reform of the EU's DCP.

Title XVII of the Maastricht Treaty placed international cooperation among the aims of the EU Common Foreign Policy and Security Policy (CFSP). Article 130.u states that external cooperation should foster the following goals in developing countries, especially the poorest: their sustainable economic and social development; their smooth and gradual integration into the world economy; the fight against poverty; the observance of human rights and fundamental freedoms; and the development and consolidation of democracy and the rule of law. Coordination, complementarity, coherence, and consistency are the four principles guiding the EU DCP.

Following the adoption of the OECD Development Assistance Committee (DAC) strategy paper in 1996 (OECD 1996b), the majority of the EU donors show a higher level of formal commitment to poverty reduction objectives. Most of them have formulated development cooperation strategies centred on poverty reduction and made efforts to implement them (Cox and Healey 2000, chap. 2). Poverty reduction and its eradication in all developing countries were hence made the overarching objective of the EU's development policy in the Amsterdam Treaty (art. 177). Although poverty reduction is the stated objective, the 1998 DAC peer review of the EU's DCP found that operational programming was lacking and exhorted the Commission to exploit the considerable potential to turn the goal into a more operational concept. Partly in response to these criticisms, in May 1999 the Council of EU Development Ministers invited the Commission to draw up a general policy statement on the shape a review of the EU's aid policies could take. In March 2000, the Commission adopted a White Paper on 'Reforming the Commission' (Commission 2000a), which aims to profoundly change the culture, organisation and management of the institution.

Within this broad agenda, the highest priority is given to reforming the EC's external assistance, both in terms of strategy and management.

The recommendations of the White Paper are included in the communication on the European Community's Development Policy (Commission 2000d), which set out the new framework for the EU's DCP. According to this document, besides humanitarian aid, the EU will concentrate on six areas which have been identified on the basis of the added value of the Union action and of their contribution to poverty reduction (Commission 2000d: 24–27): the link between trade and development; regional integration and co-operation; support for macro-economic policies and the promotion of equitable access to social services; transport; food security and rural development; and institutional capacity-building. Cross-cutting principles such as good governance, human rights and the rule of law, effect on poverty reduction, institutional and capacity building, gender equality, environment, must guide EU action in all these areas.

DCP is now located in the second pillar of the EU: member states have not transferred their competencies in matters of external assistance to the Commission and other EU institutions, but have committed themselves to cooperate using an intergovernmental method. Building on the principles stated in the White Paper, the Commission set in motion a reform aiming to reshape the overall EU external relations services. The new organisational structure is organised along two functional axes (see OECD 2002a). On the vertical axis, policy and key strategic decisions are kept in Brussels at the Directorate Generals and various Committees, while implementation responsibility is increasingly being delegated to the field. On the horizontal axis, two agencies, EuropeAid and the EC Humanitarian Aid Office (ECHO), manage long- and short-term implementation. The former was established in January 2001 as a department responsible for implementing the external aid instruments that are funded by the EC budget and the EDF. ECHO was created in 1992 to handle emergency aid, food aid, and aid for refugees and displaced persons.

The reform effort includes different pillars. First, a more coherent approach to relief, rehabilitation and development, so as to reduce the 'grey zone' that exists between humanitarian and development aid. Second, stronger dialogue with non-governmental organisations (NGOs), in policy formulation as well as through financial support. Third, an emphasis on decentralised cooperation, using technical, material and financial resources to boost the direct involvement of non-state actors (civil society, the private sector, local government) in the development process and promote the emergence of a democratic fabric in recipient countries. Finally, more assertive action within the UN system, where the EU has observer status and therefore enjoys little influence despite the size of its financial engagement.

How many European DCPs?

In its action the EU combines characteristics of a bilateral donor and of a multilateral institution, making it unique among development cooperation institutions. Members and the Commission also participate in the DAC, the coordination forum for donors' policies and practices. Member states, however, still control the implementation of a wide range of policies. It is hard to say if a homogenous model of a European DCP exists. Qualitative evidence and empirical studies looking at the determinants of member states' foreign assistance uncover a wide range of differences, not only between European countries and other global players (USA and Japan), but also within Europe (Breuning 1995; Schraeder, Hook and Taylor 1998; Alesina and Dollar 2000; Berthélemy and Tichit 2004).

The key question is therefore whether the EU DCP has an autonomous identity, or is simply the sum of the aid policies of individual members. The EC has always made clear that its own development assistance was neither just an addition to the bilateral aid programmes of its member states, nor aid by a disinterested international development organisation (Commission 1982), and routinely invokes complementarity and coordination with member states. However, member states have different concepts of development and different ideas about how far the development process should be carried out through the EU (Lister 1998b). DCP is seen as a key element of the external dimension of their sovereignty. So, although the pledge for coordination, consistency, and coherence is not new (Loquai 1996), both the Commission and the member states continue to be active in almost all sectors in the developing countries, still in accordance with the '15 plus 1' formula.

In fairness, the wording contained in the Treaty is general and ambiguous enough to allow for different interpretations by the member states, making it difficult to establish a consensus on principles and instruments, but also leaving room for flexible approaches. The legal provisions do not *communautairise* development cooperation, neither do they explicitly exclude the possibility of a full-fledged integration in the future.

> There is definitely a need not to confine the Community to being a sixteenth implementing actor in the area of development cooperation, but to consider it as a promoter and facilitator in the search of new forms of European governance.
>
> (Commission 2000d: 14)

The successful coordinating role of the Commission in matters such as debt relief and untying aid (OECD 2002a) indicate how it can contribute to a more systematic European approach to DCP.

Identifying VIPs in the EU DCP

Despite the slow advance of the process of Europeanisation, the Commission has reaffirmed its peculiar role with respect to the member states and the other international financial organisations. In particular, the 'special features and value added of Community policy in relation to the member states' would stem from the fact that 'Community policy pursues EU's shared objectives and interests [conveying] a certain image of Europe in the world'. Furthermore, 'European social values, the diversity of the existing social systems and the importance attached to environmental considerations, give EU policy a distinct profile as regards the quality of sustainable development' (Commission 2000d: 15–16). Such policy must be supported by a coherent trade policy and the promotion of good governance in partner countries.

What official texts say

In its Communication on Development Cooperation in the Run-up to 2000 (Commission 1992a), the EC elaborated on the principles of the European DCP stated in article 130u of the Maastricht Treaty. The Communication on the European Community's Development Policy (Commission 2000d) further clarifies them, specifying that the Community development policy is grounded on the principle of *sustainable, equitable* and *participatory* human and social development. In addition, as part of the TEU, the objective of the European DCP must be coherent with the fundamental values that underpin the Union's very existence: the promotion of world peace and the settlement of conflict through dialogue, the development and consolidation of democracy and the constitutional state, the observance of human rights and the fundamental freedoms, equity and solidarity.

> The goal of development policy is to encourage sustainable development that helps to eradicate poverty in developing countries and integrate these countries into the global economy. In addition to these economic and social objectives, there is a political plan: to help reinforce democracy and the rule of law, whilst promoting respect for human rights and basic freedoms.
> (Commission, Legislative Summary Website 'Development',
> http://europa.eu.int/scadplus/leg/en/lvb/r12000.htm)

In the same Communication the Commission identifies DCP ('policy of solidarity') as an instrument to project the European values of democracy, social justice and sustainable development:

> The global projection of European values of *democracy, social justice* and *sustainable development* calls for an *EU policy of solidarity.*
> (Commission 2000d: 10, emphasis added)

and stresses the importance of increasing the EU's presence and influence in international fora where development policies are discussed:

> One of the most critical aspects of coordination within the EU is to enhance the ability of the EU to present common positions in international bodies, thus realising the potential for increased European influence.
> (Commission 2000d: 13)

The Treaty of Maastricht also made respect for democracy and human rights a general principle of EU law, and therefore compels members to subject all of their activities, including DCP, to it. A series of regulations issued in 1991 gave democracy promotion a special status as an overarching objective of foreign aid, not only for the Community but also for its member states (Olsen 2000; Santiso 2003; Youngs 2001a, b). These regulations introduced both supportive elements – through the allocation of incentive financing to encourage democratisation – and cautions – in the form of an escape clause of partial or complete suspension of cooperation agreements in the event of grave and persistent human rights violations or the serious interruption of democratic processes. Since 1992, the Commission has inserted democracy clauses in over 120 cooperation agreements with third countries.

DCP has to be placed in the broader context of the EU external action. Therefore, this policy must contribute to the protection of the European interests and must help to enhance the EU presence on the world stage, furthering the recognition of the EU's identity by other countries and within international organisations. The increasing importance of security helps explain the changing pattern of geographical distribution of aid (see 'Geographical evolution of spending' below) since 'the EU's objective interests have led it to give priority to the stability and development of neighbouring countries and to aid for countries in crisis in the regions nearest to the EU' (Commission 2000d: 4).

The EU defines its own development mission in rather different terms than the US Agency for International Development (USAID), which explicitly refers to the importance of DCP as a means to promote national interests and exert world leadership:

> Promoting sustainable development in developing and transitional countries *contributes to U.S. national interests and is a necessary and critical component of America's role as a world leader.* It helps reduce the threat of crisis, and create the conditions for economic growth and poverty reduction, the expansion of democracy and social justice, and a protected environment. Under these conditions, *citizens in developing and transitional countries can focus on their own social and economic progress, which creates demands for U.S. goods and services and expands cooperative relationships between the U.S. and assisted countries.*
>
> (USAID Strategic Plan 2000: 1, emphasis added)

Two points are worth noting. First, there is a lot of strategic continuity in USAID principles since the 1961 Foreign Assistance Act, which stated implicitly that fostering stable democracies and prosperous economies in the developing world is in the US interest. Second, the September 2002 National Security Strategy echoes this principle and integrates long-term development considerations and the national interest. As the DAC notes,

> the concept of 'national interest' has been persistently part of foreign policy strategy and legislation since the earliest days of foreign aid, and is

considered by seasoned politicians to be the litmus test against which the
acceptability of new policy is judged.

(OECD 2002b: 14)

Institutions

The institutions and actual practices (*modus operandi*) of the EU's DCP provide an
additional important source of information to reconstruct interpretatively the
'unwritten' norms sustaining such policy and to shed some lights on the slow
process of *institutionalising principles* that seems to be central to EU foreign policy.
In particular, we look here at the institutional set up of the major cooperation
programme, the EU–ACP partnership, and the European approach to political
and economic conditionality as a way of affirming its values.

The ACP partnership: from Lomé to Cotonou

The ACP–EU partnership was based on the equality of partners, considered
development aid an explicit contract and gave ownership of development strategies to ACP countries, created joint institutions to steer the partnership and
monitor the respect of mutual obligations, included provision for the respect of
human rights and democracy, and finally expanded cooperation beyond governments, by including non-state actors and local authorities both in EU and
ACP countries. Although it was considered an innovative form of North–South
cooperation and a model to imitate, 'the Lomé co-operation was mainly based
on paternalistic, neo-colonial attitudes that undermined the principle of equality' (Lethinen 1997). EU aid was not primarily allocated according to the needs
and performance of the ACP countries, but to other interests of the EU members (Wolf and Spoden 2000). The unwillingness of the EU to adequately
empower the joint institutions and the lack of institutional capacities in ACP
countries greatly undermined the ability of ACP countries to influence the
political dialogue. The Commission's *Green Paper* on EU–ACP acknowledged
that despite the formal framework, the political dialogue and the 'partnership'
have failed (Commission 1996a: 12).

In light of the new priority set by the international community on poverty
reduction and eradication, this document highlighted the need to arrive at a
new partnership. The Cotonou agreement, the new EU–ACP convention, formally came into force on 1 March 2000 and promised to be a major break with
the past. As part of a stronger political foundation, the partnership involves a
larger set of stakeholders and covers a broader range of political issues (such as
peace and security, the arms trade, migration) than traditional development
cooperation. It also gives the 'national authorising officer' of the ACP state a key
role in the elaboration of the national development programmes and their
implementation. Finally, it makes respect for democracy, human rights and the
rule of law as 'fundamental elements' of the partnership. The emphasis that
Cotonou places on the principles of shared responsibility between the ACP

states and the EU, ACP ownership of development strategies and participation by the civil society seems to reinforce the above-mentioned vision of a principled-DCP, built around solidarism and partnership.

Conditionality and dialogue

'Conditionality' refers to the asymmetrical relationship between a donor and a recipient of development aid in which the aid is conditionalised by political or economic considerations valued by the donor. It can be imposed through positive measures related to the promotion of valued principles and sanctions in the case of violations of these principles (Lehtinen 1997).

Economic and political conditionality play an increasingly important role in EU DCP. An important step in this direction has been made with the Cotonou Agreement, which marks the end of the 'aid entitlements' (i.e. fixed allocations regardless of performance). The EU can now use the resources for the ACP in a more selective and flexible way and base aid allocations on an assessment of each country's needs and performance.

Political conditionality was firstly introduced in the mid-term revision of the Fourth Lomé Convention in 1995, which made the respect of human rights, democracy and the rule of law an 'essential element' for receiving aid. Good governance was included as a fundamental principle, but not as a legally enforceable condition, meaning that in itself it would not constitute a ground for suspension.[5] In case of violations, article 366a establishes that contracting parties should engage in a constructive dialogue that would include the analysis of the situation and could lead to the reconciliation of the problem. In case of failure of consultations, the measures of suspension of cooperation can be taken.

The European approach to political conditionality is based on the promotion of an open and constructive dialogue as set in the Resolution on Human Rights, Democracy and Development (28 November 1991):

> The Community and its member states will give high priority to a positive approach that stimulates respect for human rights and encourages democracy. An open and constructive dialogue between them and the governments of developing countries can make a very important contribution to the promotion of human rights and democracy.

The Commission has started to explicitly take measures with reference to economic conditionality in the aftermath of the 1980s debt crisis and the elaboration of structural adjustment programmes. Various Council Resolutions (in particular May 1992 and June 1995) define the European approach to structural adjustment. These resolutions acknowledged the importance of structural adjustment to 'restoring balance in crucial areas and to creating an economic environment conducive to accelerated sustainable growth' and established the obligation to combine economic reforms with the promotion of democratisation and political pluralism as a necessary condition for any economic development (see Commission 1992a and 1994). At the same time, they criticised the Bretton Woods institutions for not taking into due consideration the social impact of adjustment and lack of ownership of adjustment programmes:

> the significant reduction in public expenditure has been made to the det-riment of maintaining economic and social infrastructure, which often has no longer been kept up, and, in certain cases, to the detriment of the proper functioning of essential government bodies. [...] The real involve-ment of representatives of the countries concerned in defining the pro-grammes was inadequate.
>
> (Council of the European Union 1995, para 7)

Nevertheless, the EU is aware of the need for greater selectivity in its DCP, as stressed in the *Green Paper*:

> Twenty years' experience, however, shows the [Lomé] Convention to be an ambitious but sometimes unrealistic framework based on assumptions about the ACP countries' institutional and political capacities that have not been fulfilled. Thus, the respect for national sovereignty that once took the form of an almost boundless trust in the recipient governments is evolving into an approach guided by considerations of efficiency.
>
> (Commission 1996a: 12)

The EU approach to both political and economic conditionality is closer to a 'positive approach' based on incentives rather than a 'negative' one based on sanctions. Unfortunately, it is very difficult to judge whether this reflects a truly different stance, or rather the difficulty of implementing sanctions within the partnership agreement, due to the vagueness of the fundamental principles defined therein and the absence of criteria for applying sanctions in case of violations (Santiso 2002). In the recent, indeed ongoing, case of Zimbabwe, where the democratic deficit has been accompanied by the free fall of the economy and serious regional repercussions, the EU response has been 'char-acteristically lethargic' (Taylor and Williams 2002: 553). After much delibera-tion, 'smart' sanctions, including a travel ban on Mugabe and nineteen members of his inner circle were finally imposed on 18 February 2002, only to be circumvented when Mugabe visited Rome for an international summit four months later.

Actual disbursements

The previous two sections illustrated EU's VIPs as they emerge from official texts and declarations and by the functioning of the major institutions governing its DCP. As stated by the Commission, since DCP is part of the EU's external actions, it also reflects its geopolitical, trade, and environmental objectives. In this section we look at the actual aid disbursements, so as to perform a reality check and further explore the determinants of the EU's DCP.

Functional evolution of spending

Figure 10.1 presents a functional breakdown of EC aid commitments by major sectors over three periods: 1986–90, 1991–95, and 1996–98. The overall picture emerging from these data seems to confirm the shifting priorities of EU DCP towards poverty eradication and basic human needs, as suggested by the analysis in the previous sections. Access to 'social infrastructure and services' has gradually increased over the decade, becoming the second largest allocation at the end of the 1990s. Within this broad category, support for education and health represents the biggest contribution.

Food aid, once the largest EU aid item, has gradually declined during the 1990s, though still ranking fifth in 1998. In-kind food aid has progressively been reduced and replaced by financial aid in support of food security operations and funding allocations have shifted from indirect aid (support provided through a contract between the Commission and implementing organisations such as the UN), to direct aid (support managed directly by the recipient government as part of an agreed country support strategy). The increasingly larger share of humanitarian aid observed from the period 1991–95 reflects the response to the

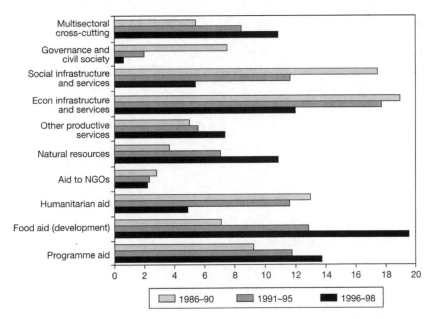

Figure 10.1 Sectoral allocation of EC external cooperation (1986–98): share of total allocable aid

Source: European Commission/ODI Database 1999 (adapted from Cox and Chapman 1999: 30)

crisis in the Balkans and the Great Lakes region in Africa. Interestingly, the sum of 'governance and civil society' and 'support to NGOs' represents more than 10 per cent of total commitments, reflecting the importance attached to good governance and popular participation particularly from the fifth Lomé Convention. While 'support to NGOs' has remained almost constant over the whole period, 'governance and civil society' registered a ten-fold increase (from 0.6 to 7.5).

Geographical evolution of spending

Although EU development policy concerns all developing countries, the Commission distinguishes three levels of poverty as the foci for directing Community aid. Under the primary poverty focus, aid is directed towards the poorest, least developed countries (LDCs). Under the secondary and tertiary poverty foci, aid is directed at the 'poorest sections' in developing, low-income countries (LICs) and middle-income countries (MICs), respectively. As regards the allocation of resources, the EU intends to give priority to the LDCs, in an approach that takes into account their efforts to reduce poverty, their needs, their performance and their capacity to absorb aid. Poverty reduction strategies are also encouraged in middle-income countries where the proportion of poor people remains high (Commission 2000d).

Table 10.1 provides evidence on the distribution of aid by income group for the EC, the EU member states and the sum of all DAC countries. Three years are considered, 1980, 1991 and 2000, in order to compare Cold- and post-Cold War era allocations. The picture is a telling one. As mentioned in the introduction, over the last ten years, while EU member states were cutting their budgets (in real terms) by almost 15 per cent, the EC increased its assistance to developing countries and transition economies by some 45 per cent. This increase, however, was not uniformly distributed. Three major trends are worth noting.

- The declining importance of low-income countries (LDC plus LIC) both in absolute and relative terms. Although ODA more than doubled in real terms from 1980 to 2000, low-income countries received a decreasing share of this larger cake, in favour of middle-income countries.
- The rising importance of CEEC/NIS countries. The share of Part II countries in total assistance increased from 34 per cent to 42 per cent. In absolute terms, Part II countries received in 2000 almost the same amount of aid granted to low- and middle-income developing countries, despite their considerably smaller number and higher average per capita incomes.
- EU member states seem to have delegated to the EC the task of taking care of CEEC/NIS countries. EU member states responded to the challenge of sustaining transition economies, but increased their share from 14 to 16 per cent only, maintaining almost unchanged their distribution to the various income groups.

development assistance by income group. Million dollars at constant prices and exchange rates (base year 2000) –

C	Other low income countries	Lower-middle income countries	Other	PART I[1]	PART II	Total Allocable[2]	ODA[3]
958	319	175	78	1,530		1,530	1,761
(63)	(21)	(11)	(0.05)	(100)			
,391	2,972	2,207	2,159	12,729		12,729	14,502
(42)	(23)	(17)	(0.17)	(100)			
,023	6,370	7,013	5,482	27,888		27,888	31,977
,213	468	825	338	2,844	1,456	4,299	3,304
(28)	(11)	(19)	(0.08)	(66)	(34)		
,009	4,431	3,790	2,836	17,066	2,755	19,821	20,839
(30)	(22)	(19)	(0.14)	(86)	(14)		
,573	12,314	20,925	6,887	50,698	5,165	55,863	58,371
(19)	(22)	(37)	(0.12)	(91)	(9)		
,071	480	1,951	438	3,940	2,907	6,847	4,763
(16)	(7)	(28)	(0.06)	(58)	(42)		
,003	3,611	3,861	915	13,389	2,459	15,848	17,734
(32)	(23)	(24)	(0.06)	(84)	(16)		
,464	10,087	10,907	1,913	31,371	5,491	36,862	42,189
(23)	(27)	(30)	(0.05)	(85)	(15)		

h-Income Countries. Part I = developing countries. Part II countries comprise more advanced developing countries, and
anced Central and Eastern European Countries and New Independent States of the former Soviet Union (see OECD 2003).
ns one to four).
OA) countries.

Shares in brackets. In order to give a truer idea of the volume of flows over time, annual data have been adjusted to
in question and the reference year (2000), and changes in the exchange rate between the currency concerned and the
eriod.

ment Statistics Database (http://www.oecd.org/dac)

When considering the geographical distribution of development assistance (OECD 2003), two additional comments are in order. Firstly, the declining share of low-income countries in European aid mainly reflects the decreasing importance of Africa, and in particular sub-Saharan Africa (on this point see also Grilli 1993; Lister 1998b). This trend concerns more in the EC than the member states, which (for historical reasons) maintain bilateral programmes with Africa. Secondly, beside the greater effort in neighbouring Eastern European countries, the EC has considerably diversified its geographical reach, by signing partnership agreements with other regions, in particular Latin America.

The shift of geographical emphasis in the EC's development cooperation partly reflects the different perspectives brought by each new entrant to the EU. It also partly reflects the changing role of development policy. From an aid approach focused on relationship with ex-colonies, the EC has developed a broader framework of external relations encompassing political, commercial, security and humanitarian dimensions, as well as the aspiration of the EU to become a global player.

The analysis of this section showed that actual disbursements do not necessarily match official declarations. Security concerns and the perspective of the enlargement of the Union, as well as mounting dissatisfaction with the results of EU–ACP cooperation, led to significant reductions in the commitment of the EC towards the poorest countries in the world. On the other hand, the functional distribution of EC aid would suggest a shift towards basic human needs and participatory development in line with the development rhetoric. Which one of these two trends prevails in the coming years will decide if the overarching objective of poverty reduction is more than rhetoric.

EU policies in sub-Saharan Africa: do deeds match words?

The previous section helped to critically assess what are the VIPs informing the EU's DCP. In this section we perform a reality check on their relative importance by looking at the aid allocation to Africa by controlling for specific characteristics of recipient countries, capturing their needs as well as their strategic importance to donors.

Given its consistent status as one of world's poorest regions, sub-Saharan Africa has always received a considerable share of European aid. In the 1960s, it was politically important to offer the newly 'associated countries' benefits, which enabled Europe to maintain its influence in at least one continent. Africa was also seen as the natural economic complement of Europe: one rich in land and natural resources and specialised in the production of primary commodities, the other endowed with capital and skilled labour and specialised in the production of manufactured commodities. This second feature gained in importance in the 1970s following the oil crisis. But the importance of Africa has diminished ever since: first on account of the meagre results of economic growth, then because the region's strategic value diminished in the post-Cold War era, and finally when the EU searched for wider and deeper complementarities with other developing areas, in particular Central and Eastern Europe.

A simple test to clarify the relative importance of the EC's DCP goals consists in ranking recipient countries by their aid per capita and then checking the correlation with their needs, performance and commercial importance. The *ex ante* hypothesis on the correlation between aid and the recipient's characteristics is illustrated below:

Recipient needs (RN)	Performance	Donor interests (DI)
Income per capita (+)	Lagged income growth (+)	Trade interest (+)
Mortality (+)	Lagged perceived absence of corruption (+)	

Aid disbursements should be higher in countries where income per capita is lower, infant mortality is higher, economic performance (growth) is higher, good governance (absence of corruption) is higher, and the share of import from the donor in recipients' total imports is higher. No clear pattern emerges. Certainly, aid allocations do not respond to recipient needs, as proxied by income per capita or infant mortality. At the same time, other determinants fail to help in understanding the aid puzzle. As Table 10.2 illustrates, the results of a Spearman rank-correlation test show that the correlation between aid and income per capita is negative, suggesting that richer countries get larger shares of aid. The other relationships have the correct sign, but the magnitude of the correlation is quite small, and they are not statistically significant at conventional levels (95%). The only significant relationship is between aid and good governance.

In fairness, these results must be interpreted with extreme caution. First, only one of these correlations is statistically significant. Second, since these are bi-variate correlations, the analysis does not control simultaneously for the other characteristics of the donor–recipient relationship. We therefore performed a multivariate regression analysis of aid determinants estimating a standard recipient needs–donor interests (RN–DI) model applying a panel estimation method with fixed effects.[6] Before presenting the results, two remarks on the RN–DI model are in order. First, despite being widely used, this model presents an important shortcoming, in so far as it does not take into account the characteristics of the donor country, such as the economic conditions of the country, the

Table 10.2 Spearman rank-correlation test results

	GDP per capita	*Infant mortality*	*Growth*	*Corruption*	*Trade links*
ECAID pc					
Correlation coefficient	−0.16	0.08	0.11	**0.24**	0.14
one-sided significance	(0.17)	(0.32)	(0.26)	(0.09)	(0.21)
Number of countries	37	37	37	32	36

Note: statistically significant correlations in bold

political credo of the government, the preferences of the electors, but also the *values, principles*, and *images of the world* informing policy makers.[7] Second, the model was originally developed to study bilateral aid relations and therefore it only imperfectly fits to the case of the EU, which combines the features of a bilateral and multilateral donor.

The results are reported in Table 10.3. The parsimonious specification used explains 45 per cent of the variance of EC aid to Africa. It seems that the EC does not respond to RN, but rather attaches greater importance to its trade links and to the behaviour of its major member countries (surprisingly, France was not significant). The EC tends to provide larger amounts of aid to countries that: are highly dependent on EU imports, less corrupt (economic performance, on the other hand, is not significant), receive large amounts of aid from the UK and Germany, receive small amounts of aid from non-EU countries, and – surprisingly – have higher per capita income.[8]

Our results confirm previous findings by Wolf and Spoden (2000) which focus on EC aid to ACP countries and concluded that 'EU aid per capita towards ACP countries is not correlated with GDP per capita to a significant extent and it is positively correlated to the Human Development Index, which is a combined index of income, health and education indicators. ... That means that currently aid is not given according to needs'. They also found that more democratic countries (as proxied by an index of civil liberties) tend to receive more aid.

Concluding, the analysis of European aid to Africa lends only limited support to the ranking of values suggested by the textual analysis, which placed poverty

Table 10.3 EC aid to Africa: Regression Results. Dependent Variable: Log of EC aid to African countries (per-capita)

Variable	Coefficient	Std. Error	t-Statistic	Prob.
Log(GDP pc)	1.29	0.41	3.15	0.00
Growth	−0.01	0.01	−0.95	0.34
Log(POP)	0.93	0.61	1.51	0.13
Corruption	0.20	0.09	2.38	0.02
Trade links	0.01	0.00	2.83	0.00
LOG(AID others)	−0.36	0.09	−3.93	0.00
LOG(GER AID)	0.29	0.08	3.65	0.00
LOG(UK AID)	0.16	0.08	2.06	0.04
R-squared	0.45	Mean dependent var		1.06
Adjusted R-squared	0.40	S.D. dependent var		1.31
S.E. of regression	1.02	Sum squared resid		398
F-statistic	45.7	Durbin-Watson stat		1.72
Prob(F-statistic)	0			

Note: Sample: 1985–2000. Country effects not reported. Corruption is proxied by the ICRG index which takes higher values in less corrupt countries. 'Aid others' refers to aid disbursed by all DAC countries excluding the EC and the three major European donors, France, Germany and UK.

reduction as the overarching objective of development cooperation. This comes as no surprise, since rhetoric and policy behaviour seldom coincide. The results, however, must be interpreted with caution. The analysis, in fact, is an aggregate one that does not allow us to take into account the functional distribution of aid in each country. Assuming that priority in aid allocation is given to countries that have historical linkages or strategic importance, a more detailed analysis should be conducted to assess how this aid is spent within those countries. Unfortunately, data availability does not allow us to perform this kind of analysis.

Conclusions

This chapter's main aim has been to investigate the VIPs informing the EU DCP. Different DCP models exist, both within and between European and non-European countries. We have mainly focused on development cooperation at the Community level – abstracting from individual member countries' behaviour – an area that has been only marginally considered in the aid litera-ture. Furthermore, since the EU is often considered the most advanced form of institutionalisation of inter-state cooperation, the closer approximation to what a post-Westphalian international order would look like (Held 1995; Linklater 1998), our analysis has been guided by the exploratory hypothesis that the 'dif-ferent' nature of its DCP might be explained by the 'different' nature of the EU itself. In other words, it can be argued that this Community of states, which have rejected the logic of anarchy and military might as the regulating principle of their relationships and made the principle of economic cooperation the cor-nerstone of a new model of international coexistence, projects externally the values specific to its polity in the form of a DCP as a 'policy of solidarity'. This thesis, however, needs qualifications and cautions.

First of all, our textual analysis revealed that the promotion of sustainable development, social justice, democracy and human rights are the fundamental principles of the EU's DCP, whose overarching objective is the eradication of poverty. The respect of these fundamental principles as well as the concrete effort to make aid more effective, have in recent years increasingly become defining conditions of the EU's development cooperation programmes. The EC itself defines its DCP as a 'policy of solidarity' conveying a certain image of Europe, while acknowledging that foreign policy goals, commercial interests and strategic concerns that have no intrinsic connection with development have always played a role in the European DCP.

The reality check performed on actual disbursements showed that rhetoric and policy behaviour are often different, i.e. deeds do not always meet words. Confirming the findings of the existing empirical studies, both the simple descriptive analysis and the econometric estimation of the determinants of EC aid showed that aid is not necessarily directed towards the poorest countries, and that, at least in the case of Africa, commercial interest, the recipient gov-ernance stance (as imperfectly measured by the index of perceived corruption) and the behaviour of other donors influence the EC's aid giving.

It is difficult to establish to what extent these above-mentioned values and principles are specifically European insofar as they emerged simultaneously with a political consensus within the UN Conferences of the 1990s and the DAC over development goals and instruments. Certainly, the greater emphasis on people-oriented development, poverty reduction, gender equality and sustainable development have always been at the core of some EU member states' development cooperation and can probably be traced back to their solidaristic tradition. According to this view, the establishment and development of foreign aid programmes have been the natural international projection of the domestic income-redistribution mechanism – i.e. the welfare state – that emerged in the developed world (Nöel and Thérein 1995). The few attempts that have been made to model the determinants of multilateral donors, however, do not provide conclusive results, finding that some agencies tend to respond to humanitarian needs more than others (Neumayer 2003; Thacker 1999; Barro and Lee 2002; Wolf and Spoden 2000).

At the same time, external interaction with other donors did influence the way today's EU DCP principles were shaped. According to aid practitioners, the role the EU had in influencing the definition of the shared development goals was rather limited, due to the lack of a clear and coherent strategy.[9] However 'shared' these principles may be, differences clearly exist in the way they are translated into policy as well as how they are ranked. In this respect, official declarations offer limited guidance. We therefore tried to uncover the 'European way' or 'interpretation' of these shared principles by looking at the norms that are embedded in the institutional set up. Partnership, dialogue, and constructive engagement appeared as salient features of the EU's policy of solidarity.

The EU–ACP cooperation has been on a partnership basis founded on the principles of shared responsibility since its beginning in 1975. Of course, the existence of joint institutions, ACP ownership of development strategies, and participation of non-state actors and civil society give the agreement a rather unique – albeit historically determined by the colonial past – feature. Conditionality, both economic and political, is the other important aspect of this institutional set up. In this respect, the European approach is best described as one of 'constructive engagement' rather that of 'negative sanctions'. This is confirmed by the 'bottom-up' approach to promotion of democracy, which is characterised by a strong preference for funding advocacy NGOs. If the institutions governing the agreement seem to respond to the EU rhetoric – partnership and positive conditionality – their actual functioning is not completely satisfactory. The new Cotonou Agreement aims at giving a stronger political foundation to the partnership, so as to make it more effective.

As far as the EU identity is concerned one tentative conclusion can be drawn. The values and principles embedded in the EU DCP are those of a *policy of solidarity* and could represent an important part of the *ethos* guiding the global action of the EU as a 'civilian power'. In practice, however, the EU DCP does not produce the expected return in terms of EU identity formation because of the EU structural incapability to politicise it by first capitalising on its symbolic asset externally and second linking it to a convergent internal process of identity building.

In fact, as seen in section two of this chapter, the Commission often makes reference to a European image based on shared values, which should be projected through its DCP. The ability of projecting such an image, however, greatly depends on two related factors. First, greater coherence and coordination of the EU DCP with those of member states and with other EU policies. Second, greater influence in international development fora. On the latter point, it has to be recognised that the EU's large-scale disbursements do not entail proportional influence within international development organisations. The EU, as a whole, financed for example 64 per cent of the cost of the structural adjustment programmes in Africa, while the cumulated voting right of the member states in the IMF is only 27 per cent. Such lack of influence stems from the absence of a unique EU position in these organisations. As former EU Trade Commissioner Pascal Lamy argued, the Eurozone needs to speak with one voice at bodies like the IMF and World Bank to make its external economic policy more effective.

At the same time, the process of identity building with respect to development cooperation also entails raising the awareness of EU citizens about development issues. Ongoing research within the OECD shows that, over the last decade, public support had appeared to remain strong in most EU member countries (McDonnell *et al.* 2003). This support, however, is not matched by awareness on the EU DCP. According to the 1998 Eurobarometer surveys, most European citizens are not aware of the existence of the EU's development co-operation programmes. In response to this lack of public awareness, the EC has begun to make special efforts in the area of information, communication and development education to inform and educate European citizens about its activity in developing countries.

We did not look at the 'others' perceptions of the EU. Anecdotal evidence from field interviews conducted in Ethiopia seems to suggest that recipient countries identify Europe as a distinct donor when it finances projects that are visible, such as big infrastructure. This is not new, as the experience of the latecomers to the EU (Greece, Portugal, and Spain) shows. The EU's identity would therefore be linked to its size, more than to a particular image. Non-EU aid practitioners, on the other hand, suggested that the peculiar feature of the EU DCP was its explicit reference to a 'policy of solidarity'. In both cases, however, the question remains as to what this external perception amounts to in terms of identity building if it is not sustained by an active process of politicisation – perhaps only to a further confirmation of the well-known expectation–capability gap as the best fitting identity description of the EU.

Notes

1 The term DCP refers to the set of policies aiming at creating the conditions for the sustainable economic and social development of partner countries. A key element of these policies is the transfer of financial and non-financial resources to finance

projects in poor countries and increase their institutional capacity. The loans and grants allotted to developing countries by governments of developed countries constitute official development assistance (ODA). See http://www.oecd.org/dac for details and OECD (1996a) for an historical review of official development assistance.

2 Revised four times since 1974, the Convention now links the EU and 70 ACP countries representing some 500 million people.

3 These conferences are: Rio 1992 (environment and development), Vienna 1993 (human rights), Cairo 1994 (population and development), Copenhagen 1995 (social development), Beijing 1995 (women and development), Rome 1996 (food), Istanbul 1996 (Habitat II), Geneva 2000 (social development). The strategic prominence of the 'campaign against poverty' and people-oriented development was set out in OECD (1996b), which led to the adoption of the Millennium Development Goals (MDGs) by the UN.

4 Clare Short, former British Secretary of State for International Development, said 'The European Commission's programmes have huge potential to do good, but they are much less effective than they should be. (...) the Commission is the worst development agency in the world. The poor quality and reputation of its aid brings Europe into disrepute. (...) The commission can improve its aid management, but to achieve more it must do less', in 'Aid that doesn't help', *Financial Times*, 23 June 2000, speaking on the day of the signature of the Cotonou Agreement.

5 The EU initially wanted good governance to be included as an 'essential element', whose violation could lead to a suspension of aid. The negotiation led to the inclusion of good governance as a 'fundamental element' and an agreement was reached on the possibility of using the suspension of aid as a measure of last resort in serious cases of corruption.

6 The fixed effect model introduces a country-specific term that should capture the specificity of the donor–recipient relationship, such as colonial past, strategic importance, cultural similarity and the like. On the RN–DI model see McKinlay and Little (1977).

7 Very few are, indeed, the studies that incorporate these elements into the analysis. Mosley (1985) finds that aid disbursements are only mildly responsive to the state of the domestic economy and that different donors react in different ways to the domestic demand for development assistance. In particular, governments such as Sweden, Germany, and Canada seem to react to public demand and adjust the supply of aid either through changes in quantities or adjusting the quality of aid provided. Lahiri and Raimondos-Møller (2000) develop a political-economic model of foreign aid allocation between competing recipient countries where not only international political variables but also domestic factors such as lobbying by ethnic groups in the donor country explain the foreign aid puzzle, i.e. only a small proportion of total foreign aid goes to the LDCs.

8 Per capita income is highly correlated with infant mortality. Using the latter variable produces the same results.

9 'Inside the EC's DG VIII the 1996 Strategy for the 21st century came as somewhat of a revelation to the senior management (...) they knew it was an important document, but did not know quite what to do with it, and there was no systematic internal reflection on the implications. As the pressure to reform mounted on the EC, I think the senior management started to look more systematically at the International Development Goals, and the poverty reduction goals especially, as an important organising principle. Whether this was pushed by the member states or was the usual reflection of the interaction with the member states I am not sure, but the end result was that the Goals now figure centrally in the EC's policy statements. So, I do not think the EC influenced the definition of the goals in 1996.' Interview with a senior EU official, September 2002.

11 European Union regulatory capitalism and multilateral trade negotiations

Adrian van den Hoven

International relations scholars have developed a strong interest in the study of the European Union's (EU's) trade policy at the World Trade Organization (WTO) because it is one of the rare external domains of exclusive EU competence. They have focused essentially on the influence of institutional processes (Hanson 1998: 61–65; Meunier 2000; Meunier and Nicolaïdis 1999) or economic interests (Messerlin 2001: 17) on the direction of EU trade policy at the WTO. Most of these studies are rather critical of EU trade policy and warn of the dangers of the potential for protectionism in the EU political system. Meunier and Nicolaïdis (1999: 498) warn that the fragmented EU decision-making process could encourage member states to 'log-roll' protectionist concessions for one another in the Council of Ministers.[1] Messerlin (2001: 42) criticises the high degree of EU protectionism in twenty-two agricultural and industrial sectors. Yet, despite this criticism, some scholars consider EU trade policy to be rather liberal in nature.

Hanson (1998) argues that the EU did not become a protectionist 'fortress', as many warned it would become, because it chose to progressively liberalise the Single Market to international trade. Hanson basically reverses Meunier and Nicolaïdis's thesis by arguing that the decision-making process in the Council of Ministers strengthens the hand of 'liberal' northern member states relative to the 'protectionist' southern member states of the Union. However, Hanson's thesis presents major flaws. First, it is difficult, if not impossible, to classify EU member states as 'liberal' or 'protectionist' because all member states have offensive and defensive interests in trade negotiations. Moreover, a drawn out conflict between 'liberal' and 'protectionist' member states in the Council of Ministers would inevitably lead to deadlock in multilateral trade negotiations where the legal standing of the Luxembourg Compromise veto has never been clarified (Teasdale 1993). Finally, if the 'liberal' member states dominated the Council of Ministers, they would have liberalised the EU agricultural market long ago. However, the level of protectionism in the EU agricultural market has remained remarkably stable over the years (Paarlberg 1997: 416).

In contrast to what has often been stated in EU trade policy literature, liberalism appears to be the primary economic value underpinning the European project. With the notable exception of the agriculture sector, the EU has progressively liberalised its economy and is expected to continue to do so in the future because of the multilateral trading system. Indeed, GATT and WTO multilateral trade rounds have been closely associated with the EU integration process. The Kennedy Round (1964–67) reduced the European common external tariff (CET) just a few years before it was applied in 1969 (Preston 1997: 168). The Tokyo Round (1973–79) also reduced the CET following enlargement to the UK, Denmark and Ireland in 1973. The Uruguay Round (1986–94) reduced it further following the Greek (1981), Iberian (1986) Nordic and Austrian (1995) enlargements. Finally, the Doha Development Agenda (DDA) will reduce tariffs after the enlargement to the East (2004–07).

Despite this link between EU integration and multilateral trade rounds, EU participation in GATT/WTO negotiations was not automatic and the EU strategy toward multilateral trade negotiations has evolved considerably over the years. While US leadership drove most of the multilateral trade rounds from 1947 to 1994, the DDA is an EU inspired round. Since the creation of the WTO in 1995, the EU has been the strongest supporter of a new round of trade negotiations (van den Hoven 2004). Leon Brittan was the first EU Trade Commissioner to call for a 'Millennium Round' in 1996 (Gavin 2001: 1). When Pascal Lamy was nominated Trade Commissioner in 1999, he announced that his priority would be the launch of a new WTO Round (Lamy 1999a) and his essential role in launching the DDA was underlined by the US Trade Representative, Robert Zoellick (AFP 2001). Similarly, Peter Mandelson declared upon being nominated in November 2004 that concluding the DDA would be his priority as Trade Commissioner (Mandelson 2004).

It would seem that economic interests alone could not explain the EU commitment to multilateral trade liberalisation. There is no denying that the EU has offensive commercial interests for industrial products and services. Yet, the US and Japan, which have similar economic interests, have been less active in the DDA negotiations. The EU commitment to WTO negotiations is best explained by political rather than economic interests. The EU has limited powers in international relations. At best, the EU exercises 'soft power' through trade negotiations and its (limited) ability to grant development assistance to poor countries. Therefore, the EU's power in the WTO contrasts markedly with its lack of power in international relations more generally. As a result, trade policy has become a kind of foreign policy through which the EU can project its own values and principles on the world stage.

Recent studies of EU trade policy have therefore begun exploring the links between trade policy and more intrinsic values of the EU system. Young (2001) and Young, Holmes and Rollo (2000) have studied the influence of the EU's domestic regulatory regime on multilateral trade negotiations. This chapter builds on these ideas by arguing that values are increasingly important in explaining the EU position in the WTO.

Although liberal economic theory posits that trade liberalisation increases the economic welfare of countries that open their markets by increasing static and dynamic efficiency, trade policy remains heavily influenced by mercantilism

because the benefits of freer trade are diffuse while the economic rents generated by protectionism tend to be concentrated among a limited group of producers. Hence, protectionists have a strong interest in criticising, for instance,
EU proposals in the WTO to liberalise the internal market (Messerlin 2001: 8).
To counter this criticism and to legitimise trade policy, it is therefore important
to frame it as pursuing broader political objectives. This chapter argues that EU
trade policy is framed within a broader European free trade ideology.

A European approach to free trade

In a landmark study, Goldstein (1993: 2) demonstrated that America's belief in 'free
and fair' trade remained unchallenged as a foreign policy idea at a time when the
US economy was facing increased competitive pressures and appeared to be in
relative decline and therefore could have reverted to a protectionist trade policy.
In opposition to Helen Milner (1988), who argues that trade policy reflects the
balance of economic forces supporting or opposing trade liberalisation, Goldstein
explains that liberalisation and protectionism are framed within general, value-
based conceptions of how the international trading system should be organised.

Applying this type of value-based analysis to the EU is difficult given that it is
still a regional organisation composed of 25 countries. However, to the extent
that the EU is engaged in a process of progressively deepening integration from
a custom's union (1962), to a common market (1993) and now to an economic
union (2002), it can be argued that the EU project is also being built on
common values. Majone (1996) has argued that the EU is primarily developing
as a regulatory authority – which differentiates it from a classical state organisation based on coercion or military authority. There are two reasons that
explain why the EU is primarily a regulatory authority.

The first reason is associated with the limited budgetary powers of EU institutions. As the cost of regulations is generally borne by the persons or groups
that are regulated and not by the public institutions that adopt them, they are
an inexpensive policy tool. Laura Cram (1993) has warned that the EU adopts
regulations precisely because it does not have to pay the costs. Claudio Radaelli
(1998) has also demonstrated that this may be problematic because EU institutions assume that regulations have no cost when, in fact, they impose variable
costs on industries and firms.

The second reason is of greater interest to this chapter because regulations
are also associated with a European view of capitalism. Critics of the EU project
claim that it is nothing more than a deregulated common market (Balanya *et al.*
2000). However, internal liberalisation has been accompanied by increasing
regulation of markets at the European level. For instance, the deregulation
measures of the Single European Act (SEA) were supplemented by increasing
EU-level regulation of competition matters, EU-level funding of high technology
research and development and EU environmental policy that goes far beyond
dealing with cross-border environmental problems. Thus, the EU market is far
more 'regulated' than 'liberal', in the classical sense of non-intervention.

This spillover of the EU regulatory approach to capitalism on to the multilateral trading system could fundamentally alter its functioning. Traditionally, while the trading system has removed barriers to trade (negative integration), the EU would like the WTO to promote common rules (positive integration) to regulate the global economy. Hence, the WTO could become 'less and less centred on trade rather than domestic regulation and legal systems' (Ostry 2000: 2; see also Brenton 2000).

This approach to globalisation was best exemplified under the leadership of Pascal Lamy, Trade Commissioner from 1999 to 2004. Indeed, some may argue that Lamy's policy of regulating globalisation through stronger multilateral trade rules was purely a reflection of his personal views on the need to 'harness' globalisation. However, the ideas behind transforming the WTO into a global regulator actually began under the leadership of his predecessor, Leon Brittan, who promoted a broad agenda of regulatory issues to be negotiated in the WTO – including investment, competition and transparency rules. In fact, Lamy inherited the EU mandate for the DDA negotiations from his predecessor and made little attempt to modify it during his tenure. This suggests that the EU regulatory approach to the WTO, although exemplified by Pascal Lamy, has deeper roots in the EU system itself. Indeed, the European business federation UNICE calls for a strengthened WTO system aimed at 'preventing and reducing the negative and destabilising effects that globalisation and liberalisation inevitably entail, while at the same time releasing tremendous opportunities in terms of economic growth and employment' (UNICE 2001a: 5). Public opinion in the EU also appears to support stronger global regulation to address concerns over the possible negative effects of globalisation (Commission 2001c: 2–29).

The shift to a more values-based EU position in the WTO

Since 1996, the EU has called for a 'comprehensive round' of trade negotiations at the WTO, which focuses on more than just eliminating barriers to trade by also calling for new rules that are related to trade or to deal with issues that are affected by the globalisation of the economy. From a general negotiating perspective, it seems clear that this 'comprehensive round' approach is based on EU interests in multilateral trade negotiations.

The EU has found itself in a defensive position at the WTO on issues related to trade in agriculture and textiles. The Common Agricultural Policy (CAP) is widely perceived to be a protectionist policy for EU farmers (Oxfam 2001) and the EU refusal to accept that export subsidies for agriculture be eliminated in a new round of negotiations was at the centre of debates at the Doha ministerial conference in November 2001. The EU offer to eliminate export subsidies for agricultural goods in May 2004 was therefore a major concession in the DDA negotiations. Similarly, the EU has been slow to implement its Uruguay Round commitments on textiles. Although the Multifibre Agreement[2] was meant to be dismantled from 1995 to 2005, the EU had only removed the quotas affecting 20 per cent of textile imports by 2002 (WTO 2002: 10; WTO 2000b: 29) –

leaving the lion's share to be removed from 2003 to 2005. The EU will almost certainly be required to liberalise its agriculture and textiles sectors during the DDA negotiations. However, if the new round were restricted to the removal of barriers to trade in agriculture and textiles, the EU would have little to gain.

Clearly, the EU insistence on a 'comprehensive round' was partly a strategy to offset demands to reduce agricultural subsidies and protectionism in textiles. While this is commonly acknowledged (CAFOD 2001), the EU also needs to show that it has received concessions from its trading partners in order to build up domestic support for a trade agreement. As barriers to trade in industrial goods are generally low worldwide, with the exception of a few emerging countries, tariff concessions alone would be insufficient in comparison to the concessions that the EU will eventually have to give on agriculture or textiles. Therefore, the EU also needed concessions in areas where it would make obvious gains.

From an economic perspective, the EU's comprehensive agenda also corresponds to Europe's comparative advantage in services. To make progress in international trade negotiations, it needs the support of pro-liberalisation groups to legitimise a new round. However, groups will only mobilise to support a trade agreement if they are sure to gain some special advantage from it (Gilligan 1997). This explains why the EU relies on services providers to build a pro-round coalition at the member state level. In addition, the 'comprehensive agenda' at the WTO allows the EU to project its stricter (and costlier) regulatory structure at the international level and thereby limits the possibility for other states to compete by lowering environmental or labour standards in a 'race to the bottom'. It is hoped that this will reduce the risk of multinational corporations transferring production facilities abroad to take advantage of lower regulatory standards and hence keep more jobs in Europe.[3]

While the EU's 'comprehensive round' approach to WTO negotiations clearly adheres to its economic interests, a more detailed analysis of its position sector by sector reveals that values are increasing in importance in EU trade policy. Table 11.1 describes the EU position at the WTO on key issues in relation to domestic interests and values.

Values inform the EU position on sector negotiations in the WTO in different ways. They can serve as a cover for defending or promoting EU economic interests in WTO negotiations, as is the case with agriculture and services negotiations. The EU can also defend certain positions in the WTO based almost solely on value considerations and may even go as far as to sacrifice its own economic interests. This is the case with the EU position on TRIPs, development, social and competition rules. In some cases, the EU may avoid referring to values when it is preparing to liberalise a protectionist industry as has been the case with textiles. Finally, on some issues, the EU's economic interests are intertwined with values to the extent that it is difficult to distinguish which inform its position. This is the case with investment and environmental rules.

If we look at the EU's position on agriculture in the WTO from an interest perspective, it is amazing to see how little it has changed over the years. In the

Table 11.1 Interests and values in the EU position at Doha

Issue	EU position	Interest	Value/concern
Agriculture	Defend the CAP	Protect EU farmers	Sustain rural economy
Textiles	Delay removal of quotas	Protect industry	Avoid shocks to industry (unemployment)
Other goods	Free trade	Promote exports	Liberalisation
Services	Liberalisation	Promote exports/ internationalisation	Improve services in developing countries
Investment	Liberalisation	Protect investment interests	Encourage development
Intellectual Property Rights	Weakening (access to medicines) and strengthening (against counterfeiting)	Protect investment interests	Encourage development
Environment	Strengthen rules	Export strict environmental regulations	Sustainable development
Consumer rights	Strengthen rules	Export strict regulations	Promote public health
Social standards	Strengthen rules	Export strict social standards	Sustainable development
Competition rules	Strengthen rules	N/A	Prevent cartels
Development	Promote development	Protect ACP countries dependent on EU markets	Sustainable development

negotiations leading up to the launching of the Uruguay Round negotiations of the GATT (1986–94) in 1985, the EU position was to refuse any commitments on eliminating export subsidies (Vahl 1997: 73–74). In 2001, the EU defended the exact same position at the Doha ministerial conference (Lamy and Fischler 2001). This incredible stability seems to show that farm groups still heavily influence the CAP. However, the EU has begun substantially reforming the CAP (Commission 2001d) with the objective of reducing spending on trade distorting subsidies while maintaining farm incomes to sustain rural economies. Although it is possible to question whether CAP reform will completely decouple subsidies from production (Messerlin 2001: 79–83), the overall approach is framed within EU values about managing the environment, sustaining rural economies and providing farmers with reasonable incomes (redistributive justice).

The EU's position on services liberalisation in the WTO is also primarily an interest-based position. The EU has a comparative advantage in a number of service industries, notably financial services, telecommunications, water, electricity and other public services. In addition, the service industry has actively mobilised to support the EU in its push for a new round of trade negotiations at the WTO.[4] Despite this obvious link to its economic interests, the EU argues that services liberalisation is primarily geared toward promoting development. While there are clearly good economic arguments to support developing countries opening their markets, this requires substantially improved regulation as well. Thus, the EU argues that the promotion of harmonised rules for services regulations at the WTO could enable developing countries to gain access to a higher level of services. Although the EU position on services liberalisation is clearly interest-based, it is also associated with improving market regulation at the multilateral level.

In contrast to agriculture or services liberalisation, the EU's position on the WTO TRIPs agreement is astonishing from an interest point of view. At the Doha Ministerial meeting in November 2001, the EU ignored the interests of its own pharmaceutical industry by supporting developing country demands that the agreement be made more flexible in cases of health crises. Despite warnings from the EU pharmaceutical industry that the weakening of the TRIPs agreement would threaten European economic interests without significantly improving the health situation in developing countries, the Commission fought hard for the Doha declaration on TRIPs and health emergencies.[5] On this issue, the EU seems to have been convinced by humanitarian NGOs such as Médecins Sans Frontières (MSF *et al.* 2001) that a WTO agreement would contribute to lowering prices for life-saving drugs.[6]

At the Doha Ministerial Conference, the EU found itself alone in defending a position on integrating social standards into WTO affairs but it was unable to make any progress on this issue because developing countries consider trade unions to be the voice of industrialised country protectionism (O'Brien 2000: 99). The interest-based explanation of the EU position on labour rights in the WTO is clear. The EU has the world's strictest and most expensive labour laws and it therefore has an interest in exporting these laws to countries with lower standards. However, Michel Rainelli (2001: 227) questions whether it would be appropriate to impose European social standards at the international level, when these standards were developed over a 100-year period of economic development. Moreover, economists who believe that trade liberalisation can have a negative effect on unskilled workers (by lowering wages or eliminating their jobs) do not call for Western social standards to be applied in developing countries (Rodrik 1997: 76–77).[7]

This may explain why the EU's position on this issue is far more balanced than either economists or developing countries claim. The EU accepts the idea that developing countries need to achieve a higher standard of living before adopting higher social standards. Consequently, the EU relies primarily on 'positive inducements' to encourage developing countries to abide by basic labour standards rather than resorting to trade sanctions. Under the EU's Generalised System of Preferences (GSP), developing countries can apply for lower tariff duties on certain products, if they can prove that they abide by certain core labour and international standards (WTO 2000b: 36). Although this system can be applied in a discriminatory manner, the EU is not imposing its social standards on developing countries.

Surprisingly, EU economic interests did not drive the EU's promotion of regulatory cooperation in competition matters at the WTO. Indeed, business interests (the most likely affected group) have been only moderately supportive of negotiations on this issue. UNICE cautioned that competition rules at the WTO should only target 'hardcore cartels' (UNICE 2003). The Commission's vigorous promotion of this issue in the WTO, in spite of developing country opposition, could only be explained by its belief in regulation. Indeed, Commissioner Lamy had been a strong advocate of 'regulating the global market' (Lamy 2002) to reassure EU citizens that are fearful of the activities of multinational corporations. Regulatory cooperation on competition rules is an obvious way for the EU to regulate multinational corporations at the global level.

The EU's strong position on development issues is also difficult to argue from an interest perspective. Although the EU has a strategic interest in convincing developing countries to support its position in the WTO and to launch a new round of trade negotiations, its direct material interests are not evident. When assessing the reasons for the failure of the WTO Ministerial in Seattle (November 1999) before the European Parliament, Commissioner Lamy (1999b) felt that there were two major problems related to development. First, developing countries were critical of industrialised WTO members' record in implementing their Marrakech Agreement liberalisation commitments in textiles and agriculture.[8] Second, developing countries felt that the WTO decision-making structure was too heavily weighted in favour of industrialised countries and they feared an expansive trade agenda to new issues, such as investment, financial services, competition, environmental or labour standards for which they are ill prepared.

This was quite a self-critical assessment for Commissioner Lamy to make, since he basically conceded that the EU's position in the WTO was partly to blame for the breakdown.[9] Therefore, the EU's assessment acknowledges its share of responsibility in the Seattle failure through what Thomas Risse (2000) calls 'truth-seeking': 'when actors engage in a truth-seeking discourse, they must be prepared to change their own views of the world, their interests, and sometimes even their identities'. By acknowledging that its position in WTO negotiations contributed to the failure in Seattle, Commissioner Lamy was advocating that the EU would have to change its policy or face failure again. However, by structuring the debate in this way, the Commissioner was proposing a policy shift that would seem to contradict the interests of the EU in WTO negotiations by arguing that it needed to moderate its own demands and to offer more concessions to satisfy developing country demands in the WTO. We have seen in the above sections on TRIPs, that the EU made concessions to developing countries against its own economic interests. The EU was able to make these concessions mainly by referring to economic justice for developing countries.

In contrast to most other issues, the EU's slow phasing out the Multifibre Agreement ahead of schedule (Libération, AFP and Reuters 2001) relates almost solely to the EU's economic interests. Yet there is no underlying value-based argument for protecting this industry in the future. For instance, in December 2000, Pascal Lamy promised the French textiles industry in December 2000 that the EU would only dismantle the Multifibre Agreement 'intelligently' because the EU did not want to give developing countries any 'unnecessary gifts' (Lamy 2000). At the same time, he refused to adopt new trade policy measures to mitigate the effects of the dismantling of the MFA on the EU textiles industry.

On the other hand, EU textiles importers, NGOs (Oxfam 2001) and member states have used moral arguments that the EU unfairly restricts access to its textiles market for developing countries.[10] Given the strong moral arguments in favour of textiles market liberalisation, it is not surprising that Commissioner Lamy agreed to speed up the implementation of the EU's Uruguay Round commitments on textiles at the Doha Ministerial meeting. However, this values-based approach also created problems for the EU in the DDA negotiations when developing countries dependent on preferential access to the EU market (e.g. Mauritius, Sri Lanka) began warning that they would be unable to compete in a liberalised EU textiles market with more competitive developing country producers such as China and India. Thus the EU was stuck in a values quandary over textiles liberalisation. It feels obligated to liberalise the sector to promote developing country exports while it is desperately trying to improve its preferential trading regime to allow weaker developing countries to maintain their competitiveness in the EU textiles market.

The EU's position on the environment at the WTO may be interpreted from an interest perspective, but there is also evidence that there are basic values underlying its approach to environmental regulation. The EU has been criticised on several occasions for masking the pursuit of its economic interests behind a veil of good intentions, such as environmental protection. For instance, the US negotiator of the Kyoto Protocol has argued that the EU's principled position during the negotiations, which eventually led to a US withdrawal, was simply a way of protecting Europe's heavily regulated corporations from foreign competition (Reilly 2000). A similar argument can be made for the EU's position on the precautionary principle, which would authorise restrictions on the import of goods without clear scientific evidence that they are less safe than conventional farm products.

The EU has been reluctant to allow the use of genetically modified organisms (GMOs) in agriculture due to fears that GMOs would considerably raise productivity and lead to overproduction in the agriculture sector. However, this policy could also put EU producers at a competitive disadvantage on world markets relative to US farmers that do use GMOs. For this reason, the EU has been actively seeking ways to protect its market from GMO exporting countries. In 2000, the EU signed the biosafety protocol in Montreal, which authorises import restrictions and the labelling of GM products. However, it cannot use this agreement to restrict US GM crops from entering the European market under WTO law because the US refused to ratify the protocol (Gavin 2001: 83).

Consequently, the EU has been pushing for a clarification of the relationship between multilateral environmental agreement (MEA) and WTO rules to ensure that environmental rules take precedence over trade rules.

Although there are economic interests associated with the EU's position on the environment, we can also make a value-based interpretation of this position. Article VI of the Treaty of Amsterdam requires the EU to integrate environmental concerns into all community policies (Gavin 2001: 188), including trade policy. This legal mandate reflects the EU's commitment to sustainable development (Article II of the treaty). The EU has also embarked on a policy of adopting much stricter regulations for environmental matters over the past ten years. An interesting example of this change is found in the EU's regulation of potential health risks.

David Vogel argues that there has been a reversal in the way American and European governments perceive health risks over the past fifteen years (Vogel 2001). In short, European regulatory policies have become more risk-averse than American policies. He argues that there are three reasons for this.

1 Northern European concerns about health and environmental issues have spread from Northern Europe to the rest of the continent.
2 The EU allows more participation by civil society representatives in policy making.
3 Food crises that have weakened the EU's credibility as a regulator.

Nevertheless, there are two problems with the EU's value-based position on the precautionary principle. First, the EU has been unable to provide very much credible scientific evidence that some of the foods it bans are actually unsafe (Messerlin 2001: 119–120; Bailey 2002). Second, EU invocations of the precautionary principle and food safety bans have been far from transparent. For instance, the Commission's Directorate General for Agriculture, often subject to pressure from farmers, plays an important role in determining food safety rules. Similarly, on several occasions, EU member states have banned imports of beef and GMOs from other EU member states despite EU authorisation to allow the export of these foods (Messerlin 2001: 118; Balanya, *et al.* 2000: chap. 6). This makes the EU's food safety policy inconsistent and subject to the whims of interest groups and public opinion.

This brief description of the EU's position in WTO negotiations has shown that values are important in the definition of the EU's trade policy. While interests are certainly not absent from the EU's position, they are always associated with certain important values. Moreover, and perhaps more fundamentally, the EU recently adopted positions against its own economic interests (in textiles and pharmaceuticals) in support of broader values.

EU and US disagreements at the WTO

EU–US relations in the WTO have changed markedly since the launch of the DDA negotiations in 2001. During the Uruguay Round (1986–1993), the EU and the US were in conflict in agricultural negotiations but cooperated on a number of other issues (TRIPs, industrial market access, services liberalisation). Surprisingly, the EU and the US have been cooperating closely on agricultural issues in the DDA. For instance, they presented a common position on agricultural negotiations in August 2003, which provoked a strong negative reaction from other agricultural exporters and ultimately caused the breakdown of negotiations at the Cancun Ministerial meeting.

However, cooperation on other issues such as industrial market access, services liberalisation is weaker in the DDA and was almost non-existent on the so-called Singapore issues. Economic interests cannot explain this lack of cooperation in the WTO between the two trading giants. Indeed, the EU and the US have very similar offensive and defensive interests in the DDA negotiations and both are facing increasing competitive pressures from the rapidly emerging countries of Asia and Latin America. Indeed, there appear too be more fundamental disagreements regarding the future and current role of the WTO system.

It is not clear whether the EU approach to the WTO can be reconciled with US views of the multilateral trading system. Judith Goldstein (1993: 2) has argued that US trade policy is based on the idea that trade should be both 'free and fair'. Trade policy scholars will be quick to point out the fundamental contradiction in 'free and fair' trade. 'Fair trade' is considered to be a form of disguised protectionism because it would be impossible for countries to have the same level of social or environmental norms to make trading 'fair' (Bhagwati 1996: 9–40).

EU trade policy is no less contradictory because it is based on the idea that trade should be 'free and regulated'. Of course, 'free' and 'regulated' are, in a certain sense, opposites. Freedom means having no rules to follow, whereas regulations are rules. This contradiction between 'free' and 'regulated' markets is also found in the EU treaties. The EU's commitment to free trade is found in Article IV of the treaties which states that common policies should be developed in accordance with the principle of 'an open market with free competition' (Brenton 2000: 4). However, Article II also requires the EU to promote 'a harmonious, balanced and sustainable development of economic activities, a high level of employment and of social protection, equality between men and women [and] economic and social cohesion'.

According to trade scholars, the differences between US and EU trade policy are linked to deeper values held by their societies. The US places greater emphasis on fairness because it is a more unrestricted society that seeks to grant fair access to the economic system for all. On the other hand, Europe is a more hierarchical and immobile society that emphasises redistributive justice (Rainelli 2001: 219). While the EU believes that markets should be liberalised for economic efficiency, there is a general distrust of the market to deliver 'justice' or a fair distribution of the economic gains. Consequently, government regulations should enforce this fair distribution. In the US, the focus on 'free and fair' trade is based on the value of 'fairness' – that everyone should have a fair chance to reap the economic gains from trade. However, while US citizens generally trust the market to be fair, they distrust government intervention in the market. This explains why US trade policy focuses on reciprocity in trade negotiations and US 'unfair' trade legislation (antidumping and countervail legislation) to counter intervention by foreign governments.

Table 11.2 summarises the differences in approaches toward the WTO as reflected in the values emphasised in statements by the EU Trade Commissioner and the United States Trade Representative (USTR).

Table 11.2 EU and US interpretations of the trading system

	EU	US
Reference Values	Free and regulated trade 1. Justice 2. Distrust of markets 3. Faith in governments	Free and fair trade 1. Fairness 2. Faith in markets 3. Distrust of governments
Effect on trade policy	1. Markets need to be liberalized but also regulated to prevent market failures. 2. Need harmonization/ convergence of regulations.	1. Domestic liberalization requires reciprocal liberalization by trade partners. 2. Need enforcement of reciprocity.
Statements by Trade Officials (*emphasis added*)	Pascal Lamy (Trade Commissioner): • 'Internally, we have opted for a *combination of market opening with the necessary regulation* in the economic, social and environmental field, accompanied by some (limited) redistribution of the gains of openness.' • 'My premise is that today, we have a *deficit of global rules*: the globalization of markets has progressed far more rapidly than the evolution at global level of the institutions and mechanisms that are needed to shape market forces so as to produce outcomes that are compatible with the *values held by our societies*.' (Lamy 2002)[1]	Robert Zoellick (USTR): • 'Given *America's relative openness*, we can only maintain domestic support for trade if we retain strong, effective laws against *unfair practices*. Although some nations are critical of the U.S. application of these rules, other countries are using them to an increasing degree – and without the transparency and standards applied by the United States. *So we will continue to insist that any consideration of WTO rules focus first on getting the practices of others up to U.S. standards so that American businesses and workers can compete on a level playing field.*' • 'The WTO *is not an international regulatory body*; it has no independent power to develop regulations; it cannot force any government to change its laws.' (Zoellick 2001)

Note: 1 Pascal Lamy 'Europe's Role in Global Governance: The Way Ahead', Speech delivered at Humbolt University, Berlin, 6 May 2002, DG Trade website, speeches and articles

Although Table 11.2 only provides summary information on the differences between these two WTO members, it shows that countries with similar levels of economic development do not necessarily share the same views on how the multilateral trading system should function. These different approaches also shed light on some of the differences in negotiating positions at the WTO. Indeed, over the years, the EU has adopted a greater leadership role in the WTO by trying to infuse its negotiating positions within a broader framework of values. In turn, this has provoked major disagreements with its main trading partner – the US.

The four Singapore issues – investment, competition, trade facilitation and transparency in government procurement – have been on the WTO agenda since 1996. However, there have been fundamental disagreements among WTO Members regarding the decision to launch negotiations on these issues in the DDA. While the EU has been the leading advocate of negotiations, India and Malaysia have been firm opponents. The US, which presumably has similar interests in these fields as the EU, did not support the EU's quest for negotiations.

This lack of EU–US cooperation can be explained by the absence of a common understanding of the purpose of the Singapore issues. For the EU, the Singapore issues have a 'systemic' value because they aim to strengthen and clarify multilateral rules governing investment, competition, government procurement and customs (trade facilitation) in order to improve global economic governance. On the other hand, the US never fully supported the four Singapore issues because it preferred to focus its demands on improving market access for its producers and it did not see the need for new WTO rules. When the WTO agreed to drop three of the four Singapore issues (investment, competition and transparency in government procurement), it was hailed as a victory for developing countries. In reality, it reflected contrasting EU and US views on the possible expansion of the WTO rules. This disagreement may be associated with current appreciations of the functioning of the WTO as a trade rules enforcer.

Governments and trade policy scholars have been surprised by the transformation of the old policy-driven GATT multilateral trading system and the new rules-based WTO system. The large number of high profile trade disputes and their sometimes controversial settlement have led some scholars to question the political viability of the WTO system. Goldstein and Martin (2000) have argued that the increasing legalisation of the multilateral trading system and the resulting limited flexibility in applying trade rules may undermine public and governmental support for trade liberalisation in the future. Consequently, they have called for greater flexibility in the application of WTO trade rules.

This flexibility has been applied in practice by the US with respect to trade disputes. The US Congress has often refused to abide by WTO dispute panel decisions in which US laws have been found to be incompatible with WTO rules (FSC, Byrd Amendment, 1916 Antidumping Act). Only the threat of retaliatory trade sanctions by the EU and others has pressured the US to align its laws with its WTO commitments.

Although the EU's record on the implementation of WTO panel rulings is not spotless, there has been a conscious effort to comply. In the field of anti-dumping, the EU has systematically amended its legislation to comply with WTO panels by abandoning the use of 'zeroing' in the calculation of dumping margins for instance. Surprisingly, the EU has placed its trade defence regime under the strict and rather transparent rules of the WTO (Chambre de commerce et d'industrie de Paris 2003: 18) even though scholars have warned that this could provoke a negative reaction from EU member states (Coleman 2004: 67). In more contentious areas, such as the import ban of hormone-treated beef from Canada and the US, the EU eventually modified its legislation in 2003 to comply with a WTO ruling even though it has not lifted the ban.

These differences in US and EU approaches to WTO panel disputes are clearly linked to their divergent views on legalisation. While Goldstein and Martin's arguments for greater flexibility in applying WTO rules have been generally accepted in the US, they have been firmly rejected in the EU (Petersmann 2002: 15). This was clearly demonstrated when the former Trade Commissioner, Pascal Lamy, proposed to allow greater flexibility in the application of WTO rules to 'collective preferences' (Lamy 2004b) to the dismay of the trade policy community in Brussels. In essence, the Trade Commissioner was looking to allow exceptions to WTO rules in areas considered to be 'collective preferences' (agriculture, health measures, cultural measures, etc.) (Laidi 2004). The strong reaction of the Brussels trade policy community against this proposal led to it being permanently shelved.[11]

Conclusion

This chapter argues that EU values have a growing impact on trade policy in the WTO. Although we cannot claim that these values are totally interest free, there is evidence that in certain cases values take precedence over interests in trade policy. This is most clearly the case in evaluating the EU's overall vision of how the WTO should function as a system and in cases where the EU has adopted a position in trade negotiations that goes against its own economic interests.

The EU vision of the WTO system is that it should regulate the global economy to ensure that the economic gains from trade are redistributed fairly. This is based on the EU's belief in justice and its lack of trust in the market to deliver equitable distribution of economic gains. To demonstrate the impact of this value-based conception of the WTO system, this chapter analysed the growing influence of values in EU positions in WTO DDA negotiations. On some issues (agriculture, services liberalisation), it seems clear that the EU defends its economic interests at the WTO. However, on other issues (TRIPs, competition) the EU is primarily occupied with promoting values such as justice or global regulation. Moreover, the EU has adopted value-based positions on certain issues (TRIPs, textiles) that clearly go against well-organised domestic economic interests. This seems to show that the EU will only defend its economic interests in cases where it believes there is a value-based argument to do so.

These arguments are further strengthened through a comparison of EU and US approaches to WTO negotiations and the WTO system itself. Acceptance of WTO rules is very different in the EU and the US. While the former strives, sometimes with great difficulty, to comply with WTO rules, the latter needs to be forced to comply with the threat of retaliatory sanctions. Similarly, the EU has been a partisan of expanding the WTO's remit to a host of new trade issues (investment, competition) while the US has been rather lukewarm toward expanding the role of the multilateral trading system in global economic governance.

We may also question how values in the EU's trade policy fit in with larger debates over the EU's role in the international system. The evidence presented in this chapter shows that there is a link between defending values and exercising power in international relations. First, the EU is exporting its own values into the multilateral trading system by promoting the transformation of the WTO into the regulator of the global economy. To a certain extent, the EU is trying to shape the WTO in its own image, just as the US created the GATT-system in its own image. Second, the EU defends its interests (or refuses to defend its interests) in the WTO based on fundamental values primarily linked to social justice. This can also be linked to exercising power in the international system because it limits the ability of domestic groups to prevent the EU from offering trade concessions to (mainly) developing countries and because it convinces developing countries to support the EU conception of the WTO as a global regulatory authority. Thus, we can argue that the EU's value-based position in trade policy also strengthens its control over the multilateral trading system.

Notes

1 Case studies have shown, however, that log-rolling is less frequent in the Council of Ministers than Meunier and Nicolaïdis suggest. See Coleman (2004: 69–74).
2 A system of quotas for textile products from developing countries.
3 There is little evidence that multinational corporations are actually doing this, but as most EU countries want to protect the so-called 'European social model', this requires the EU to promote stricter labour and environmental standards at the international level.
4 The Financial Leaders' Group and the European Services Forum are the most active business interest groups in the EU on WTO issues along with the generalist business federation – UNICE.
5 Due to strong media pressure, the pharmaceutical industry played down its opposition to the declaration on TRIPs. The International Federation of Pharmaceutical Manufacturers Associations said the declaration was 'ambiguous' and needed further study. (AFP 2001) The European pharmaceutical industry was more vocal in its opposition to the Declaration, however. See De Filippis and Losson (2001).
6 Pascal Lamy recently acknowledged that he opposed his 'domestic constituency – the EU pharmaceutical industry' on this issue. See Guptka (2005)
7 For Rodrik, the solution seems to lie with insuring those displaced by trade with more social policy or with temporarily maintaining current levels of protectionism.
8 This was evident in the concluding remarks by the Chairperson responsible for the WTO Trade Policy Review of the EU (WTO 2000b: ix-x).

9 Although Pascal Lamy also tried to shift much of the blame on the US (Lamy 1999b).
10 Sweden and the Netherlands were lead countries pushing for textiles liberalisation (Pagrotsky *et al.* 2000).
11 At a conference organised on the issue on 15 September 2004, Pascal Lamy's proposal was roundly rejected by all of the participants (scholars, business and NGO representatives). The proposal has been shelved.

12 Conclusion

Valuing principles in European Union foreign policy

Sonia Lucarelli and Ian Manners

... it is now clear that European Union is the best example in the history of the world of conflict resolution and it is the duty of everyone, particularly those who live in areas of conflict to study how it was done and to apply its principles to their own conflict resolution.

(Hume 1998)

Africa and the problems of that continent afford us a chance in Europe to re-describe ourselves, what we're about, our values system, our technology, our capabilities. In the end this is our neighbour that's in a crisis. And I think this can be as much for us as for them, in terms of believing in Europe. My kids, and their friends, and the people that come to our shows want to believe in Europe. But they want to believe in Europe that has beliefs, that has values, that has a vision.

(Bono 2005)

We have sought to understand how values and principles shape, and are shaped by, EU foreign policy relations with the rest of the world. Nobel peace prize laureate, John Hume, argued that it is the duty of everyone to understand the principles of the EU in order to resolve conflict worldwide. African aid campaigner, Bono, has reversed this argument in order to advocate that addressing the problems of Africa would give the EU a chance to re-describe its values system in a more positive way. Both of these voices from outside of academic debate remind us of the importance of valuing principles in the study of EU foreign policy. To conclude, we will try to value principles by considering what our analysis of EU foreign policy tells us about the EU as a normative political and social system. As stated at the outset, this book was aimed at providing some answers to these under-researched questions of the relationships between values, principles, foreign policy, the international identity of the EU (i.e. the way in which the EU is constituted, constructed and represented internationally), and the political identity of the Europeans.

In the book we have explored, through three conceptual chapters and eight case studies, the way in which a core set of values, principles and images of the world emerges through EU foreign policy, and thus constitutes the international identity of the EU. At the same time, we argue that such emergence reflects back into the identity-formation processes *within* the Union in mutually-constitutive routines and practices of political union. In the rest of this chapter we aim to bring together the ways in which principled foreign policy links to the overall processes of polity-building in the EU in five sections. We will start by briefly summarising specific values, principles and images of the world that we believe have emerged from the analysis of EU foreign policy in the case studies. Second, we consider the differences between universal and particular interpretations of values and principles in EU foreign policy. Third, we will look at the way in which values and principles are put into practice in EU foreign policy. Fourth, we will briefly reconsider the inter-relationships between 'foreign' policy and the 'self' of the European integration process. Finally, we will reflect on what we have learned about values, images and principles of the EU.

Summary – VIPs in EU foreign policy

The analysis of EU foreign policy, broadly defined to include relations between the EU and the rest of the world, confirms the emergence of a number of fundamental **values** found in the case studies. These include the prime value of *peace*, as well as the core values of *human dignity/rights, freedom/liberty, democracy, equality, justice/rule of law*, and *solidarity*. In addition to these prime and core values, the case studies suggest a number of derived or more recent values, such as *regulated liberalism/capitalism* and *ecological modernisation*. If we read *regulated liberalism/capitalism* and *ecological modernisation* as being complex interpretations of 'good governance' and 'sustainable development', then what is interesting about the case studies is the relative match with the constitutive values and principles identified in chapter two.

Clearly, none of these values are unique to the EU and its foreign policy, although the relative importance given to them is of central interest to this book. However, what is of greater interest and has been explored in the case studies is the way in which particular EU interpretations of these values have been translated into guiding **principles** of EU policy. These principles include conflict prevention principles in *peace*; conditionality principles (essential and fundamental elements clauses) for *human rights, democracy, rule of law*, and *good governance*; mainstreaming principles for *equality*; the precautionary and preventative principles for *ecological modernisation*; as well as associated principles such as UN authorisation, multilateralism, and 'free and regulated trade'.

The **images of the world** that underlie the EU interpretation of its values and their translation into principles (and thus policies) seem to be broadly transformative, with a clear faith in human progress and in the power of legal frameworks. This EU image is based on a liberal understanding of foreign policy that combines the Kantian recipe for 'perpetual peace' – domestic democracy, an international *foedus* of democratic countries, and the development of cosmopolitan law (Kant 1795/1991) – with a Grotian faith in the positive effects of regulation and international law. According to this image the opportunity for pacific transformation of international relations into a world politics for the better is still possible. Conflict prevention through structural foreign policy is understandable only within this worldview.

Universal and particular – the specificity of VIPs

From our brief summary of the VIPs found in the book, it should become clear that of paramount importance are the ways in which particular EU interpretations of universal values shape the relationships between VIPs and foreign policy. Each of the values and principles considered in the book illustrate this specificity of VIPs in foreign policy, as the examples considered here will illustrate.

Peace is probably the most universally-recognised value and it would seem impossible to see it as a particularly EU value. However, the specific link that the EU has made between *peace* and the other values mentioned here is a particular feature of the EU. As Lucarelli and Menotti discussed in chapter nine, achieving lasting peace involves an understanding of the complex causes of conflict, alongside more conventional conflict prevention and crisis management. In this respect, the translation of other values into the principles of democracy promotion, international law promotion, sustainable development etc., are all seen as central to achieving peace. However, this imposes a broad understanding of peace which cannot be limited to the absence of war that is in tension with the use of 'preventative intervention'.

Human dignity and *human rights* would also appear to be values of universal reach, but as we discussed in the introduction, and is made explicit in the EU Charter of Fundamental Rights, there are particular EU interpretations of these values. As Welsh discussed in chapter four, human dignity involves the sanctity of the citizen particularly in biotechnology (see also article 3: right to the integrity of the person in the Charter). As chapters seven to ten illustrated, human rights are valued principles in foreign policy relations with near and far neighbours, in conflict prevention and cooperation policy. However, what these chapters also suggest is that human dignity and human rights are not isolated values, but are interpreted within the context of other values and principles such as justice/rule of law.

Freedom and *liberty* are also seen to be universal values, understood as an absence of restraints and the possession of rights respectively. Again, the EU does appear to exercise particular interpretations of these values. As Balfour discussed in chapter seven, the EU's foreign policy with its near neighbours involves broadly liberal interpretations of freedom and liberty, but with considerable emphasis placed on minority rights. In chapter eleven van den Hoven appears to support this broadly liberal reading of EU values, but qualifies it in the area of trade by arguing that the EU is far more regulated than liberal when it comes to freedom from regulatory intervention. Thus, EU interpretations of freedom and liberty are also shaped by their interplay with other values such as human rights (for minorities) and regulated liberalism (for trade).

Democracy is increasingly accepted as a universal aspiration, although substantial parts of the world have yet to experience it. As chapters seven to ten suggest, there is a particular EU interpretation of the value of democracy, including an emphasis on parliamentary government; a preference for proportional systems of representation; and a separation of the roles of head of state and head of government. In chapter seven Balfour argues that the value of democracy is compromised in regions (such as the Southern Mediterranean and the Middle East) where stability is a concern, particularly since the 11 September agenda has displaced human rights and democracy. In chapter nine Lucarelli and Menotti distinguished the EU's support for humanitarian intervention from the US's support for pre-emptive action (which may lead to democratisation). Interestingly, it seems to be the case that the EU now appears to be in favour of intervention on humanitarian grounds, but not for the promotion of democracy. However, democracy, human rights, and the rule of law are all clearly interlinked values in the EU's use of essential elements clauses, as chapters seven and ten suggested.

Equality should be a universal value, but is rarely practised. In this respect, the particular EU interpretation of equality is one that seeks to advocate the value of equality in the absence of widespread international support. As Pető and Manners suggested in chapter six, the EU's support for gender equality has led to the establishment of principles of equal pay, equal treatment, and equal opportunity within the EU, culminating in the mainstreaming principle. As this chapter illustrates, gender equality is also pursued in foreign policy through enlargement and development policy, although somewhat unevenly. In chapter ten Bonaglia, Goldstein, and Petito identified equality as a value to be promoted as part of the EU's human and social development policy. Again like the previous values, equality in both gender equality and development cooperation policy is not independent of other values such as solidarity and human rights.

Justice and the *rule of law* are held to be universal values, although their interpretation often reflects predominant power relations. As briefly suggested within the EU images of the world (above), the particular EU interpretation of these values places great faith in the importance of justice and law through both the *acquis communautaire* and international law more broadly. All of the case study chapters place considerable emphasis on the role of justice and law in ensuring the other values and principles are upheld, whether that be the precautionary principle (Welsh and Baker), gender equality (Pető and Manners), relations with near and far neighbours (Balfour and Panebianco), UN authorisation for intervention (Lucarelli and Menotti), good governance and trade regulation (Bonaglia, Goldstein and Petito; and van den Hoven).

Solidarity is a cosmopolitan universal value, but not one that has been often shared in a world of states. The particular EU interpretation of this value is controversial because of the inherent tension between solidarity within the EU (through common policies, for example), and solidarity across the world (through development policies, for example). The EU value of solidarity in foreign policy can be found in chapters ten and eleven where the policy of solidarity and the issue of regulated versus fair trade feature prominently. In chapter ten Bonaglia, Goldstein and Petito identified the development cooperation policy of solidarity as being important in projecting EU values of democracy, social justice and sustainable development. In chapter eleven van den Hoven contrasted the EU emphasis on free and regulated trade with that of the US on free and fair trade (fair to the US), but concluded that the EU promotes trade values at the WTO linked to social justice.

Regulated liberalism/capitalism was identified as an EU value by van den Hoven in chapter eleven, although it was made clear that this is by no means a universal value. This value should undoubtedly be understood in close relation to the values of justice/rule of law and solidarity already discussed. This relationship results in the operating principles of the EU, including the emphasis placed on good governance, multilateralism, and international coordination within the framework of the UN/WTO systems. As van den Hoven argues, the EU faith in international regulation emphasises that gains from economic trade should be redistributed. The value of regulation in EU foreign policy clearly extends beyond the WTO and the Doha development agenda, as agreements such as the European Security Strategy and the Constitution for Europe illustrated in 2003–04. Both these documents placed considerable emphasis on good governance, effective multilateralism, and the role of the United Nations.

Ecological modernisation was identified as an EU value by Baker in chapter five, although again this is not a universal value. Similar to regulated liberalism/capitalism, the value of ecological modernisation should be understood in close relations to the values of justice/rule of law and solidarity. This interplay between values leads to the crucial policy aim of mainstreaming sustainable development across all sectors of EU activity (TEU article 2, TEC articles 2 and 6). Baker suggests that the value of ecological modernisation leads to the EU operating principles of the polluter pays principle; the preventative principle, and the precautionary principle. Both Welsh in chapter four and van den Hoven in chapter eleven agree that the precautionary principle is central to EU foreign policy in the areas of science, foodstuffs, trade and the environment.

What this brief review of the specificity of EU VIPs suggests is that there are two identifiable relationships between the universal and the particular in EU interpretations of values and operating principles. The first relationship involves a particular interpretation of a generally held value, such as human dignity/rights, freedom/liberty and democracy. Such an interpretation takes place either because a universal value is translated by the EU into a specific principle, or because of the specific interpretation of a certain value in the light of other values or principles, that then produces a new value (e.g. regulated liberalism/capitalism and ecological modernisation). The second relationship involves attempts to promote such new values to a universal status, an attempt which meets resistance from a variety of directions, and thus involve interpretation and advocacy in foreign policy.

Principles and practice – VIPs in action

Having discussed the specificity of the EU value interpretation and operating principles, we will now turn to reflect on the ways in which VIPs are put into practice in foreign policy, including some of the limitations on action. Here we will briefly discuss six of the most common ways in which VIPs shape the conduct of principled foreign policy actions, together with five of the most common limitations and problems association with these actions.

Structural prevention – the case studies suggest that the EU places a premium on addressing the causes rather than the symptoms of problems, through structural foreign policy characterised by transformation rather than conservation. This strategy becomes apparent throughout the case studies, although appears particularly acute in Baker, Balfour, Lucarelli and Menotti's chapters on the environment, relations with near neighbours, and coercive intervention. Keukeleire has argued that structural foreign policy is a central feature of EU foreign policy, and within this book we have found several ways in which VIPs shape structural prevention in policy practice, including institutionalisation, regulation, multilateralism, partnership, and solidarism.

Institutionalisation – the case studies suggest that the EU slowly institutionalises principles through policies, treaties and legal arrangements. Thus we can notice the steady institutionalisation of policies, in particular through a variety of attempts at mainstreaming. Baker looks at sustainable development mainstreaming since the 1997 Amsterdam Treaty, while Pető and Manners discuss the role of gender mainstreaming, and Lucarelli and Menotti look at conflict prevention mainstreaming since the 2001 Gothenburg Council.

Regulation – the case studies illustrate the way in which the EU shows a particular faith in regulation. This emphasis on regulation within the EU leads to championing of international and global attempts to create and strengthen regulatory authorities. All the case studies examined the way in which EU treaties, conventions, and policy principles lead to different forms of regulation in foreign policy. Examples of such regulation include the way in which the introduction of regulations concerning human rights and democracy have led from Luxembourg 1970 to the EU Charter of Fundamental Rights 2000, and the impact this has had on foreign policy.

Multilateralism – the case studies also illustrate the way in which the EU's attempts at international regulation take the form of the creation and support of multilateral institutions. As discussed, the relevance of multilateralism for the EU had been reinforced in 2003 by Solana's 'European Security Strategy' and by the Commission's communication to the Council and the European Parliament on the EU's relations with the UN (Commission 2003e). In chapter nine Lucarelli and Menotti explored the way in which, in the post-2003 period, multilateralism has become a constitutive feature of the EU.

Partnership – the case studies also suggest that the EU tends to try to work in partnership with other actors, states, and institutions, in particular by emphasising political dialogue, constructive engagement and positive conditionality.

The EU seems particularly opposed to the use of sanctions and negative conditionality, although there are many examples of their use. Chapters eight and ten both encountered the way in which EU foreign policy tried to work in partnership with other parts of the world. Panebianco engaged with the troubled question of the EU's strategic partnership with Russia in chapter eight. In a different context Bonaglia, Goldstein and Petito considered the partnership agreements the EU has developed with the ACP countries as part of its development cooperation policy.

Solidarism – finally, the case studies show that the EU tends towards solidarist solutions with a focus on individuals, rather than pluralist claims of national/cultural exceptions, as discussed by Jørgensen in chapter three. Thus implementation is often bottom-up (focused on individual needs), rather than top-down (focused on governmental role). Such a solidarist approach usually entails working closely with civil society, NGOs, social movements and the 'social partners' both within and without the EU. In chapter seven Balfour examines the emphasis placed on the EU bottom-up approach to encouraging democracy, including support for local development and 'ownership'. Interestingly, Balfour juxtaposes the merits and tensions inherent in EU practices of a bottom-up approach to democracy assistance with a top-down approach to partnership and political dialogue.

Problems of inconsistency – alongside the common strategies of VIPs in foreign policy are five problems encountered in policy actions, the first of which are the problems of inconsistency. The case studies suggest that there is a central tension in EU foreign policy between the need for consistency in the application of principles, and the need for pragmatism in dealing with different issues and actors. This tension manifests itself in a whole range of global relations where, on one hand, horizontal coordination and consistency demand one approach (i.e. negative conditionality), but where, on the other hand, constructive engagement and pragmatism demand another approach (i.e. positive conditionality). A further complicating tension exists between the EU foreign policy and the member states' foreign policies. This produces further inconsistencies, not only over time but also over cases (see double standards). The EU's inconsistency is particularly denounced in the case of EU's democracy and human rights promotion policy, as both Balfour and Panebianco's chapters illustrated in this book.

Problems of double standards – these are frequently raised in the areas of democracy and human rights promotion, but are also relevant in the interpretation and relevance of international law. The construction of an EU international identity distinctively shaped by claims of normative power cannot afford to dismiss problems of inconsistent support and respect for international law. Any such inconsistencies, as sometimes seen in the debates over the use of force, undermine the normative power of EU foreign policy. For example, the EU has adopted two different positions in regard to armed interventions in Kosovo 1999 and Iraq 2003. In the first case, the intervention was considered acceptable and 'legitimate' because it was pursued in order to stop severe violations of human rights, despite being illegal without UN authorisation. In the second case, intervention was considered unacceptable and illegal because it was without UN authorisation. This is a clear example of the most problematic aspect of a 'full spectrum' EU foreign policy and its acquisition of the use of force. As Lucarelli and Menotti explore in chapter nine on the use of force, there is a clear need for a VIPs-informed EU to clarify the relationship between structural foreign policy and humanitarian intervention if it is to develop its normative power in world politics.

Problems of efficacy – as Jørgensen (1998) has previously argued, measuring the success of EU FP is a highly complicated task, which is made more difficult by the observation that it is easy to see when it fails, but difficult to spot when it succeeds. It is precisely because the principled foreign policy valued by the EU has such high aspirations that questions regarding efficacy have been raised since the entry into force of the Treaty on European Union. As Manners interrogated in chapter two, the Constitution for Europe defined the Union's objectives as the promotion of peace, its values and the well-being of its peoples, as well as contributing to the greater good in the wider world. Could EU foreign policy ever be able to achieve these objectives? Clearly, valuing principles in foreign policy creates objectives which are both bold and open-ended in their aspirations, but could the EU ever be effective in achieving goals such as peace, the sustainable development of the earth, the eradication of poverty, or the promotion of human rights? Clearly these are some of the most important issues to be addressed in the twenty-first century, but the challenge for the EU is to demonstrate the relevance and efficacy of its principled foreign policy in ways which are satisfactory and credible in the overall creation of a European *polis*.

Problems of multilateralism and the value of solidarity – multilateralism has undoubtedly represented one of the pillars of the Cold War world order during which multilateral institutions such as the UN and Bretton Woods were created and developed (Ikenberry 1996). The end of the Cold War has not yet brought an end to multilateralism, but problems associated with the role of the US as benevolent leader and good transatlantic relations are threatening the continued success of multilateralism. As many of the chapters explore in this book, the crisis of US unilateralism and subsequent consequences for EU support of multilateralism cover almost the entire spectrum of EU foreign policy from the external consequences of internal policies (Walsh, Baker, Pető and Manners) to external actions in world politics (Lucarelli and Menotti, Bonaglia, Goldstein and Petito, van den Hoven). However, as van den Hoven argued in chapter eleven, the breakdown of the WTO negotiations in Cancun was caused not by the failure of multilateralism, but the success of EU–US bilateralism and their absence of solidarity with the rest of the world's agricultural exporters. Thus the problems of multilateralism in the post-Cold War world are clearly related to the changing value given to solidarity, and whether that solidarity is limited to the state, the union, the transatlantic, or the world.

Problems of structural prevention through democracy promotion – the idea of structurally preventing conflict through the spread of democracy is certainly not unique to the European Union. In the post-Second World War period the Wilsonian tradition of American foreign policy led the USA to use democracy as a foreign policy tool (Chomsky 1992; Mead 2001). Similar to multilateralism, in the post-Cold War period the interpretation of this tradition on the two sides of the Atlantic has now dramatically diverged. This inevitably draws a dividing line between an EU and US understanding of the relationship between the two core values of peace and democracy and their interpretation into foreign policy. This became evident in chapters seven and eight where Balfour and Panebianco looked at the limits of the EU's democracy promotion policy with its near and far neighbours. In the present global conditions of promoting security concerns over the values of democracy and human rights, the EU clearly needs the help of both its member states and the US in promoting sustainable peace through democracy and human rights.

Foreign and self – VIPs in the integration process

> The proposition of this article is that, as a working assumption, the European Union has an identifiable and coherent international identity that is not a synonym for 'foreign policy' or 'external relations'. ... In defining the concept of international identity there is an interrelated requirement to explore how this international identity is both constructed and represented.
>
> (Manners and Whitman 1998: 246)

We have so far considered the specificity and practices of VIPs in EU foreign policy, without reflecting on their impact on the EU itself. Drawing on the arguments of Manners and Whitman from the 1990s, it is clear that we need to understand how VIPs contribute to the integration process itself through constructing and representing the international identity of the European Union (see also Manners and Whitman 2003). Our analyses of the specificities and practices of VIPs in foreign policy suggest a close relationship between valuing principles in foreign policy and self-constructions of the EU polity. The theory and case study chapters seem to point to two processes at work in the construction of the international identity of the EU involving a self-learning process and an identity-construction process.

The European Union's self-learning process

The first aspect of VIPs in the integration process brought out by the chapters emphasises the self-learning process which the EU experiences in engaging in principled foreign policy. By this we mean that through attempting to innovate and conduct principled foreign policy, the EU institutions, members, and participants find themselves developing mutually constitutive routines and practices, many of which may never have been intended. The chapters identified three types of self-learning processes linking together principles from different policy areas and arenas that we term externalising, transferring, and reconstituting.

Externalising principles involve a process in which principles that were developed in internal policy areas are applied in EU foreign actions in the related policy area. The chapters included many examples of externalising principles, but Baker's chapter five illustrates keenly the example of the preventative principle in the area of environmental protection. The principle was first spelt out in the Commission's first Environmental Action Programme of 1973–76; it was then introduced in the Treaties with the Single European Act, then mainstreamed with the Treaty on European Union together with sustainable development. The process of externalising principles involves self-learning because it is often unintended, has consequences for the EU polity as a whole, and involves different areas of the EU learning a little more about themselves.

Transferring principles involve a process in which principles that were developed in one policy area are applied in other policy areas, both internally and externally. As previously discussed under the practice of 'institutionalisation', the practice of mainstreaming involves transferring values and principles from the area and arena in which they were developed in order to spread them across the EU. As Baker, Pető and Manners, and Lucarelli and Menotti considered in this book, transferring policy areas through the mainstreaming of sustainable development, gender, and conflict prevention is a particularly contentious self-learning process as differing areas of EU policy are encouraged to confront prejudices in the process of learning a little more about the rest of the EU.

Reconstituting principles involve a process in which principles that were developed in response to a particular problem become far more important than was originally intended as concerns regarding inconsistency and double standards contribute to the reconstitution of other policy areas. For example the way in which the Copenhagen Criteria for enlargement have come to reconstitute the EU's habitus and international identity. In instrumentalist terms this process where principles, even if enunciated in rhetorical terms, have the effect of changing policy in a range of areas have been thought about in terms of 'rhetorical action' (Schimmelfennig 2003). Similarly, the role which networks of transnational advocacy activists play in mobilising around policy principles in order to bring about change in other areas or arenas has been thought about in terms of a 'boomerang effect' (Keck and Sikkink 1998). The case studies suggest that the process of reconstituting the EU through self-learning is less instrumental and more reflexive than rhetorical action and the boomerang effect advocate. On this basis we argue that values and principles have the effect of reconstituting the EU 'habitus' by changing the way in which socially acquired and embodied systems of cultural reproduction adapt to innovation and advocacy of values and principles in one area of policy making (see Bourdieu 1977).

Clearly the EU's self-learning process in constructing its international identity involves constant and complex interplay between externalising, transferring, and reconstituting processes at the interfaces of self and foreign. This is no more clearly illustrated than by the values of democracy, human rights, and rule of law which run through most of the chapters of the book. Left implicit in the early decades of the Community, they are only explicitly mentioned in reference to the Federal Republic of Germany. During the era of détente, the Helsinki process, and enlargement from the 1970s onwards, these values become more explicit signifiers of the EC and its identity. With the end of the Cold War, these values have transgressed their original context to become both criteria for membership and conditions for aid, as Balfour, Panebianco, Bonaglia, Goldstein and Petito explored. By the Amsterdam Treaty these values have come to reconstitute the EU and are constitutionalised as article 6 principles. This then leads to their pronouncement as the Union's values in article I-2 of the Constitution for Europe. Finally, as this book has explored, the processes of externalising, transferring, and reconstituting ensure that democracy, human rights, and the rule of law have become constitutive values of the EU's international identity in the twenty-first century.

EU foreign policy and identity

If values, principles, and self-learning processes influence EU foreign policy, so also do policy failures or omissions of policies feed back into EU self-perceptions and constructions. In this respect the EU's self-representation has been constantly challenged by perceived disagreements or failures of common foreign policy, most clearly with the conflicts in Yugoslavia 1991–95, and Iraq 2003. Conflicts and political crises such as these have probably done more to initiate public debate and awareness about the existence of an EU international identity than have any attempts to cultivate common cultural roots (for examples, see Lucarelli 2000; Levy, *et al.* 2005). As Lucarelli, Manners, and Jørgensen discussed in the theory chapters, the reason for this impact of EU foreign policy on its identity has to do with the peculiarities of the processes of identity building in the complex and evolving political system of the EU. As Lucarelli argued in chapter one, EU political identity is clearly a constructed phenomenon that does not need to rely on the recognition of common cultural roots. Indispensable elements of this phenomenon are the politics, policies and common historical experiences of the EU (Cerutti 2001a, 2001b, 2003).

The EU experiences legitimacy and credibility crises when the Union does not perform the foreign policy its citizens expect it to perform. In these cases, regardless of the complexity of the EU foreign policy decision-making system, any inaction which implies stepping back from the EU's proclaimed principles and values is often perceived as representing a challenge to the EU's identity. In adopting a post-national perspective, we believe that there is a clear relationship between values and principles in EU foreign policy on the one side, and EU identity on the other. For this reason we would suggest that the two huge current challenges to the EU – connecting the Union to its citizens and developing its international presence – are deeply interlinked. The first aspect of this challenge involves constructing an EU polity that extends democratic accountability and legitimacy for its institutions – well beyond any populist or academic perceptions of a 'democratic deficit'. The second aspect is shaped by EU citizens' awareness of the EU as a political entity which involves their recognition of a set of EU values and principles as being representative of themselves. Such awareness needs the interpretation of seemingly abstract values into more concrete principles of action and, ultimately, effective policies. As we have seen throughout the book, similar values can have very different interpretations into principles and ultimately policies, and it is only by looking at these interpretations that we fully understand the set of social and political values and principles that constitute the core of EU identity.

Drawing these arguments over the processes of self-learning and identity construction together, we would suggest that VIPs play an important part in the integration process, but one that is undoubtedly constrained by the difficulties of connecting citizens and the public sphere together in an understanding of the EU polity itself. It is unfortunately the case that while the self-learning processes have resulted in a fairly agreed settlement on some core values and principles, these are largely outside the EU public sphere. Similarly, while high-profile problems of common EU policy capture the public attention in crises such as Yugoslavia or Iraq, there is rarely any recognition or understanding of why the EU polity is unable to deal with such disagreements between member governments. These combinations of EU-level processes, international crises, vacant public sphere, and absence of citizens' comprehension unfortunately ensures that while the EU may have an identifiable and coherent identity in world politics, it is probably one that is clearer to non-citizens (see Rifkin 2004) than EU citizens.

On reflection – what we have learned

We started our study by asking, like Chris Patten, 'do we have in Europe any remaining value-driven visions of the world?' and have began to conclude, like John Hume and Bono, that the EU has principles and values but perhaps not one vision. Through the book we have seen many examples and illustrations of the way in which the EU values principles in its foreign policy, stretching from science, environment, and gender policies to conflict, development, and trade policies. On the basis of these contributions we argue that principled foreign policy is not simply the external actions of a consolidated polity, but in the case of the EU is part of constituting the political and international identity of the Union itself. On reflection, we suggest that there are a number of aspects to this political constitution which we need to think about, including rethinking EU foreign policy itself, identifying the specificities and practices of VIPs, the habitus of EU foreign policy, normativity and pragmatism, and the question of EU visions of the world. Furthermore, departing from this study, we can speculate about the exportability of the research model here employed.

Rethinking EU foreign policy itself is no longer a methodological choice but an analytical necessity. The idea that foreign policy analysis should be constrained to studying the traditional role of member states, with an emphasis on executive actions and sharp distinction between internal and external policies is rendered obsolete in the study of EU foreign policy (see a similar discussion of member state foreign policy in Manners and Whitman 2000). As recent works on EU foreign policy concur, the study of the EU in world politics must go beyond the simple study of CFSP, ESDP, and external relations (see H. Smith 2002; K. Smith 2003; Carlsnaes, *et al.* 2004; Bretherton and Vogler 2006; Elgström and Smith 2006). At the same time, also the traditional distinction between EU foreign/external relations experts and EU public policy experts should be overcome. As we have shown, EU foreign policy cannot be understood without reference to both the EU integration process and EU public policies, both due to the externalisation and transferral of values and principles from domestic to foreign sectors and across time, and because of the close, reconstitutive relationship between the process of identity building within the EU and its international role.

Our analysis of this rethought EU foreign policy has argued that a number of values are shared with other international actors, but have a particular interpretation and translation into principles and policies. This translation helps us better understand the character of the EU and the relationships between its foreign policy and the process of European integration. In this way we believe we can shed more light on the relationship between the EU as a process and as an actor in order to make sense of the links between process and actorness. This linkage is particularly important in the study of EU foreign policy because, as we have discussed, the co-constitution of self and foreign in the integration process is not shared with many other polities.

In developing these linkages between values, principles and policies, as well as between process and actorness, we have argued that VIPs are important in our understanding of the habitus of EU foreign policy. In this respect we have suggested that there are tensions between VIPs and the way they are put into practice, such as problems of inconsistency, double standards, and efficacy, all of which are part of challenging the existing socio-political system of dispositions regarding the 'ethicacy' and efficacy of discrete foreign policy actions. Secondly, we have also suggested that values and principles discretely developed in one policy area often externalise, transfer or reconstitute themselves into other areas or arena. It is this combination of both critical reflection on the problems of practice and translation from one area or arena to another that contributes to a more reflexive EU (see Bourdieu 1990).

Encouraging the construction of a more reflexive EU habitus will not necessary lead to any simple resolution of tensions between normativity and pragmatism in EU foreign policy. As most of the case studies illustrated, there are always tremendous normative difficulties involved in attempting to engage in principled foreign policy, as EU relations with Bosnia, Kosovo, and near neighbours Russia and China make clear. However, as Jørgensen argued in chapter three such tensions should not cause us to continue any detour away from the study of VIPs. Indeed, as Balfour picks up in chapter seven, the EU seems to show a strong tendency towards a 'flexible adherence to principles', as scholars such as Jack Donnelly and Chris Brown advocate. We argue that simply because the EU may be starting from a poor position in international relations, this should never stop it from trying to head towards a better direction – that it should profess normative values and practice pragmatic principles.

We should also reflect on the question of EU visions and images of the world, be they plural and contradictory. As Jørgensen discussed in chapter three, there are many images of the world held in international relations generally, so we should not be surprised if the EU reflected this plurality of perspectives. In chapter two Manners argued that EU images of itself were also plural and were to be found somewhere in between a Europe of states, a European state, and Europe as a participant in the state of humanity. It is this continuing disagreement and confusion over what the EU itself is that leads to a lack of consistency and continuity of the activities it carries out – national, supranational, and international policy practices continue to coexist. As we have discussed above, this plurality of images and visions seems broadly transformative in combining Kant's three articles of peace with a series of values that seek to strike a balance between individualist liberal democracy and collectivist social democracy. Hence, EU images of the world seek to accommodate a world of democratic states, a European supranational federation, and global cosmopolitan law, with all the contradictions which this sometimes involves, ranging from communitarian particularisms to cosmopolitan universalisms. We do not consider this absence of one, overarching EU vision or image of the world to be a bad thing *per se* – if Europeans have learnt anything during the last 100 years of brutal history, it must be that any totalising vision, ideology, or metanarrative is inherently dangerous. However, we believe that the failure on the side of political elites to shape a *public–political discourse* around different, even competing, visions of the EU/Europe is highly problematic. The current political debate on the EU presents elements of competing visions (e.g. liberal EU vs social EU) which, however, fail to produce alternative political programmes around which public debate could be articulated. Such a failure allows for national public debates to prevail on a genuine European one, slowing down the development of a European public sphere and inhibiting progress in the integration process, as the 2005 referenda on the approval of the Constitution in France and the Netherlands have shown.

Finally, we conclude with a reflection on what we have learned from this study as far as general research on foreign policy is concerned: is the research framework applicable to other cases? What are the lessons with which other studies could start working? We believe that studying VIPs in the foreign policy of other relevant international actors such as the China, India, the US, Japan, or Iran would not just be possible but highly necessary in that it would contribute to providing content to a lively debate on clashes among values and cultures which so far has not been substantiated by close analytical scrutiny. There are at least three lessons from which such studies could start.

The first lesson is the importance of the relationship between domestic and foreign policy not only in the rationalistic sense of the formation of interests in a two-level game, but also in the sense of looking at the dynamic interrelationship between a political community and the external world, with the aim of investigating the degree of mutual influence. The second lesson is the observation that in the relationships between values, political identity and politics, values do not count much in isolation from the normative framework in which they are embedded. Rather, they assume meaning, give sense to the political identity of the members of the community, and finally influence policy on the basis of how they stand in relation to other values and principles of the normative framework in which they are embedded. Most frequently, what differentiates political communities is not a list of values, but the relationship that a political community constructs among these values, their hierarchical order, and their peculiar translation into guiding principles. Finally, the last lesson concerns the framework in which a specific translation takes place. Such a context is highly influenced by historical experiences but also by the cultural identity of the community of reference. Cultural identity is a relevant element of foreign and international policy, but in order to understand the way it operates it is indispensable to analyse its impact on the political identity of the group, through its influence on values inter-pretation and translation into political practices.

Bibliography

AFP (1999) 'UE: Pas de levée de l'embargo sur le boeuf aux hormones', *Agence France Press*, 4 May.

—— (2001) 'Pascal Lamy et Robert Zoellick, une amitié à l'épreuve des négociations OMC', *Agence France Presse*, 4 November.

Aggestam, L. (1999) 'Role Conceptions and the Politics of Identity in Foreign Policy', Oslo, Arena Working Paper 99/8.

Agriculture and Environment Biotechnology Commission (2003) *GM Nation? The Findings of the Public Debate*, Available online: http://www.gmnation.org.uk/docs/gmnation_finalreport.pdf (accessed 14 July 2005).

Alesina, A. and Dollar, D. (2000) 'Who Gives Foreign Aid to Whom and Why?', *Journal of Economic Growth*, 5: 33–63.

Allen, D. and Smith, M. (1990) 'Western Europe's presence in the international contemporary arena', *Review of International Studies*, 16(1): 19–37.

—— (1998) 'The European Union's Security Presence: Barrier, Facilitator or Manager?', in C. Rhodes, (ed.) *The European Union in the World Community*, Boulder/London: Lynne Rienner: 45–63.

—— (2002) 'External Policy Development', *Journal of Common Market Studies*, vol. 40, Annual Review: 97–115.

Amato, G. and Batt, J. (1999) *The Long-Term Implications of EU Enlargement: The Nature of the New Border*, Florence: Robert Schuman Centre for Advanced Studies.

Amnesty International [AI] (2001) Advocats Sans Frontières, Euro-Med Human Rights Network, International Federation for the Leagues of Human Rights, International Service for Human Rights, Observatory for the Protection of Human Rights Defenders, Reporters without Borders, World Organization against Torture, *Open letter to the EU Foreign Minister, EU High Representative for CFSP and the European Commissioner Chris Patten*, 29 March. Available online: http://www.amnesty.org (accessed 4 January 2005).

—— (2002) *Algérie: Quand les gestes symboliques ne sont pas suffisant: Le droit humain et l'accord entre l'Union européenne et l'Algérie*, Document Public, London, April.

Ancarani, V. (1995) 'Globalizing the World: Science & Technology in International Relations', in S. Jasanoff, *et al.* (eds) *Handbook of Science and Technology Studies*, London: Sage: 652–670.

Anderson, B. (1983; 2nd edn 1991) *Imagined Communities*, London: Verso.

Anderson, S. (1995) 'EU, NATO, and the CSCE Responses to the Yugoslav Crisis: Testing Europe's New Security Architecture', *European Security*, 4: 328–352.

Andrews, R. N. L. (2003) 'Risk-Based Decision Making', in N. J. Vig and M. E. Kraft (eds) *Environmental Policy: New Directions for the Twenty First Century*, Washington DC: CQ Press, fifth edition.

Archibugi, D. (ed.) (2003) *Debating Cosmopolitics*, London: Verso.

Associated Press [AP] (2001) 'France Threatens to Bolt WTO Talks', *Associated Press*, 13 November 2001.

Attinà, F. and Guichang, Z. (2001) 'Security Culture and the Construction of Security Partnerships: the European Union and China compared', *Mediterranean Journal of Human Rights*, 5: 85–110.

Bacevich, A. (2002) *American Empire: The Realities and Consequences of US Diplomacy*, Cambridge MA: Harvard University Press.

Bäckstrand, K. (2001) *What can Nature Withstand? Science, Politics and Discourses in Transboundary Air Pollution Diplomacy*, Lund: Lund University Press.

Badie, B. (1999) *Un monde sans souveraineté: Les états entre ruse et responsabilité*, Paris: Fayard.

Bailey, R. (2002) 'The Looming Trade War over Plant Biotechnology', *Trade Policy Analysis*, no.18, Center for Trade Policy Studies, Cato Institute, Washington DC, 1st August 2002. Available online: http://www.cato.org (accessed 4 January 2005).

Baker, P. (2002) 'Human Rights, Europe and the People's Republic of China', *The China Quarterly*, 169: 45–63.

Baker, S. (1997) 'The Evolution of European Union Environmental Policy: From Growth to Sustainable Development?', in S. Baker, M. Kousis, D. Richardson and S. Young (eds) *The Politics of Sustainable Development: Theory, Policy, and Practice within the European Union*, London: Routledge.

—— (2000) 'The European Union: Integration, Competition, Growth – and Sustainability', in W. M. Lafferty and J. Meadowcroft (eds) *Implementing Sustainable Development: Strategies and Initiatives in High Consumption Societies*, Oxford: Oxford University Press.

—— (2003) 'Environmental Policy in the European Union: Towards Sustainable Development?', The Norman Vig Lecture, presented at Carlton College, USA, February.

Baker, S. and McCormick, J. (2004) 'Sustainable Development: Comparative Understandings and Responses', in N. J. Vig, and M. C. Faure (eds) *Green Giants? Environmental Policy of the United States and the European Union*, Cambridge MA: MIT Press.

Baker, S. and Welsh, I. (2000) 'Differentiating Western Influences on Transition Societies in Eastern Europe: A Preliminary Exploration', *Journal of European Area Studies*, 8: 79–103.

Balanya, B., Doherty, A., Hoedeman, O., Ma'anit, A. and Wesselius, E. (2000) *Europe Inc: Regional and Global Restructuring and the Rise of Corporate Power*, London: Pluto Press/Corporate European Observatory.

Barling, D. (2000) 'Regulating GM foods in the 1980s and 1990s', in D. F. Smith and J. Phillips (eds) *Food, Science, Policy and Regulation in the Twentieth Century: International and Comparative Perspectives*, London: Routledge.

Barro, Robert J. and Jong-Wha Lee (2002) 'IMF Programs: Who is Chosen and What Are the Effects?,' NBER Working Papers 8951, http://www.nber.org/papers/w8951.pdf (accessed 10 January 2006).

Batt, J. (1997) 'The International Dimension of Democratization in Hungary, Slovakia and the Czech Republic', in G. Pridham, E. Herring and G. Sanford (eds) *Building Democracy? The International Dimension of Democratization in Eastern Europe*, London: Leicester University Press.

Bauer, M. W. and Gaskell, G. (2002) *Biotechnology: The Making of a Global Controversy*, Cambridge: Cambridge University Press.

Bauman, Z. (2004) *Europe: An Unfinished Adventure*, Cambridge: Polity.

Beck, U. (1992) *Risk Society: Towards a New Modernity*, London: Sage.

—— (2003) 'Understanding the Real Europe', *Dissent*, Summer: 32–38.

Beitz, C. R. (1999) *Political Theory and International Relation*, revised edition, Princeton: Princeton University Press.

Berenskoetter, F. (2004) 'Mapping the Mind Gap: A Comparison of US and EU Security Strategies', *Working Paper 3*, Fornet – European Foreign Policy Research Network. Available online: http://www.fornet.info/CFSPforumworkingpapers.html (accessed 20 March 2005).

Berthélemy, J. C. and Tichit, A. (2004) 'Bilateral donors' aid allocation decisions – a three dimensional panel analysis', *International Review of Economics and Finance*, 13: 253–274.

Beveridge, F., Sue, N. and Kylie, S. (2000) 'Mainstreaming and the Engendering of Policy: a Means to an End?', *Journal of European Public Policy*, 7: 385–405.

Bhagwati, J. (1996) 'The Demands to Reduce Domestic Diversity among trading nations', in J. Bhagwati, and R. Hudec, (eds) (1996) *Fair Trade and Harmonization. Prerequisites for Free Trade?*, vol. 1 Economic Analysis, vol. 2 Legal Analysis, Cambridge MA: MIT Press.

Bodansky, D. (2002) 'US Climate Policy After Kyoto: Elements for Success', paper presented at the BP Transatlantic Programme Workshop, *The Kyoto Protocol without America: Finding a Way forward after Marrakech*, European University Institute, Florence, 21–22 June.

Boehmer-Christiansen, S. A. (1995) 'Britain and the International Panel on Climate Change: The Impact of Scientific Advise on Global Warming', *Environmental Politics*, 4: 1–18.

Bonanate, L. (1992) *Ethics and International Politics*, Oxford: Polity.

—— (2001) '2001: la politica interna del mondo', *Teoria politica*, 17: 3–26.

Bono (2005) European Commission Press Conference on the 9th July 2005 with President Barroso & Bono.

Booth, C. and Bennett, C. (2002) 'Gender Mainstreaming in the European Union: Towards a New Conception and Practice of Equal Opportunities?', *The European Journal of Women's Studies*, 9: 430–446.

Bourdieu, P. (1977) *Outline of a Theory of Practice*, Cambridge: Cambridge University Press.

—— (1990) *In Other Words: Essays toward a Reflexive Sociology*, Cambridge: Polity Press.

Bowring, F. (2003) *Science, Seeds & Cyborgs: Biotechnology and the Appropriation of Life*, London: Verso.

Bratton, S. P. (1984) 'Christian Ecotheology & the Old Testament', *Environmental Ethics*, 6: 195–209.

Brenton, P. (2000) 'The Changing Nature and Determinants of EU Trade Policies', *CEPS Working Document*, 150, October.

Bretherton, C. (1996) 'Universal Human Rights: Bringing People into Global Politics?', in C. Bretherton and G. Ponton (eds) *Global Politics. An Introduction*, Oxford: Blackwell Publishers: 247–273.

—— (1999) 'Women and Transformation in CEEC: Challenging the EUs Women's Policy?', in M. Mannin (ed.) *Pushing Back the Boundaries: The EU and Central and Eastern Europe*, Manchester: Manchester University Press.

—— (2001) 'Gender Mainstreaming and EU Enlargement: Swimming against the Tide?', *Journal of European Public Policy*, 8: 60–81.

—— (2002) 'Gender Mainstreaming and Enlargement: The EU as Negligent Actor?', paper presented to conference on *The European Union in International Affairs*, National

Europe Center, Australian National University, 3–4 July, National Europe Center Paper no. 23.

Bretherton, C. and Vogler, J. (1999) *The European Union as a Global Actor*, London: Routledge.

—— (2006) *The European Union as a Global Actor*, 2nd edition, London: Routledge.

Breuning, M. (1995) 'Words and Deeds: Foreign Assistance Rhetoric and Policy Behavior in the Netherlands, Belgium, and the United Kingdom', *International Studies Quarterly*, 39: 235–254.

Brown, C. (1997) *Understanding International Relations*, Basingstoke: Macmillan.

—— (2001) 'Ethics, Interests and Foreign Policy', in K. E. Smith and M. Light (eds) *Ethics and Foreign Policy*, Cambridge: Cambridge University Press.

—— (2002) 'On Morality, Self-Interest and Foreign Policy', *Government and Opposition*, 37: 173–189.

Brundtland, G. H. (1987) *Our Common Future: Report of the World Commission on Environment and Development*, Oxford: Oxford University Press.

Bryner, G. (2000) 'The United States: Sorry, Not Our Problem', in W. M. Lafferty and J. Meadowcroft (eds) *Implementing Sustainable Development: Strategies and Initiatives in High Consumption Societies*, Oxford: Oxford University Press.

Bull, H. (1966) 'International Theory: The Case for the Classical Approach', *World Politics*, 38: 361–377.

—— (1968) 'The Grotian Conception of International Society', in H. Butterfield and M. Wight (eds) *Diplomatic Investigations*, Cambridge MA: Harvard University Press.

—— (1977) *The Anarchical Society: A Study of Order in World Politics*, London: Macmillan.

Bulletin of the EC, (1990) *Declaration of the European Council on the Environmental Imperative*, 23: 16–18.

Burgess, P. (2002) 'What's so European about the European Union?', *European Journal of Social Theory*, 5(4): 467–481.

Burgoon, B. (2001) 'Partnership and Competition of US and European Embedded Liberalisms', *The International Spectator*, 36: 61–76.

Bush, G. W. (2001) 'Restoring US Leadership in Support of Free Trade', speech to the Farm Journal Forum in Washington, DC, 28 November. Available online: http://www.uswheat.org/wheatLetter/doc/69D8FAE7C07983CF85256F8100589583?OpenDocument (accessed 14 July 2005).

—— (2002) *The President's State of the Union Address*, The United States Capitol, Washington DC, 29 January. Available online: http://www.whitehouse.gov/news/releases/2002/01/20020129–11.html (accessed 25 January 2005).

—— (2005) *Second Inauguration Speech*, 20 January. Available online: http://www.whitehouse.gov/news/releases/2005/01/20050120–1.html (accessed 25 January 2005).

Buttel, F. (2000) 'The recombinant BGH controversy in the United States: towards a new consumption politics of food', *Agriculture and Human Values*, 17: 5–20.

Buzan, B. (1991) *People, States, and Fear: An Agenda for International Security Studies in the Post-Cold War Era*, London: Harvester Wheatsheaf.

—— (2001) 'The English School: An Underexploited Resource in IR', *Review of International Studies*, 27: 471–488.

Buzan, B. and Waever, O. (2003) *Regions and Powers: The Structure of International Security*, Cambridge: Cambridge University Press.

Buzan, B., Waever, O. and de Wilde J. (1998) *Security: A New Framework for Analysis*, Boulder CO: Lynne Rienner.

CAFOD (2001) 'The World Trade Organisation: The EU Mandate Post-Seattle', CAFOD Submission to the House of Lords European Union Committee, 12 October

2001. Available online: http://www.cafod.org.uk/policy/policyeurunion.shtml (accessed 11 January 2006).

Cahill, A. (2003a) 'Third World planning programmes under threat', *Irish Examiner*, 6 May.

—— (2003b) 'EU says condoms are best way to fight AIDS', *Irish Examiner*, 21 October.

Calhoun, C. (2001) 'The Virtues of Inconsistency: Identity and Plurality in the Conceptualization of Europe', in L. E. Cederman (ed.) *Constructing Europe's identity: the external dimension*, Boulder CO: Lynne Rienner Publishers.

Caplan, R. (1998) 'International Diplomacy and the Crisis in Kosovo', *International Affairs*, 74: 745–761.

Carlsnaes, Walter, Sjursen, Helene, and White, Brian (2004) *Contemporary European Security Policy*, London: Sage.

Carpenter, T. G. (2000) 'Kosovo as an Omen: the Perils of the "New NATO"', in T. G. Carpenter (ed.) *NATO's Empty Victory: a Postmortem on the Balkan War*, Washington DC, Cato Institute.

Cederman, L. E. (ed.) (2001) *Constructing Europe's Identity: the External Dimension*, Boulder & London: Lynne Rienner.

Cerutti, F. (2001a) 'Towards the Political Identity of the Europeans: an Introduction', in Furio Cerutti and Enno Rudolph (eds) *A Soul for Europe*, Volume I: *On the Political and Cultural Identity of the Europeans. A Reader*, Leuven: Peeters.

—— (2001b) 'Peace and War in the European Conscience', in Furio Cerutti and Enno Rudolph (eds) *A Soul for Europe*, Volume I: *On the Political and Cultural Identity of the Europeans: A Reader*, Leuven: Peeters.

—— (2003) 'A Political Identity of the Europeans?', *Thesis Eleven*, 72: 26–45.

—— (2005) 'Constitution and Political Identity in Europe', in U. Liebert (ed.) *Postnational Constitutionalisation in the Enlarged Europe: Foundations, Procedures, Prospects*, Baden-Baden: Nomos.

Cerutti, F. and Rudolph, E. (eds) (2001a) *A Soul for Europe*, Volume I: *On the Political and Cultural Identity of the Europeans. A Reader*, Leuven: Peeters.

—— (2001b) *A Soul for Europe*, Volume II: *On the Cultural and Political Identity of the Europeans. An Essay Collection*, Leuven: Peeters.

Chambre de commerce et d'industrie de Paris (2003) 'Antidumping: Quelles améliorations pour cet instrument de défense nécessaire aux entreprises', Rapport de la Commission du commerce international.

Cheah, P. and Robbins, B. (1998) *Cosmopolitics: Thinking and Feeling beyond the State*, Minneapolis MN: University of Minnesota Press.

Chesters, G. C. and Welsh, I. (2005) 'Complexity and Social Movement: Process and Emergence in Planetary Action Systems', *Theory Culture and Society*, 25(5): 187–211.

Chomsky, N. (1992) *Deterring Democracy*, New York: Vintage Books.

Ciampi, C. A. (2002) Speech of the President of the Republic at the European University Institute of Florence, 26 September 2002.

Claude, I. (1993) 'The Tension Between Principle and Pragmatism in International Relations', *Review of International Studies*, 19: 215–226.

Coleman, A. (2004) 'Transparency Trap: Antidumping and the Pursuit of Closer Trade Cooperation with the EU and the WTO', *Collegium Revue*, 29: 49–78.

Coles, J. (2000) *Making Foreign Policy. A Certain Idea of Britain*, London: John Murray.

Collins, H. and Pinch, T. (1996) *The Golem: What Everyone Should Know about Science*, Cambridge: Cambridge University Press.

Common Foreign and Security Policy [CFSP] (1998) *Common Position 98/240/CFSP*, Brussels, 19 March.

Commission (1973) 'First Programme of Action on the Environment', *Official Journal*, vol. 16, no. C112, 20.12.73.

—— (1982) *Memorandum on the Community's Development Policy*, COM (82) 640 final, Brussels: European Commission.

—— (1987) 'Fourth Environmental Action Programme', *Official Journal*, C 328. 7.12.87.

—— (1992a) *Development Cooperation in the Run-up to 2000*, SEC (92) 915 final, Brussels: European Commission: May. Available online: http://europa.eu.int/comm/development/body/legislation/recueil/en/en01/en011.htm (accessed 4 January 2005).

—— (1992b) *Towards Sustainability: A European Community Programme of Policy and Action in Relation to the Environment*, (1992–2000) COM (92) 23 final.

—— (1994) *Community Support for Structural Adjustment in ACP countries: Towards the Consolidation and Strengthening of a Realistic and Concerted Approach*, COM (94) 447 final, Brussels: European Commission: October.

—— (1995a) *A long-term policy for China–Europe relations*, Communication from the Commission, COM (95) 279.

—— (1995b) *On the inclusion of respect for democratic principles and human rights in agreements between the Community and third countries*, COM (95) 216 final, Brussels, 23 May.

—— (1996a) *Green Paper on the EU–ACP Relations: A New Partnership for the 21st Century – Challenges and options for a new partnership*, Brussels: European Commission: November. Available online: http://europa.eu.int/comm/development/body/publications/l-vert/lv_en.htm (accessed 4 January 2005).

—— (1996b) *Progress Report from the Commission on the Implementation of the European Community Programme of Policy and Action in relation to the Environment and Sustainable Development 'Toward Sustainability'*, COM (95) 624 final.

—— (1997a) *Agenda 2000: For a Stronger and Wider Europe*, DOC 97/6, Strasbourg, 15 July.

—— (1997b) *Agenda 2000: Commission Opinion on Romania's Application for Membership of the European Union*, DOC 97/18, Brussels, 15 July.

—— (1997c) *Agenda 2000: Commission Opinion on Slovakia's Application for Membership of the European Union*, DOC 97/20, Brussels, 15 July.

—— (1997d) *Ritt Bjerregaard Speech*, no. 275, 8 December, Commission Spokesman Services.

—— (1997e) *The EU Approach for Kyoto*, Brussels, Commission of the European Communities.

—— (1997f) *The Energy Dimension of Climate Change*, COM (97) 196.

—— (1998) *Building a Comprehensive Partnership with China*, Communication from the Commission, COM (98) 181 final.

—— (2000a) *White Paper on Reforming the Commission*, COM (2000) 200, Brussels: European Commission: March.

—— (2000b) 'DG Enlargement', *PHARE Annual Report 2000*, Available online: http://europa.eu.int/comm/enlargement/pas/phare/programmes/index.htm (accessed 11 January 06).

—— (2000c) *Towards a European Climate Change Programme*, COM (2000) 88 final.

—— (2000d) *The European Community's Development Policy*, COM (2000) 212 final, Brussels: European Commission: April.

—— (2000e) *Communication on the Precautionary Principle*, COM (2000) 1 final.

—— (2000f) *Reinvigorating the Barcelona Process*, COM (2000) 497 final, Brussels, 6 September.

—— (2000g) *On the Implementation of Measures Intended to Promote Observance of Human Rights and Democratic Principles in External Relations for 1996–1999*, COM (2000) 726 final, Brussels, 14 November.

—— (2001a) *Environment 2010: Our Future, Our Choice*, COM (2001) 31 final.

—— (2001b) *The European Union's Role in Promoting Human Rights and Democratization in Third Countries*, Communication from the Commission to the Council and the European Parliament, 8 May 2001, COM (2001) 252 final.

—— (2001c) 'Etude qualitative des perceptions de la mondialisation par les citoyens de 7 Etats-Membres de l'Union européenne (France, Allemagne, Espagne, Royaume-Uni, Grèce, Irlande, Suède)', OPTEM, study commissioned by DG Trade.

—— (2001d) 'EU Farm Commissioner Fischer: Strong backing from over 40 countries for non-trade concerns in agriculture', DG Agriculture Press Release, IP/01/1542, 10 November 2001.

—— (2001e) *Annual Report of the Meda programme 2000*, COM (2001) Document number and date unavailable, Brussels, Available: http://europa.eu.int/comm/europeaid/reports/meda_2000_en.pdf (accessed 4 January 2005).

—— (2001f) *On Conflict Prevention*, COM (2001) 211 final, Brussels, 11 April.

—— (2001g) *The European Union's Role in promoting human rights and democratization in third countries*, COM (2001) 252 final, Brussels, 8 May.

—— (2001h) *Report on the Implementation of the European Initiative for Democracy and Human Rights in 2000*, SEC (2001) 801, Brussels, 22 May.

—— (2001i) *Communication from the Commission: European Climate Change Programme: Action Plan*, COM (2001) 580.

—— (2001j) 'Programme of Action for the mainstreaming of gender equality in Community Development Co-operation', COM (2001) 295 final.

—— (2002a) *Communication from the Commission: European Governance: Better Law Making*, COM (2002) 275, final.

—— (2002b) *Communication from the Commission on Impact Assessment*, COM (2002) 276, final.

—— (2002c) *Communication from the Commission Consultation Document: Towards a reinforced culture of consultation and dialogue-proposal for general principles and minimum standard for consultation of interested parties by the Commission*, COM (2002) 277 final.

—— (2002d) *Communication from the Commission: Action Plan 'Simplifying and improving the regulatory environment'*, COM (2002) 277, final.

—— (2002e) *Communication: Life Sciences and Biotechnology – A Strategy for Europe*, COM (2002) 27 final, 23.1.2002, Brussels.

—— (2002f) *The Stabilisation and Association Process for South East Europe*, First Annual Report, COM (2002) 163 final, Brussels, 4 April.

—— (2003a) *A maturing partnership – shared interests and challenges in EU–China relations*, Commission Policy paper to the Council and the European Parliament, COM (2003) 533 final.

—— (2003b) *Wider Europe-Neighbourhood: A New Framework for Relations with our Eastern and Southern Neighbours*, Communication from the Commission to the Council and the European Parliament, 11 March 2003, COM (2003) 104 final.

—— (2003c) *Russian Federation: Country Strategy Paper 2004–2006*, Commission Working Document, 21 May 2003.

—— (2003d) *Communication: Life Sciences and Biotechnology – A strategy for Europe Progress Report and Future Orientations*, COM (2003) 96 final, 5.3.2003, Brussels.

—— (2003e) *The European Union and the United Nations: The choice of multilateralism*, Communication from the Commission to the Council and the European Parliament, Brussels, COM (2003) 526 final.

—— (2004) *Communication from the Commission to the Council and the European Parliament on relations with Russia*, Communication to the Council and the European Parliament, COM (2004) 106.

Common Market Law Review [CMLR] (1993) 'Are European Values being Hoovered Away?', Editorial Comment, *Common Market Law Review,* 30: 445–8.

Conference on Security and Cooperation in Europe [CSCE] (1990) *Document of the Copenhagen meeting of the Conference on the Human Dimension of the CSCE.* Available online: http://www.osce.org/documents/odihr/1990/06/13992_en.pdf (accessed 11 January 2006).

Cooper, R. (2003) 'The New Liberal Imperialism', *Guardian Unlimited – The Observer Special Reports.* Available online: www.observer.co.uk/worldview/story/0,11581,680095,00.html (accessed 25 January 2005).

Council of the European Union (1995) *Resolution on Structural Adjustment,* June. Available online: http://europa.eu.int/comm/development/body/legislation/recueil/en/en12/en122.htm (accessed 4 January 2005).

—— (1997) *Application of Conditionality with a view to developing a Coherent EU-Strategy for the Relations with the Countries in the Region,* Annex to Annex III to Council Conclusions, Luxembourg, 29–30 April 1997.

—— (2003) *European Union Annual Report on Human Rights: 2003,* Luxembourg: Office for Publications of the European Communities.

Cox, A. and Chapman, J. (1999) *The European Community external co-operation programme,* Overseas Development Institute/European Commission, Brussels. Available online: http://europa.eu.int/comm/europeaid/evaluation/odi_report_en/index_en.htm (accessed 4 January 2005).

Cox, A. and Healey, J. (2000) *European Development Cooperation and the Poor,* London: Macmillan Press.

Cox, S. (1993) 'Equal Opportunities', in M. Gold (ed.) *The Social Dimension: Employment Policy in the European Community,* London: Macmillan.

Cram, L. (1993) 'Calling the Tune without Paying the Piper? Social Policy Regulation – The role of the Commission in European Community Social Policy', *Policy and Politics,* 21: 135–146.

—— (2001) 'Governance "to Go": Domestic Actors, Institutions and the Boundaries of the Possible', *Journal of Common Market Studies,* 39: 595–618.

Crawford, G. (1996) *Promoting Democracy, Human Rights and Good Governance Through Development Aid: A Comparative Study of the Policies of Four Northern Donors, Leeds,* Centre for Democratisation, University of Leeds.

—— (2001) *Evaluating EU promotion of human rights, democracy and good governance: towards a participatory approach,* DSA European Development Policy Study Group, *Discussion Paper,* no. 20, February.

Cremona, M. (1998) 'The European Union as an International Actor: The Issues of Flexibility and Linkage', *European Foreign Affairs Review,* 3: 67–94.

Daalder, I. H. and O'Hanlon, M. E. (2000) *Winning Ugly: NATO's War to Save Kosovo,* Washington DC: Brookings Institution Press.

Danish Council of Ethics (2004) *Patenting Human Genes and Stem Cells,* Copenhagen.

De Filippis, V. and Losson, C. (2001) 'L'OMC cale à Doha: Confusion hier soir sur la suite à donner à la Conférence', *Les Echos,* 14 November.

Delanty, G. (1995) *Inventing Europe: Idea, Identity, Reality,* London: Macmillan.

Dent, C. (1997) *The European Economy: The Global Context,* London: Routledge.

Desgagné, R. (1995) 'Integrating Environmental Values into the European Convention on Human Rights', *The American Journal of International Law,* 89: 263–294.

Dittmer, L. (2002) 'Globalization and the Twilight of Asian Exceptionalism', in C. Kinnvall and K. Jönsson (eds) *Globalization and Democratization in Asia: The Construction of Identity,* London: Routledge.

Donaldson, T. (1995) 'International Deontology Defended: A Response to Russell Hardin', *Ethics and International Affairs*, 9: 147–154.

Doyle, M. W. (1983) 'Kant, Liberal Legacies and Foreign Affairs', Part 1, *Philosophy and Public Affairs*, 12(3): 205–235.

Duchêne, F. (1972) 'Europe's Role in World Peace', in R. Mayne (ed.) *Europe Tomorrow: Sixteen Europeans Look Ahead*, London: Fontana.

—— (1973) 'The European Community and the Uncertainties of Interdependence', in M. Kohnstamm and W. Hager (ed.) *A Nation Writ Large? Foreign Policy Problems before the European Community*, Basingstoke: Macmillan.

Dunne, T. (1999) *Inventing International Society: A History of the English School*, Basingstoke: Macmillan.

Elgström, O. (2000) 'Lomé and Post-Lomé: Asymmetric Negotiations and the Impact of Norms', *European Foreign Affairs Review*, 5: 175–195.

Elgström, O. and Smith, M. (eds) (2006) *New Roles for the EU in International Politics?*, London: Routledge.

Eliassen, K. A. (ed.) (1998) *Foreign and Security Policy in the European Union*, London: Sage.

Ellul, J. (1964) *The Technological Society*, New York: Vintage Books.

Elman, C. (1996) 'Horses for Courses: Why Not a Neorealist Theory of Foreign Policy?', *Security Studies*, 6: 7–53.

Euro-Mediterranean Conference (1995) *Barcelona Declaration*, Barcelona, 27–28 November.

European Council (1993) *Presidency Conclusions*, Copenhagen European Council, 21–2 June.

—— (1999) *Presidency Conclusions*, Cologne European Council, 3–4 June.

—— (2001) *Laeken Declaration on the Future of Europe*, Attachment to the Presidency Conclusions, European Council Meeting in Laeken, 14–15 December 2001 (SN300/01 ADD1).

—— (2003) *A Secure Europe in a Better World: European Security Strategy*, European Council Meeting in Brussels, 12 December 2003.

European Environment Agency (EEA) (2001) *Late Lessons from Early Warnings: The Precautionary Principle 1896–2000*, Copenhagen: European Environment Agency.

European Group on Ethics in Science and New Technologies [EGE] (2000) *Citizens Rights and New Technology: A European Challenge*, European Group on Ethics in Science and New Technologies, Brussels.

—— (2002) *A History of Patenting Life in the United States with Comparative Attention to Europe and America*, European Group on Ethics in Science and New Technologies, Brussels.

European Parliament (1988) *Criteria for the Assessment of European Fusion Research*, vols I & II, European Parliament-STOA-F1/F2, Luxembourg.

—— (2001) *Report on the Commission Communication on relations between the EU and the Mediterranean region: reinvigorating the Barcelona Process*, Committee on Foreign Affairs, Human Rights, Common Security and Defence Policy, Rapporteur Sami Naïr, A5–0009/2001 final, Brussels 22 January.

—— (2002a) *Human Rights in the World in 2001 and European Union Human Rights Policy*, Annual Report, A5–0106/2002 final.

—— (2002b) *Report on the Commission Communication on Life Sciences and Biotechnology – A Strategy for Europe*, Committee on Industry, External Trade, Research & Energy, A5–0359/2002 FINAL, 23.10.2002.

—— (2002c) *Report on the Commission communication on an EU Strategy towards China*, A5–0076/2002 final.

European Political Cooperation [EPC] (1991) *Guidelines on the Recognition of New States in Eastern Europe and in the Soviet Union*, statement by an extraordinary EPC Ministerial Meeting, Brussels and The Hague, 16 December.

European Union (2005) *Treaty establishing a Constitution for Europe*, as signed in Rome on 29 October 2004 and published in the *Official Journal of the European Union* on 16 December 2004 (C series, No. 310).

Evans, R. (1999) *Macroeconomic Forecasting: A Sociological Appraisal*, London: Routledge.

Eve, R., Horsfall, S. and Lee, M. (1997) *Chaos, Complexity, and Sociology: Myths, Models, and Theories*, London: Sage.

Falk, R. (1995) *On Humane Governance: Towards a New Global Politics*, Cambridge: Polity Press.

Fearon, D. (1998) 'Domestic Politics, Foreign Policy, and Theories of International Relations', *Annual Reviews of Political Science*, 1: 289–213.

Forsberg, T. (2004) 'The EU–Russia Security Partnership: Why the Opportunity was Missed', *European Foreign Affairs Review*, 9: 247–267.

Freeman. A. M. (2003) 'Economics, Incentives, and Environmental Policy', in N. J. Vig and M. E. Kraft (eds) *Environmental Policy: New Directions for the Twenty First Century*, Washington DC: CQ Press, fifth edition.

Frost, M. (2001) 'The Ethics of Humanitarian Intervention: Protecting Civilians to Make Democratic Citizenship Possible', in K. E. Smith and M. Light (eds) *Ethics and Foreign Policy*, Cambridge: Cambridge University Press.

Fuller, G. (1995) 'The Next Ideology', *Foreign Policy*, 98: 145–158.

Functowicz, S. O. and Ravetz, J. (1993) 'Science for the Post-Normal Age', *Futures*, September: 739–755.

Galison, O. and Hevly, B. (eds) (1992) *Big Science: The Growth of Large Scale Research*, Stanford: Stanford University Press.

Garde, P. (1996) 'Après Dayton, le déluge?', *Politique internationale*, 72: 145–166.

Garnett, J. C. (1984) *Commonsense and the Theory of International Politics*, Basingstoke: Macmillan.

Gavin, B. (2001) *The European Union and Globalisation: Towards Global Democratic Governance*, Cheltenham UK: Edward Elgar Publishing.

Geertz, C. (1973) *The Interpretation of Cultures*, New York: Basic Books.

Giddens, A., (1979) *Central Problems in Social Theory: Action, Structure and Contradictions in Social Analysis*, London: Macmillan.

—— (1990) *The Consequences of Modernity*, Cambridge: Polity.

—— (1991) *Modernity and Self Identity*, Cambridge: Polity.

Gilligan, M. (1997) 'Lobbying as a Private Good with Intra-Industry Trade', *International Studies Quarterly*, 41: 455–474.

Ginsberg, R. (2001) *The European Union in International Politics: Baptism by Fire*, Lanham/Boulder CO: Rowman & Littlefield.

Glasner, P. and Rothman, H. (2001) 'New Genetics, new ethics? Globalisation and its discontents', *Health, Risk & Society*, 3: 245–259.

Gnesotto, N. (1994) *Lessons of Yugoslavia*, Chaillot Paper 14, Paris: The Institute for Security Studies of the Western European Union.

Goldstein, J. (1993) *Ideas, Interests, and American Trade Policy*, Ithaca: Cornell University Press.

Goldstein, J. and Keohane, R. (1993) 'Ideas and Foreign Policy: An Analytical Framework', in J. Goldstein and R. Keohane (eds) *Ideas and Foreign Policy: Beliefs, Institutions and Political Change*, Ithaca: Cornell University Press.

Goldstein, J. and 'Keohane, R. (eds) (1993) *Ideas and Foreign Policy. Beliefs, Institutions and Political Change*, New York: Cornell University Press.

Goldstein, J. and Martin, L. (2000) 'Legalization, Trade Liberalization, and Domestic Politics: A Cautionary Note', *International Organization*, 54(3): 603–632.

Gong, G. W (1984) *The Standard of 'Civilization' in International Society*, Oxford: Clarendon Press.

Gough, I. (1998) 'Social Aspects of the European Model and its Economic Consequences', in W. Beck, L. van der Maesen, A. Walker (eds) *The Social Quality of Europe*, Bristol: Polity Press.

Graham, J. D. and Hsia, S. (2002) 'Europe's Precautionary Principle: Promise and Pitfalls', *Journal of Risk Research*, 5: 371–390.

Green, D. and Griffith-Jones, R. (1984) *Eurofutures: The Challenge of Innovation*, London: Butterworth.

Grieco, J. (1990) *Cooperation among Nations: Europe, America and Non-Tariff Barriers to Trade*, Ithaca and London: Cornell University Press.

Griffin, G. and Braidotti, R. (eds) (2002) *Thinking Differently: A Reader in European Women's Studies*, London: Zed Books.

Grilli, E. (1993) *The European Community and the Developing Countries*, World Bank and Johns Hopkins University Press.

Grubb, M. and Gupta, J. (2000) 'Climate Change, Leadership and the EU', in J. Gupta and M. Grubb, (eds) *Climate Change and European Leadership: A Sustainable Role for Europe*, Dordrecht: Kluwer.

Guptka, M. (2005) 'Lamy Seeks Consensus Pitch for WTO Job', *Business Standard India*, 26 February 2005.

Guzzini, S. (1998) *Realism in International Relations and International Political Economy*, London: Routledge.

Haarscher, G. (2001) 'Europe's Soul: Freedom and Rights', in F. Cerutti and E. Rudolph (eds) *A Soul for Europe*, Volume I: *On the Political and Cultural Identity of the Europeans. A Reader*, Leuven, Peeters.

Habermas, J. (1998) *Die postnationale Konstellation und die Zukunft der Demokratie*, Frankfurt am Main: Suhrkamp.

—— (2001) 'Why Europe Needs a Constitution', *New Left Review*, 11: 5–26.

—— (2003a) 'Toward a Cosmopolitan Europe', *Journal of Democracy*, 14: 86–100.

—— (2003b) *The Future of Human Nature*, Oxford: Polity Press.

Haigh, N. (1996) 'Climate Change Policies and Politics in the European Community', in T. O'Riordan and J. Jäger (eds) *Politics of Climate Change: A European Perspective*, London: Routledge.

Halliday, F. (1998) 'Morality in International Affairs: a Case for Robust Universalism', in B. McSweeney (ed.) *Moral Issues in International Affairs: Problems of European Integration*, London: Macmillan Press.

Hampel J., Pfenning, U. and Peters, H. P. (2000) 'Attitudes toward Genetic Engineering', *New Genetics and Society*, 19: 233–249.

Hanson, B. (1998) 'What Happened to Fortress Europe? External Trade Policy Liberalization in the European Union', *International Organization*, 52: 55–85.

Haraway, J. D. (1995) 'Situated Knowledges: the Science Question in Feminism and the Privilege of Partial Perspective', in A. Feenberg and A. Hannay, *Technology and the Politics of Knowledge*, Indiana: Indiana University Press.

Hardin, R. (1995) 'International Deontology', *Ethics and International Affairs*, 9: 133–143.

Havelkova, H. (2000) 'Abstract Citizenship? Women and Power in the Czech Republic', in B. Hobson (ed.) *Gender and Citizenship in Transition*, London: Macmillan.

Hedemann-Robinson, M. (2000) 'Defending the Consumer's Right to a Clean Environment in the Face of Globalisation', *Journal of Consumer Policy*, 23: 25–61.

Held, D. (1995) *Democracy & the Global Order: From the Modern State to Cosmopolitan Governance*, Cambridge: Polity Press.

Hempel, L. C. (2003) 'Climate Change on the Instalment Plan', in N. J. Vig and M. E. Kraft (eds) *Environmental Policy: New Directions for the Twenty First Century*, Washington DC: CQ Press, fifth edition.

Henderson, K. (1999) 'Slovakia and the Democratic Criteria for EU Accession', in K. Henderson (ed.) *Back to Europe: Central and Eastern Europe and the European Union*, London: University College London Press.

Hilgartner, S. (2000) *Science on Stage: Expert Advice as Public Drama*, Stanford: Stanford University Press.

Hill, C. (ed.) (1983) *National Foreign Policies and European Political Co-operation*, London: Allen & Unwin.

—— (1993) 'The Capability – Expectations Gap, or Conceptualizing Europe's International Role', *Journal of Common Market Studies*, 31(3): 305–328.

—— (1998) 'Closing the capability–expectations gap?', in J. Peterson and H. Sjursen, (eds) *A Common Foreign Policy for Europe? Competing visions of the CFSP*, London: Routledge: 18–38.

Hill, J. (1994) 'The Precautionary Principle and Release of Genetically Modified Organisms (GMOs) to the Environment', in T. O'Riordan and J. Cameron (eds) *Interpreting the Precautionary Principle*, London: Earthscan.

Hoffmann, S. (1996) 'In Defence of Mother Teresa: Morality in Foreign Policy', *Foreign Affairs*, 75(2): 172–175.

—— (1998) *World Disorders: Troubled Peace in the Post-Cold War Era*, Lanham MD: Rowman & Littlefield.

Holland, M. (ed.) (1991) *The Future of European Political Co-operation: Essays on Theory and Practice*, London: Macmillan.

Hollis, M. and Smith, S. (1990) *Explaining and Understanding International Relations*, Oxford: Clarendon Press.

Holsti, K. (1970) 'National Role Conceptions in the Study of Foreign Policy', *International Studies Quarterly*, 14: 233–309.

Holton, R. J. (1998) *Globalization and the Nation-State*, London: Macmillan.

Hoogvelt, A. (2001) *Globalization and the Postcolonial World: The Political Economy of Development*, 2nd edition, Basingstoke: Palgrave.

Hoskyns, C. (1994) 'Gender Issues in International Relations: the Case of the European Community', *Review of International Studies*, 20: 225–239.

—— (1996) *Integrating Gender: Women, Law and Politics in the European Union*, London: Verso.

—— (2004) 'Gender Perspectives', in A. Wiener and T. Diez (eds) *European Integration Theory*, Oxford: Oxford University Press: 217–236.

Howorth, J. (2001) 'European Defence and the Changing Politics of the European Union: Hanging Together or Hanging Separately?', *Journal of Common Market Studies*, 39: 765–789.

—— (2004) 'Discourse, Ideas and Epistemic Communities in European Security and Defence Policy', *West European Politics*, 27: 211–234.

Hubel, H. (2004) 'The EU's Three-level Game in Dealing with Neighbours', *European Foreign Affairs Review*, 9: 347–362.

Human Rights Watch (1999) *Human Rights Watch World Report 1999*, New York: Human Rights Watch.

Hume, J. (1998) The Nobel Lecture given by The Nobel Peace Prize Laureate 1998 – John Hume, Oslo, 10 December 1998. Available online: http://www.nobel.no/eng_lect_98h.html (accessed 11 January 06).

Huntington, S. (1993) 'The Clash of Civilizations?', *Foreign Affairs*, 72: 22–49.

—— (1996) *The Clash of Civilizations and the Remaking of World Order*, New York: Simon and Schuster.

Hutton, W. (2002) *The World We Are In*, London: Little Brown.

Ifestos, P. (1987) *European Political Co-operation: Towards a Framework of Supranational Diplomacy?*, Aldershot: Gower.

Ikenberry, J. (1996) 'The Myth of Post-Cold War Chaos', *Foreign Affairs*, 75(3): 79–91.

International Commission on the Balkans [ICB] (1996) *Unfinished Peace*, New York: Carnegie Endowment for International Peace.

ISA Consult, European Institute, Sussex University, and GJW Europe (1997) *Evaluation of the PHARE and TACIS Democracy Programme 1992–1997: Final Report*, Brighton and Hamburg.

Jackson, R. H. (2000) *The Global Covenant: Human Conduct in a World of States*, Oxford: Oxford University Press.

Jasanoff, S. (1993) 'Bridging the Two Cultures of Risk Analysis', *Risk Analysis*, 13: 123–129.

Jiaxuan, T. (2000) 'China in a Changing World', *World Affairs*, 4(3): 14–30.

Johnston, A. (1996) 'Cultural Realism and Strategy in Maoist China', in Katzenstein P. J. (ed.) *The Culture of National Security: Norms and Identity in World Politics*, New York: Columbia University Press: 216–268.

Jones, R. E. (1981) 'The English School of international Relations: A Case for Closure', *Review of International Studies* 7: 1–13.

Jørgensen, K. E. (ed.) (1997) *European Approaches in Crisis Management*, The Hague: Kluwer Law International.

—— (1998) 'The European Union's Performance in World Politics: How Should we Measure Success?', in J. Zielonka (ed.) *Paradoxes of European Foreign Policy*, The Hague: Kluwer Law International.

Jupille, J. and Caporaso, J. A. (1998) 'States, Agencies and Rules: The European Union in Global Environmental Politics', in C. Rhodes (ed.) *The European Union in the World Community*, London: Lynne Rienner.

Kagan, R. (2003) *Paradise & Power: America and Europe in the New World Order*, London, Atlantic Books.

Kaldor, M., Anheier, H. and Glasius, M. (eds) (2004) *Global Civil Society 2004*, Oxford: Oxford University Press.

Kant, I. (1795/1991) *Political Writings*, Cambridge: Cambridge University Press.

Karatnycky, A. (2004) 'The 2003 Freedom House Survey: National Income and Liberty', *Journal of Democracy*, 15(1): 82–93.

Karkutli, N. and Bützler, D. (1999) *Evaluation of the MEDA Democracy Programme 1996–1998: Final Report*, Brussels, April.

Keck, M. and Sikkink K. (1998) *Activists Beyond Borders: Advocacy Networks in International Politics*, Ithaca NY: Cornell University Press.

Kennan, G. F. (1995) 'On American Principles', *Foreign Affairs*, 74(2): 116–126.

Keohane, R. (1989) *International Institutions and State Power. Essays in International Relations Theory*, Boulder CO: Westview Press.

Keukeleire, S. (2000) *The European Union as a Diplomatic Actor*, Discussion paper 71, Centre for the Study of Diplomacy, University of Leicester.

—— (2001) 'Directorates in the CFSP/CESDP of the European Union: A Plea for "Restricted Crisis Management Groups"', *European Foreign Affairs Review*, 6: 75–101.

—— (2002) 'Reconceptualizing (European) Foreign Policy: *Structural Foreign Policy*', paper presented at the first pan-European Conference on European Union Politics, Bordeaux, 26–28 September 2002. Available online: http://soc.kuleuven.be/iieb/docs/ECPR-UACES-Keukeleire.pdf (accessed 11 January 2006).

Kinnvall, C. (2002) 'Analyzing the Global–Local Nexus', in C. Kinnvall and K. Jönsson (eds) *Globalization and Democratization in Asia: The Construction of Identity*, London: Routledge.

Kleinman, M. (2002) *A European Welfare State? European Union Social Policy in Context*, Basingstoke: Palgrave.

Klintman, M. and Boström, M. (2004) 'Framing of Science and Ideology: Organic Food Labelling in the US & Sweden', *Environmental Politics*, 13: 612–634.

Knudsen, T. B. (1999) *Humanitarian Intervention and International Society*, PhD thesis, Aarhus: Department of Political Science.

Koyre, A. (1957) *From the Closed World to the Infinite Universe*, Baltimore: John Hopkins Press.

Kraft, M. E. and Vig, N. (2003) 'Environmental Policy form the 1970s to the Twenty-First Century', in N. J. Vig and M. E. Kraft (eds) *Environmental Policy: New Directions for the Twenty First Century*, Washington DC: CQ Press, fifth edition.

Krämer, L. (2002) 'Development of Environmental Policies in the United States and Europe: Convergence of Divergences?', paper presented at the *Green Giants? Environmental Policy of the United States and the European Union*, Conference, European University Institute, Florence.

Krasner, Stephen (1982) 'Structural Causes and Regime Consequences: Regimes as Intervening Variables', *International Organization*, 36(2): 185–205.

Kratochwil, F. (1982) 'On the Notion of "Interest" in International Relations', *International Organization*, 36: 1–30.

Kratochwil, F. and Ruggie J. G. (1986) 'International Organization: A State of the Art on the Art of the State', *International Organization*, 40: 753–775.

Kyi Aung, S. S. (1995) 'Freedom, Development and Human Worth', *Journal of Democracy*, 6: 11–19.

Lahiri S. and Raimondos-Møller P. (2000) 'Lobbying by Ethnic Groups and Aid Allocation', *Economic Journal*, 110: 62–79.

Laidi, Z. (2004) 'Quand le patronat libéral s'insurge contre le Commissaire Pascal Lamy à propos de l'OMC et du Social: Choisir les preferences collectives', *Libération*, 11 May 2004.

Lamy, P. (1999a) 'US–EU Relations – Bilateral and Multilateral Issues', European American Business Council, Washington DC, October 1999.

—— (1999b) 'World Trade Organisation Ministerial Conference in Seattle Appraisal and prospects', speech to the European Parliament Plenary Session in Strasbourg, France, 13 December 1999. Available online: http://europa.eu.int/comm/archives/commission_1999_2004/lamy/speeches_articles/spla08_en.htm (accessed 11 January 2006).

—— (2000) 'Le textile est un secteur majeur de l'économie européenne', Speech delivered at the Groupe d'études sur l'Industrie Textiles Habillement, Assemblée Nationale, Paris, 12 December 2000.

—— (2002) 'Europe's Role in Global Governance: The Way Ahead', Speech delivered at Humbolt University, Berlin, 6 May 2002, DG Trade website, speeches and articles.

—— (2004a) 'Europe and the Future of Economic Governance', *Journal of Common Market Studies*, 42, 1: 5–21.

—— (2004b) 'The Emergence of Collective Preferences in International Trade: Implications for Regulating Globalisation', article by Pascal Lamy for the DG Trade Conference of 15 September 2004.

Lamy, P. and Fischler, F. (2001) 'The 4th WTO Ministerial Conference, 9–14 November 2001, Doha, Qatar – Assessment of the results for the EU', information note to the European Commission, 19 November 2001.

Lan, Y. (2004) 'The European Parliament and the China–Taiwan Issue: An Empirical Approach', *European Foreign Affairs Review*, 9: 115–140.

Lane, J. and Ersson, S. (2002) *Culture & Politics: A Comparative Approach*, Aldershot: Ashgate.

Lehtinen, T. (1997) 'The Development Cooperation of the European Union between Conditionality and Dialogue: The Convention of Lomé', University of Helsinki, mimeo. Available online: http://www.valt.helsinki.fi/kvtok/1997/2581.htm (accessed January 2005).

—— (2001) 'Reforming European Development Co-operation: What do the Practitioners Think?', ECDPM, *Discussion Paper*, no. 23.

Levidow, L. and Carr, S. (1999) 'Biotechnology Regulation: De/Politicizing Uncertainty', in Fairweather *et al.* (ed.) *Environmental Futures*, London: Macmillan: 153–168.

Levidow, L., Carr, S. and Weild, D. (2000) 'Genetically Modified Crops in the EU: Regulatory Conflicts as Precautionary Opportunities', *Journal of Risk Research*, 3: 261–270.

Levy, D., Pensky, M. and Torpey, J. (eds) (2005) *Old Europe, New Europe, Core Europe: Transatlantic Relations After the Iraq War*, London: Verso Books.

Lia, B. (1999) 'Security Challenges in Europe's Mediterranean Periphery – Perspectives and Policy Dilemmas', *European Security*, 8: 27–56.

Libération, AFP and Reuters (2001) 'Projet de déclaration finale: Des accords sur les médicaments et le textile', *Libération*, 13 November.

Linklater, A. (1998) *The Transformation of Political Community*, Cambridge: Polity Press.

Lister, M. (1997) *The European Union and the South: Relations with Developing Countries*, London: Routledge.

—— (1998a) *The EU and the Developing World*, Basingstoke: Palgrave.

—— (1998b) 'Europe's New Development Policy', in M. Lister (ed.) *European Union Development Policy*, London: St. Martins Press.

—— (2003) 'Gender, Development and EU Foreign Policy', in British Overseas NGOs for Development (BOND) *Europe in the World: Essays on EU Foreign, Security and Development Policies*, London: BOND: 95–97.

Löfstedt, R. (2004) 'The Swing of the Regulatory Pendulum in Europe: From Precautionary Principle to Regulatory Impact Analysis', *The Journal of Risk and Uncertainty*, 28: 237–260.

Lombardo, E. (2003) 'EU Gender Policy: Trapped in the "Wollstonecraft Dilemma"?', *European Journal of Women's Studies*, 10: 159–180.

Loquai, C. (1996) 'The Europeanisation of Development Co-operation: Coordination, Complementarity, Coherence', ECDPM, *Working Paper*, no. 13.

Luard, E. (1986) *War in International Society*, London: Tauris.

Lucarelli, S. (2000) *Europe and the Breakup of Yugoslavia: A Political Failure in Search of a Scholarly Explanation*, The Hague: Kluwer Law International.

—— (2002a) *Peace and Democracy: The Rediscovered Link. The EU, NATO and the European System of Liberal-Democratic Security Communities. Final Report*, NATO Euro-Atlantic Partnership Council Individual Research Fellowships, 2000–02 Programme. Available online: http://www.nato.int/acad/fellow/00–02/f00–02.htm (accessed 26 January 2005).

—— (2002b) 'Unione Europea, NATO e la costruzione di comunità di sicurezza demo-cratiche in Europa Centro-orientale', *Teoria Politica*, 18: 87–120.

—— (2003) 'La politica estera di un attore in via di definizione. L'Unione e la guerra nella ex Jugoslavia', in S. Lucarelli (ed.) *La Polis europea: L'Unione europea oltre l'Euro*, Trieste: Asterios.

Lukic, R. and Lynch, A. (1996) 'La paix américaine pour les Balkans', *Études Internationales*, 27: 553–570.

MacNaghten, P. and Urry, J. (1998) *Contested Natures*, London: Sage.

Macrory, M. and Hession, R., (1996) 'The European Community and Climate Change', in T. O'Riordan and J. Jäger (eds) *Politics of Climate Change: A European Perspective*, London: Routledge.

Mahncke, D. (2001) 'Russia's Attitude to the European Security and Defence Policy', *European Foreign Affairs Review*, 6: 427–436.

Majone, G. (1996) *Regulating Europe*, London: Routledge.

—— (2001) 'What Price Safety? The Precautionary Principle and its Policy Implications', unpublished paper from the European University Institute, Florence.

Mandelson, P. (2004) 'European Parliament Hearings: Answers to Questionnaire for Commissioner Designate Mr Peter Mandelson (Trade) Part B – Specific questions', European Parliamentary Hearings, 15 November 2004.

Mangott, G. (2001) 'Farewell to Russia: The Decay of a Superpower', in Gärtner, H., Hyde-Pryce, A. and Reiter, E. (eds) *Europe's New Security Challenges*, London: Lynne Rienner: 379–406.

Manners, I. (2000a) *Normative Power Europe: A Contradiction in Terms?*, Copenhagen Peace Research Institute (COPRI) working paper 38.

—— (2000b) *Substance and Symbolism: An Anatomy of Cooperation in the New Europe*, Aldershot: Ashgate.

—— (2002) 'Normative Power Europe: A Contradiction in Terms?', *Journal of Common Market Studies*, 40, 2: 235–258.

—— (2005) 'The Value of Peace', in M. Aziz and S. Millns (eds) *Values in the Constitution of Europe*, Aldershot: Dartmouth.

—— (2006) *Europe and the World: Between Regional Integration and Globalisation*, Basingstoke: Palgrave.

Manners, I. and Whitman, R. (1998) 'Towards Identifying the International Identity of the European Union: A Framework for Analysis of the EU's Network of Relationships', *Journal of European Integration*, 21: 231–249.

—— (eds) (2000) *The Foreign Policies of European Union Member States*, Manchester: Manchester University Press.

—— (2003) 'The "Difference Engine": Constructing and Representing the International Identity of the European Union', *Journal of European Public Policy*, 10: 380–404.

Mazey, S. (1998) 'The European Union and Women's Rights: From the Europeanization of National Agendas to the Nationalization of a European Agenda', *Journal of European Public Policy*, 5: 131–152.

—— (2000) 'Introduction: Integrating Gender – Intellectual and "Real World" Mainstreaming'. *Journal of European Public Policy*, 7(3): 333–345.

—— (2002) 'Gender Mainstreaming Strategies in the EU: Delivering on an Agenda?', *Feminist Legal Studies*, 10: 227–240.

McDonnell, I., Solignac Lecomte, H. B. and Wegimont, L. (2003) *Public Opinion and the Fight Against Global Poverty*, Paris: OECD Development Centre.

McKinlay, R. D. and Little, R. (1977) 'A Foreign Policy Model of U.S. Bilateral Aid Allocation', *World Politics*, 30: 58–86.

McMurty J. (2002) *Value Wars: The Global Market Versus the Life Economy*, London: Pluto.

McSweeney, B. (ed.) (1998) *Moral Issues in International Affairs: Problems of European Integration*, Basingstoke: Macmillan.

Mead, W. R. (2001) *Special Providence: American Foreign Policy and How it Changed the World*, New York: Knopf.

Meadowcroft, J. (2003) *The Next Step: A Climate Change Briefing for European Decision Makers*, Florence: European University Institute, Robert Schuman Centre, Policy paper, 02/13.

Médecins Sans Frontières, Oxfam, Third World Network, Consumer Project on Technology, Consumers International, Health Action International, The Network (2001) 'Green Light to Put Public Health First at WTO Ministerial Conference in Doha', Joint Statement by Médecins Sans Frontières, Oxfam, Third World Network, Consumer Project on Technology, Consumers International, Health Action International, The Network, 20 November.

Menon, A. (2004) 'From Crisis to Catharsis: ESDP After Iraq', *International Affairs*, 80: 631–648.

Menotti, R. and Balfour R. (2001) *La sicurezza europea dopo il Kosovo*, Gaeta: Artistic & Publishing Company.

Merchant, C. (1983) *The Death of Nature: Women, Ecology and the Scientific Revolution*, San Francisco: Harper & Row.

Messerlin, P. (2001) *Measuring the Costs of Protection in Europe: European Commercial Policy in the 2000s*, Washington: Institute for International Economics.

Meunier, S. (2000) 'What Single Voice? European Institutions and EU–US Trade Negotiations', *International Organization*, 54: 103–135.

Meunier, S. and Nicolaïdis, K. (1999) 'Who Speaks for Europe? The Delegation of Trade Authority in the EU', *Journal of Common Market Studies*, 37: 477–501.

Miaofa, W. (2001) 'Role of China in Establishing a Multipolar World', *World Affairs*, 5(4): 46–57.

Milner, H. (1988) *Resisting Protectionism: Global Industries and the Politics of International Trade*, Princeton: Princeton University Press.

Missiroli A. (2000) *CFSP, Defence and Flexibility*, Chaillot Paper 38, Paris: Institute for Security Studies of the Western European Union.

—— (2001) 'European Security Policy: The Challenge of Coherence', *European Foreign Affairs Review*, 6: 177–196.

—— (2003a) 'La PESC tra Comunità, politiche nazionali e Alleanza Atlantica', in S. Lucarelli (ed.) *La polis europea: L'Unione Europea oltre l'euro*, Trieste: Asterios.

—— (2003b) 'ESDP – Post-Iraq. Building a European Security and Defence Policy: What are the Priorities ?', Lecture given at the International Seminar for Experts, *The Common Foreign and Security Policy of the European Union – What Lessons Can Be Learned from the Iraq Crisis?*, The Cicero Foundation, Paris, June. Available at the Cicero Foundation's website: www.cicerofoundation.org.

Moeller, K. (2002) 'Diplomatic Relations and Mutual Strategic Perceptions: China and the European Union', *The China Quarterly*, 169: 10–32.

Monar, J. (1997) 'Mostar: Three Lessons for the European Union', *European Foreign Affairs Review*, 2: 1–5.

Moravcsik, A. (1998) *The Choice for Europe: Social Purpose and State Power from Messina to Maastricht*, London: UCL Press.

Mosley, P. (1985) 'The Political Economy of Foreign Aid: a Model of the Market for a Public Good', *Economic Development and Cultural Change*, 33: 373–393.

Mushaben, J. M. (2003) 'Girl Power and Gender Mainstreaming: Looking for Peace in New Places through an EU Lens', paper presented to 8th Biennial Conference of the European Union Studies Association, Nashville, TN, 27–29 March.

Myers, R. (1990) 'Metatheoretische und methodologische Betrachtungen zur Theorie der internationalen Beziehungen', in V. Rittberger (ed.) *Theorien der Internationalen Beziehungen, Bestandaufnahme und Forschungsperspektiven*, Opladen: Westdeutscher Verlag.

National Aeronautics and Space Administration (2004) 'NASA Announces Space Radiation Materials Research Grants', press release 04–255, 3 August. Available online: http://www.nasa.gov/home/hqnews/2004/aug/HQ_04255_radiation_grants.html (accessed 14 July 2005).

Nau, H. (2002) *At Home Abroad: Identity and Power in American Foreign Policy*, Ithaca and London: Cornell University Press.

Nelkin, D. (1995) 'Science Controversies: the Dynamics of Public Disputes in the United States', in S. Jasanoff *et al.* (eds) *Handbook of Science and Technology Studies*, London: Sage: 444–456.

Neumann, I. (1997) 'Russia as Europe's Other: Barbarians at the Gate, Gatekeeper and Golden Gate to the Future', in P. J. Burgess (ed.) *Cultural Politics and Political Culture in Postmodern Europe*, Amsterdam: Rodopi: 119–153.

Neumayer, E. (2003) 'The Determinants of Aid Allocation by Regional Multilateral Development Banks and United Nations Agencies', *International Studies Quarterly*, 1: 101–122.

Nielson, P. (2001) *Fighting Poverty and Promoting Development: the EU Strategy*, speech delivered at the Japan National Press Club, Tokyo, 23 January. Available online: http://jpn.cec.eu.int/home/speech_en_Speech200101.php (accessed 4 January 2005).

—— (2003) 'Commission response to queries regarding the establishment of a special unit to monitor anti-abortion activists as reported in Irish Examiner article of 6 May 2003', press statement.

Nöel, A. and Thérein, J. Ph. (1995) 'From Domestic to International Justice: The Welfare State and Foreign Aid', *International Organization*, 49: 523–553.

Novak, M. (1999) 'Human Rights "Conditionality" in Relation to Entry to, and Full Participation in, the EU', in P. Alston (ed.) *The EU and Human Rights*, Oxford: Oxford University Press.

Nuttall, S. (1992) *European Political Co-operation*, New York: Oxford University Press.

O'Brien, R. (2000) *Contesting Global Governance: Multilateral Economic Institutions and Global Social Movements*, Cambridge: Cambridge University Press.

OECD (1996a) *The Story of Official Development Assistance*, Paris.

—— (1996b) *Shaping the 21st Century: The Contribution of Development Co-operation*, Paris.

—— (1998) *Peer Review of the European Community*, OECD Development Co-operation Review Series.

—— (2002a) *Peer Review of the European Community*, OECD Development Co-operation Review Series, June, Paris. Available online: http://www.oecd.org/dac (accessed 27 January 2005).

—— (2002b) *Peer Review of the United States*, OECD Development Co-operation Review Series, September, Paris. Available online: http://www.oecd.org/dac (accessed 27 January 2005).

—— (2003) *Development Co-operation 2002 Report*, The DAC Journal, Paris.

Offen, K. (1992) 'Defining Feminism: A Comparative Historical Approach', in G. Bock and S. James (eds) *Beyond Equality and Difference*, London: Routledge.

—— (2000) *European Feminisms: A Political History, 1700–1950*, Stanford University Press.

Olsen, G. R. (2000) 'Promotion of Democracy as a Foreign Policy Instrument of "Europe": Limits to International Idealism', *Democratization*, 7: 142–167.

Open Society Institute (2002) *Monitoring the EU Accession Process: Equal Opportunities for Women and Men, an Overview*, Budapest: Open Society Institute.

Ostry, S. (2000) 'WTO: Institutional Design for Better Governance, Efficiency, Equity and Legitimacy: The Multilateral Trading System at the Millennium', paper presented at the Kennedy School of Government, Harvard, 2–3 June.

Ott, H. (2003) 'Warning Signs from Delhi: Troubled Waters Ahead for Global Climate Policy', *Yearbook of International Environmental Law*, vol. 13, Oxford: Oxford University Press.

Owen, D. (1995) *Balkan Odyssey*, London: Victor Gollancz.

Oxfam (2001) 'Eight Broken Promises – Why the WTO isn't Working for the World's Poor', Oxfam International Briefing Paper, 9 November.

Paarlberg, R. (1997) 'Agricultural Policy Reform and the Uruguay Round: Synergistic Linkage in a Two-Level Game?', *International Organization*, 51: 413–444.

Padoa-Schioppa, T. (2001) *Europa, forza gentile*, Bologna: Il Mulino.

Pagrotsky, L., Ybema, G., Klingvall, M. I. and Herfkens, E. (2000) 'It's Time for EU Barriers to Fall', *The International Herald Tribune*, 17 October.

Painter, G. and Ulmer, K. (2002) *Everywhere and Nowhere: Assessing Gender Mainstreaming in European Community Development Cooperation*, Brussels: APRODEV and One World Action.

Patten, C. (1998) *East and West*, Basingstoke: Macmillan.

—— (1999) *Declaration on Chechnya*, Speech delivered at the European Parliament, Strasbourg 17 November 1999, SPEECH/99/166.

—— (2002) *China and Europe an important partnership*, Speech delivered at the Cathay Pacific China Trader Award Dinner, Kasteel de Wittenberg, 6 November 2002, SPEECH/02/540.

Patterson, L. A. (2000) 'Biotechnology Policy: Regulating Risks and Risking Regulation', in H. Wallace and W. Wallace (eds) *Policy Making in the EU*, 4th Edition, Oxford: Oxford University Press.

Payne, R. J. (1995) *The Clash with Distant Cultures: Values, Interests, and Force in American Foreign Policy*, Albany NY: State University of New York Press.

Pei, M. (2002) 'China's Governance Crisis', *Foreign Affairs*, 81(5): 96–109.

Petersmann, E.-U. (2002) 'Dispute Prevention and Dispute Settlement in the Transatlantic Partnership: A Research Agenda', Paper presented to the Second Annual Dispute Prevention and Dispute Settlement In the Transatlantic Partnership Conference, RSCAS-BP Chair, European University Institute, Florence, 3–4 May 2002.

Peterson, J. and Sjursen, H. (eds) (1998) *A Common Foreign Policy for Europe?*, London: Routledge.

Pető, A. (2003) *Hungarian Women in Politics 1945–1951*, New York: Columbia University Press.

Piening, C. (1997) *Global Europe: The European Union in World Affairs*, Boulder CO: Lynne Rienner.

Pijpers, A., Regelsberger, E., Wessels, W. and Edwards, G. (eds) (1988) *European Political Co-operation in the 1980s: A Common Foreign Policy for Western Europe*, The Hague: Martinus Nijhoff.

Pollack, M. and Hafner-Burton, E. (2000) 'Mainstreaming Gender in the European Union', *Journal of European Public Policy*, 7: 432–456.

Pollack M. A. and Shaffer, G. C. (2000) 'Biotechnology: The Next Transatlantic Trade War?', *The Washington Quarterly*, 23: 41–54.

Preston, C. (1997) *Enlargement & Integration in the European Union*, London: Routledge.

Prins, G. (2002) *The Heart of War. On Power, Conflict and Obligation in the Twenty-First Century*, London: Routledge.

Prodi, R. (2000) '2000–2005: Shaping the New Europe', Speech to the European Parliament, Strasbourg 15 February 2000, Speech/00/41.

—— (2003) *Discours à l'Université de Tunis*, 1st April. Available online: http://www.deltun.cec.eu.int/fr/interet_spe/Discours_Prodi.pdf (accessed 11 January 2006).

—— (2004) 'Senza la comunità internazionale questo intervento resta illegittimo', *Corriere della Sera*, 27 March 2004, p. 1.

Purdue, D. (2000) *Anti-GentiX: The Emergence of the Anti-GM movement*, Avebury: Aldershot.

Rabkin, J. (2000) 'Is EU Policy Eroding the Sovereignty of Non-Member States?', *Chicago Journal of International Law*, 1: 273–290.

Radaelli, C. (1998) 'Governing European Regulation: The Challenges Ahead', *Robert Schuman Centre Policy Paper*, no. 98/3, EUI, Florence.

Rainelli, M. (2001) 'Réflexions sur la loyauté dans le commerce international', M.-C. Smouts (ed.) *La loyauté dans les relations internationales*, Paris: L'Harmattan.

Raju, C. K. (2003) *The Eleven Pictures of Time: Physics, Philosophy, and Politics of Time Belief*, London: Sage.

Rawls, J. (1999) *The Law of the Peoples*, Cambridge MA: Harvard University Press.

Rees, T. (1998) *Mainstreaming Equality in the European Union: Education, Training and Labour Market Policies*, New York: Routledge.

Reilly, W. (2000) 'Europe's Air of Self-Righteousness', *Financial Times*, 19 December 2000.

Rifkin, J. (2004) *The European Dream*, New York: Polity Press.

Risse, T. (2000) 'Let's Argue!: Communicative Action in World Politics', *International Organization*, 54: 1–39.

Roberts, A. (1999) 'NATO's "Humanitarian War" over Kosovo', *Survival*, 41: 102–123.

Rodrik, D. (1997) *Has Globalization gone too far?*, Washington: Institute for International Economics.

Romeo-Casabona, C. M. (2002) 'Embryonic Stem Cell Research and Therapy: The Need for a Common European Legal Framework', *Bioethics*, 16: 557–567.

Roper, M. (1996) 'Seduction and Succession: Circuits of Homosocial Desire in Management', in D. Collinson and J. Hearn (eds) *Men as Managers, Managers as Men*, London: Sage.

Rosamond, B. (2000) *Theories of European Integration*, Basingstoke: Palgrave.

Rothman, H. (2000) 'Disseminating the principles of the Universal Declaration on the Human Genome and Human Rights', *New Genetics and Society*, 19: 89–104.

Ruggie, J. G. (1991) 'Embedded Liberalism Revisited: Institutions and Progress in International Economic Relations', in E. Adler and B. Crawford (eds) *Progress in Postwar International Relations*, New York: Cambridge University Press.

—— (ed.) (1993) *Multilateralism: The Anatomy of an International Institution*, New York: Columbia University Press.

—— (1993) 'Multilateralism: The Anatomy of an Institution', in J. G. Ruggie (ed.) *Multilateralism Matters: The Theory and Praxis of an Institutional Form*, New York, Columbia University Press.

Russell, A. and Vogler, J. (eds) (2000) *The International Politics of Biotechnology: Investigating Global Futures*, Manchester: Manchester University Press.

Saich, T. (2001) *Governance and Politics in China*, Basingstoke: Palgrave.

Salter, B. and Jones, M. (2002) 'Regulating Human Genetics: the Changing Politics of Biotechnology Governance in the European Union', *Health, Risk & Society*, 4: 325–340.

Santiso, C. (2002) 'The Reform of EU Development Policy: Improving Strategies for Conflict Prevention, Democracy Promotion & Governance Conditionality', CEPS, *Working Paper*, no. 182. Available online: http://shop.ceps.be/downfree.php?item_id=92 (accessed 4 January 2005).

—— (2003) 'Sisyphus in the Castle: Improving European Union Strategies for Democracy Promotion and Governance Conditionality', *European Journal of Development Research*, 15: 1–28.

Schama, S. (1995) *Landscape and Memory*, London: Harper Collins.

Schelling, T. C. (1980) *The Strategy of Conflict*, Cambridge: Harvard University Press.

Schimmelfennig, F. (2003) *The EU, NATO and the Integration of Europe: Rules and Rhetoric*, Cambridge: Cambridge University Press.

Schmitter, P. (1996) 'The Influence of the International Context upon the Choice of National Institutions and Policies in Neo-Democracies', in Whitehead L. (ed.) *The International Dimensions of Democratization*, Oxford: Oxford University Press, 26–54.

Scholte, J. A. (1997) *Globalization: A Critical Introduction*, London: Macmillan.

Schraeder, P. J., Taylor, B., and Hook, S. W. (1988) 'Clarifying the Foreign Aid Puzzle: A Comparison of American, Japanese, French, and Swedish Aid Flows', *World Politics*, 50: 294–323.

Schulten, T. (2002) 'A European Solidaristic Wage Policy?', *European Journal of Industrial Relations*, 8(2): 173–96.

Servaes, J. (2000) 'Reflections on the Differences in Asian and European Values and Communication Modes', *Asian Journal of Communication*, 10: 53–70.

Shaw, J. (2000) 'Integrating Gender: the Challenge of Feminism and the Analyses of EU legal Order', *Journal of European Public Policy*, 7: 406–431.

Sikkink, K. (1993) 'The Power of Principled Ideas: Human Rights Policies in the United States and Western Europe', in J. Goldstein and R. Keohane, *Ideas and Foreign Policy: Beliefs, Institutions and Political Change*, Ithaca: Cornell University Press.

Sjöstedt, G. (1976) *The External Role of the European Community*, London: Saxon House.

Smith, A. (1992) 'National Identity and the Idea of European Unity', *International Affairs*, 68: 55–76.

Smith, H. (2002) *European Union Foreign Policy: What it is and What it does*, London: Pluto Press.

Smith, K. (1998) 'The Use of Political Conditionality in the EU's Relations with Third Countries: How Effective?', *European Foreign Affairs Review*, 3: 253–274.

—— (1999) *The Making of EU Foreign Policy: The Case of Eastern Europe*, London: Macmillan Press.

—— (2000) 'The End of Civilian Power EU: A Welcome Demise or Cause for Concern?', *International Spectator*, 23: 11–28.

—— (2001) 'The EU, Human Rights and Relations with Third Countries: "Foreign Policy" with an Ethical Dimension?', in M. Light and K. Smith (2001) *Ethics and Foreign Policy*, Cambridge: Cambridge University Press.

—— (2003) *European Union Foreign Policy in a Changing World*, Cambridge: Polity Press.

Smith, K. and Light, M. (2001) 'Introduction', in K. Smith and M. Light (eds) *Ethics and Foreign Policy*, Cambridge: Cambridge University Press.

Smith M. (1998) 'The European Union and the Asia-Pacific', in A. McGrew and C. Brook (eds) *Asia-Pacific in the New World Order*, London: Routledge.

Smith, M. E. (2004) 'Institutionalization, Policy Adaptation and European Foreign Policy Coordination', *European Journal of International Relations*, 10: 95–136.

Smith, S. (1992) 'The Forty Year Detour: The Resurgence of Normative Theory in International Relations', *Millennium*, 21: 489–508.

Snyder, J. (1991) *Myth of Empire: Domestic Politics and International Ambition*, Ithaca: Cornell University Press.

Solana, J. (2003) 'Mars and Venus Reconciled: A New Era for Transatlantic Relations', A. H. Gordon Lecture by Javier Solana, EU High Representative for the Common Foreign and Security Policy at the Kennedy School of Government, Harvard University, 7 April 2003.

Strange, S. (1998) 'Who are EU? Ambiguities in the Concept of Competitiveness', *Journal of Common Market Studies*, 36: 101–114.

Strathern, M. (1992) *After Nature: English kinship in the Late Twentieth Century*, Cambridge, Cambridge University Press.

Suganami, H. (2000) 'A New Narrative, a New Subject? Tim Dunne on the "English School"', *Cooperation and Conflict*, 35: 217–226.

Taylor I. and Williams P. (2002) 'The Limits of Engagement: British Foreign Policy and the Crisis in Zimbabwe', *International Affairs*, 78: 547–565.

Teasdale, A. (1993) 'The Life and Death of the Luxembourg Compromise', *Journal of Common Market Studies*, 31: 567–579.

Telò, M. (2001a) 'Reconsiderations: Three Scenarios', in M. Telò (ed.) *European Union and New Regionalism*, London: Ashgate.

—— (ed.) (2001b) *The European Union and New Regionalism. Regional Actors and Global Governance*, London: Ashgate.

—— (2003) 'L'Unione Europea tra neoregionalismo e *governance* globale: tre scenari', in S. Lucarelli (ed.) *La polis europea. L'Unione Europea oltre l'euro*, Trieste: Asterios.

Tesh, S. N. (2000) *Uncertain Hazards: Environmental Activists and Scientific Proof*, Ithaca: Cornell University Press.

Thacker, S. C. (1999) 'The High Politics of IMF Lending', *World Politics*, 52: 38–75.

Therborn G. (2001) 'Europe's Breaks with Itself: The European Economy and the History, Modernity and World Future of Europe', in F. Cerutti, E. Rudolph, *A Soul for Europe*, Volume II: *On the Cultural and Political Identity of the Europeans: An Essay Collection*, Leuven, Peeters.

Thompson, K. W. (1992) *Traditions and Values in Politics and Diplomacy: theory and practice*, Baton Rouge: Louisiana State University Press.

Thompson, K. W. and Myers, R. J. (eds) (1984) *Truth and Tragedy: A Tribute to Hans J. Morgenthau*, New Brunswick: Transaction Books.

Thompson, M. (2001) 'Whatever Happened to "Asian Values"?', *Journal of Democracy*, 12: 154–165.

Tindemans, L., *et al.* (1996) *Unfinished Peace: Report of the International Commission on the Balkans*, Washington, DC, Aspen Institute Berlin & Carnegie Endowment for International Peace.

Toke, D. (2004) *The Politics of GM Food*, London: Routledge.

Triggs, G. (2003) 'Remembering the Life of Edward Said: A Tribute', Women for Palestine Memorial Event, *Ejournalist*, 3. Available online: http://www.ejournalism.au.com/ejournalist/triggs.pdf (accessed 16 June 2005).

UNICE (2001a) 'WTO Agricultural Negotiations – Update of UNICE Position of 1999', UNICE.

—— (2001b) 'New WTO Round – UNICE fact sheets', UNICE. Available online: http://wto.unice.org (accessed 26 January 2005).

—— (2003) 'A Multilateral Cooperation Agreement', UNICE Position 15 May 2003.

United Nations Development Programme [UNHDR] (2004) *Human Development Report 2004*, New York: UN Development Programme.

US Department of Energy (1994) *The Climate Action Plan*, Washington, DC: US DoE, March.

US Presidency (2002) *The National Security Strategy of the United States of America*, Washington: Office of the President, September 2002.

USAID (2000) USAID Strategic Plan 1997 (Revised 2000) Available online: http://www.gm-unccd.org/FIELD/Bilaterals/USA/USA5.pdf (accessed 4 January 2005).

Usui, Y. (2003) 'Evolving Environmental Norms in the European Union', *European Law Journal*, 9: 69–87.

Vahl, R. (1997) *Leadership in Disguise: The Role of the European Commission in EC Decision-Making on Agriculture in the Uruguay Round*, Aldershot: Ashgate.

van den Hoven, A. (2004) 'Assuming Leadership in Multilateral Economic Institutions: The EU's Development Round Discourse and Strategy', *West European Politics*, 27: 256–284.

Vig, N. (2003) 'Presidential Leadership and the Environment', in J. Vig and M. E. Kraft (eds) *Environmental Policy: New Directions for the Twenty First Century*, Washington DC: CQ Press, fifth edition.

Vincent, J. (1986) 'The Response of Europe and the Third World to United States Human Rights Diplomacy', in D. Newson (ed.) *The Diplomacy of Human Rights*, New York: University Press of America.

Vogel, D. (2001) *Ships Passing in the Night: The Changing Politics of Risk Regulation in Europe and the United States*, EUI Working Paper RSC No.2201/16, Florence: University Institute.

—— (2003) 'The WTO, International Trade and Environmental Protection: European and American Perspectives', in Vig, N. J. and M. C. Faure (eds) *Green Giants? Environmental Policy of the United States and the European Union*, Cambridge MA: MIT Press.

Von Moltke, K. and Rahman, A. (1996) 'External Perspectives on Climate Change: A View from the United States and the Third World', in T. O'Riordan and J. Jäger (eds) *Politics of Climate Change: A European Perspective*, London: Routledge.

Voorhoeve, J. J. C. (1979) *Peace, Profits and Principles: A Study of Dutch Foreign Policy*, Hague: Nijhoff.

Vrolojk, C. (2002) 'International Climate Change Management: The EU and Other Industrialised Countries', paper presented at the BP Transatlantic Programme Workshop, *The Kyoto Protocol without America: Finding a Way forward after Marrakech*, European University Institute, Florence, 21–22 June.

Walker, M. (2001) 'The European Union and Russia', in Guttman R. (ed.) *Europe in the New Century: Visions of Emerging Superpower*, Boulder CO: Lynne Rienner: 117–125.

Walker S. (ed.) (1987) *Role Theory and Foreign Policy Analysis*, Durham: Duke University Press.

Wall, D. (1994) *Green History*, London: Routledge.

Walt, S. M. (1987) *The Origins of Alliances*, Ithaca: Cornell University Press.

Walton, J. and Seddon, D. (1994) *Free Markets and Food Riots: The Politics of Global Adjustment*, Oxford: Blackwell.

Waltz, K. W. (1979) *Theory of International Politics*, Reading MA: Addison-Wesley.

—— (1996) 'International Politics is Not Foreign Policy', *Security Studies*, 6(1): 54–7.

Walzer, M. (1995) 'The Politics of Rescue', *Social Research*, 62: 53–70.

Ward, A. (1998) 'Frameworks for Cooperation between the European Union and Third States: a Viable Matrix for Uniform Human Rights Standards?', *European Foreign Affairs Review*, 3: 505–536.

Ward, I. (2003) 'The End of Sovereignty and the New Humanism', *Stanford Law Review*, 55: 2091–112.

Watson, P. (1993) 'The Rise of Masculinism in Eastern Europe', *New Left Review*, 198: 71–82.

—— (2000) 'Politics, Policy and Identity: EU Eastern Enlargement and East West Differences', *Journal of European Public Policy*, 7: 369–384.

Weale, A. (1992) *The New Politics of Pollution*, Manchester: Manchester University Press.

Webber, M. (2001) 'Third-Party Inclusion in European Security and Defence Policy: A Case Study of Russia', *The European Union Review*, 6: 407–426.

Weiler, J. (1998) 'Ideals and Idolatry in the European Construct', in B. McSweeney (ed.) *Moral Issues in International Affairs: Problems of European Integration*, London: Macmillan.

—— (2001) 'I rischi dell'integrazione: *deficit* politico e fine delle diversità', in A. Loretoni (ed.) *Interviste sull'Europa: Integrazione e identità nella globalizzazione*, Roma: Carocci.

Welsh, I. (1994) 'Ignored Reports: Letting the Research Tail Wag the End-User's Dog: the Powell Committee and UK Nuclear Technology', *Science and Public Policy*, 21: 43–53.

—— (1999) 'Risk, "Race", and Global Environmental Regulation', in A. Brah, M. Hickman and M. Mac an Ghail (eds) *Migration and Globalization*, London: BSA/Macmillan.

—— (2000) *Mobilising Modernity: The Nuclear Moment*, London: Routledge.

Welsh, I. and Evans R. J. (1999) 'Xenotransplantation, Risk, Regulation and Surveillance', *New Genetics and Society*, 18: 197–217.

Wendt, A. (1992) 'Anarchy is What States Make of It: The Social Construction of Power Politics', *International Organization*, 46: 393–425.

—— (1994) 'Collective Identity Formation and the International State', *American Political Science Review*, 88: 384–396.

—— (1999) *Social Theory of International Politics*, Cambridge: Cambridge University Press.

Wertz, D. (2002) 'Embryo and Stem Cell Research in the United States', *Molecular Medicine*, 8: 143–146.

Wheeler, N. (2000) *Saving Strangers: Humanitarian Intervention in International Society*, Oxford: Oxford University Press.

White, B. (1999) 'The European Challenge to Foreign Policy Analysis', *European Journal of International Relations*, 5: 37–66.

Whitman, R. (1998) *From Civilian Power to Superpower? The International Identity of the European Union*, London: Macmillan.

Wiener, J. B and Rogers, M. D. (2002) 'Comparing Precaution in the United States and Europe', *Journal of Risk Research*, 5: 317–349.

Wiessala, G. (2002) *The European Union and Asian Countries*, London: Continuum.

Wight, M. (1991) *International Theory: The Three Traditions*, Leicester: Leicester University Press/Royal Institute of International Affairs.

Winch, P. (1994) *The Idea of Social Science*, 2nd Edition, London: Routledge.

Winner, L. (1978; 2nd edition, 1985) *Autonomous Technology: Technics-out-of control as a Theme in Political Thought*, Cambridge MA: MIT Press.

Wivel, A. (2002) 'Realismen efter Waltz: Udvikling eller afvikling?', *Politica*, 34: 431–448.

Wolf, S. and Spoden, D. (2000) 'Allocation of EU Aid towards ACP-Countries', Universität Bonn, Zentrum für Entwicklungsforschung, *Discussion Papers on Development Policy*, no. 22. Available online: http://www.zef.de/fileadmin/webfiles/downloads/zef_dp/zef_dp22–00.pdf (accessed 11 January 2006).

Woodward, S. (1995) *Balkan Tragedy: Chaos and Dissolution after the Cold War*, Washington DC, Brookings Institution.

World Bank (1999) *Assessing Aid – What Works, What Doesn't, and Why*, Oxford: Oxford University Press.

World Trade Organization [WTO] (2000a) 'EU has open market, but still holds back on agriculture and textile products', first press release by the Trade Policy Review Division of the WTO, PRESS/TPRB/137, 4 July 2000.

—— (2000b) *Trade Policy Review: European Union 2000*, vol. 1, November.

—— (2002) *Trade Policy Review: European Union*, Trade Policy Review Body, WT/TPRS/102, 26 June.

World Wide Fund for Nature [WWF] (2004) *Living Planet Report 2004*, Gland, Switzerland: WWF.

Wynne, B. (1995) 'Public Understanding of Science', in S. Jasanoff, J. C. Markle, J. C. Peterson, and T. Pinch (eds) *Handbook of Science and Technology Studies*, London: Sage.

—— (2005) 'Reflexing Complexity: Post-Genomics Knowledge and Reductionist Returns in Public Science', *Theory Culture & Society*, 22(5): 67–94.

Xiang, L. (2001) 'An EU Common Strategy for China?', *The International Spectator*, 36(3): 89–99.

Yost, D. S. (1998) *NATO Transformed: The Alliance's New Roles in International Security*, Washington DC: United States Institute of Peace Press.

Young, A. (2001) 'Extending European Cooperation: The European Union and the "New" International Trade Agenda', *RSC Working Paper*, no. 2001/12.

Young, A., Holmes, P. and Rollo, J. (2000) 'The European Trade Agenda after Seattle', *Sussex European Institute Working Papers Series*, 37.

Young, B. (2000) 'Disciplinary Neoliberalism in the European Union and Gender Politics', *New Political Economy*, 5: 77–98.

Youngs, R. (2001a) *The European Union and the Promotion of Democracy*, Oxford: Oxford University Press.

—— (2001b) 'European Union Democracy Promotion Policies: Ten Years On', *European Foreign Affairs Review*, 6: 355–373.

—— (2002) 'The European Union and Democracy Promotion in the Mediterranean: A New or Disingenuous Strategy?', in R. Gillespie, and R. Youngs (eds) *European Union and Democracy Promotion: the Case of North Africa*. Special Issue of *Democratization*, 9: 40–62.

Yurlov, F. (2000) 'Russia: Problems of security in the post-Cold War Era', *World Affairs*, 4(2): 42–56.

Zinn, H. (2002) *A People's History of the United States*, Harlow: Longman.

Zito, A. (2000) *Creating Environmental Policy in the European Union*, Basingstoke: Macmillan.

Zoellick, R. (2001) 'The WTO and New Global Trade Negotiations: What's at Stake', speech for the Council on Foreign Relations, Washington DC, 30 October 2001. Available online http://www.ustr.gov/assets/Document_Library/USTR_Speeches/2001/asset_upload_file821_4260.pdf (accessed 11 January 2006).

Zucconi, M. (1996) 'The European Union in the Former Yugoslavia', in A. Chayes and A. H. Chayes (eds) *Preventing Conflict in the Post-Communist World*, Washington DC: Brookings Institution.

Index

An environmentally friendly book printed and bound in England by www.printondemand-worldwide.com

PEFC Certified

This product is
from sustainably
managed forests
and controlled
sources

www.pefc.org

PEFC/16-33-415

FSC

Mixed Sources

Product group from well-managed
forests, and other controlled sources
www.fsc.org Cert no. TT-COC-002641
© 1996 Forest Stewardship Council

This book is made entirely of chain-of-custody materials

#0435 - 270212 - C0 - 234/156/14 - PB